FOUR VIEWS ON **CREATION, EVOLUTION, AND INTELLIGENT DESIGN**

Books in the Counterpoints Series

Bible and Theology

FOUR VIEWS ON CREATION, EVOLUTION, AND INTELLIGENT DESIGN

Ken Ham

Hugh Ross

Deborah B. Haarsma

Stephen C. Meyer

J. B. Stump, general editor
Stanley N. Gundry, series editor

COUNTERPOINTS
► BIBLE & THEOLOGY ◄

ZONDERVAN®

ZONDERVAN

Four Views on Creation, Evolution, and Intelligent Design
Copyright © 2017 by Ken Ham, Hugh Ross, Deborah B. Haarsma, Stephen C. Meyer,
    J. B. Stump

This title is also available as a Zondervan ebook.

Requests for information should be addressed to:
Zondervan, 3900 Sparks Dr. SE, Grand Rapids, Michigan 49546

ISBN 978-0-310-08097-8

Cover design: Tammy Johnson
Cover photo: iStock.com

Printed in the United States of America

HB 04.23.2024

CONTENTS

CONTRIBUTORS

Ken Ham is the president/CEO and founder of Answers in Genesis–US and the highly acclaimed Creation Museum. Ham is one of the most in-demand Christian speakers in North America. His emphasis is on the relevance and authority of the book of Genesis and how compromise on Genesis has opened a dangerous door regarding how modern culture and the church view biblical authority. His Australian accent, keen sense of humor, captivating stories, and exceptional PowerPoint illustrations have made him one of North America's most effective Christian communicators.

Hugh Ross (PhD, University of Toronto) is founder and president of Reasons To Believe (www.reasons.org). He is the author of many books, including *More Than a Theory*, *Why the Universe Is the Way It Is*, and *Improbable Planet*. An astronomer, Ross has addressed students and faculty on over three hundred campuses in the United States and abroad on a wide variety of science-faith topics. From science conferences to churches to government labs, Ross presents powerful evidence for a purpose-filled universe. He lives in the Los Angeles area.

Deborah B. Haarsma (PhD, MIT) has served as the President of BioLogos since 2013. Previously, she served as professor and chair in the Department of Physics and Astronomy at Calvin College in Grand Rapids, Michigan. Haarsma is an experienced research scientist, with several publications in the *Astrophysical Journal* and the *Astronomical Journal* on extragalactic astronomy and cosmology. She is co-author (with her husband Loren Haarsma) of *Origins: Christian Perspectives on Creation, Evolution, and Intelligent Design* and co-editor (with Rev. Scott Hoezee) of *Delight in Creation: Scientists Share Their Work with the Church*. Gifted in interpreting complex scientific topics for lay audiences, Haarsma often speaks to churches, colleges, and schools about the relationships between science and Christian faith.

Stephen C. Meyer is Senior Fellow of the Discovery Institute. He received his PhD in the philosophy of science from the University of Cambridge. A former geophysicist and college professor, he now directs Discovery Institute's Center for Science and Culture in Seattle. He has authored the *New York Times* bestseller *Darwin's Doubt: The Explosive Origin of Animal Life and the Case for Intelligent Design* (HarperOne, 2013) as well as *Signature in the Cell: DNA and the Evidence for Intelligent Design* (HarperOne, 2009), which was named Book of the Year by the *Times* (of London) *Literary Supplement* in 2009.

J. B. Stump (PhD, Boston University) is Senior Editor at BioLogos, where he oversees the development of new content and curates existing content for the website and print materials. He has authored *Science and Christianity: An Introduction to the Issues* (Wiley-Blackwell, 2017) and co-authored (with Chad Meister) *Christian Thought: A Historical Introduction* (Routledge, 2010). He has co-edited (with Alan Padgett) *The Blackwell Companion to Science and Christianity* (Wiley-Blackwell, 2012) and (with Kathryn Applegate) *How I Changed My Mind About Evolution* (InterVarsity, 2016).

INTRODUCTION

J. B. STUMP

There are many substantial topics on which Christians hold different views: eternal security, eschatology, election, egalitarianism, the Eucharist—to name just a few that start with *e*. Such disagreements should not drive us to conclude that all views are equally supported by evidence and reason, nor even less that there are no correct answers to these contentious topics. But the lack of unanimity should give us some pause about the certainty with which we hold our own views, and it should encourage us to explore the ways other faithful Christians have articulated their beliefs on these topics.

This book aims to provide a path for exploring Christian views on another of the *e* words about which there is disagreement: evolution. Strictly speaking, evolution isn't a theological topic, so it may seem curious to include it in this series of books (I doubt if there will be a multiple views book in this series on quantum gravity!). But one's view on evolution and related scientific topics (like the age of the earth) is often correlated with views on the interpretation of Scripture, Adam and Eve, original sin, and the problem of evil. And sorting out one's views on these topics cannot avoid addressing the methodological issue of how theological knowledge is related to knowledge obtained through the sciences. So, evolution, or the broader topic of origins under which these other topics more properly belong, has enormous relevance for how we understand the Christian faith.

Why a New Edition?

In 1999 Zondervan published *Three Views on Creation and Evolution*, edited by J. P. Moreland and John Mark Reynolds. We might justify a new Counterpoints book on the topic by noting that there has been a change to the format (now the contributors respond to each other) and the addition of another view (Intelligent Design is now included). But an even stronger case can be made that a new edition is warranted because of the changes in the origins landscape since then.

There have been major scientific discoveries that are relevant to our understanding of origins. In cosmology, there has been detailed mapping of the cosmic background radiation, discovery of thousands of exoplanets, and empirical detection of gravity waves. To most scientists, these show impressive confirmations of theories about the age and development of the cosmos. In paleontology, preserved soft tissue in dinosaur fossils has been discovered. Does this mean our theories were wrong about how long soft tissue can survive? Or does it mean that dinosaur fossils can't be as old as they were thought to be? There have also been many more hominid fossils found that do not fit neatly into human or known ape categories. The Hall of Human Origins at the Smithsonian Museum of Natural History now reports fossils of more than 6000 such individuals. Where do these fit into our understanding of the relatedness of life and our theories of human origins? And undoubtedly the biggest of the origins-related increases in scientific data over the past two decades has been in genetics. The Human Genome Project completed its mapping of the entire human genome in 2003, and our ability to compare genetic information between species has dramatically increased.

Events that have shaped the origins conversation are not just in the realm of science. The Dover trial in 2005 shut down one avenue of influence for the intelligent design movement (public school curricula), but raised its profile in the media and public consciousness. The young-earth creationist organization Answers in Genesis opened The Creation Museum (2007) and the Ark Encounter (2016), which have been visited by hundreds of thousands of people. Francis Collins founded BioLogos in 2007 to promote the view that the science of evolution does not conflict with the Christian faith.

Of course, many relevant books have been published since 1999 from all perspectives about origins topics. The following is a sample of these (in chronological order) from the perspectives covered in this book:

Ross, Hugh. *The Creator and the Cosmos: How the Latest Scientific Discoveries of the Century Reveal God.* Carol Stream, IL: NavPress, 2001.

Rana, Fazale and Hugh Ross. *Who Was Adam? A Creation Model Approach to the Origin of Man.* Carol Stream, IL: NavPress 2005; updated Covina, CA: RTB Press, 2015.

Ham, Ken. *The New Answers Book*. Vol. 1. Green Forest, AZ: Master Books, 2006.

Dembski, William A. *The Design Inference: Eliminating Chance through Small Probabilities*. Cambridge: Cambridge University Press, 2006.

Collins, Francis. *The Language of God: A Scientist Presents Evidence for Belief*. New York: Free Press, 2006.

Mortenson, Terry and Thane H. Ury, eds. *Coming to Grips with Genesis: Biblical Authority and the Age of the Earth*. Green Forest, AZ: Master Books, 2008.

Meyer, Stephen C. *Signature in the Cell: DNA and the Evidence for Intelligent Design*. San Francisco: HarperOne, 2009.

Walton, John. *The Lost World of Genesis One: Ancient Cosmology and the Origins Debate*. Downers Grove, IL: IVP Academic, 2009.

Snelling, Andrew. *Earth's Catastrophic Past: Geology, Creation, & the Flood*. Dallas, TX: Institute for Creation Research, 2009.

Haarsma, Deborah B. and Loren. *Origins: Christian Perspectives on Creation, Evolution, and Intelligent Design*. Grand Rapids: Faith Alive Christian Resources, 2011.

Meyer, Stephen C. *Darwin's Doubt: The Explosive Origin of Animal Life and the Case for Intelligent Design*. San Francisco: HarperOne, 2013.

Ross, Hugh and Kathy. *Navigating Genesis: A Scientist's Journey Through Genesis 1–11*. Covina, CA: RTB Press, 2014.

Finally, the origins landscape has been affected by the growth and development of internet resources. Blogging, Facebook, YouTube, and Twitter have massively increased the dissemination of all kinds of information, and origins topics in particular seem to be over-represented on the internet. Without having the data up my sleeve to prove it, I'd guess that a higher percentage of people today are aware of the origins debates and have opinions on such topics than two decades ago. But where is that information coming from? And which information is correct? This book seeks to bring some organization and greater definition to what can be an overwhelming number of claims and information.

The Four Views

There are many possible positions (and nuances thereof) one might take on a complex issue like creation and evolution. To limit the options, we're not considering non-Christian positions here, and even within Christianity we're limiting the discussion to those who take the Bible seriously as a source of revelation from God. The resulting positions tend to coalesce around four views: Young Earth Creationism, Old Earth Creationism, Evolutionary Creation, and Intelligent Design.

A couple of notes on these labels: First, "creationist" is sometimes used in a narrow sense, to identify those who believe a literal reading of Scripture gives scientific details about the process of creation. In this sense, those holding to evolution would be disqualified as creationists, and there is controversy about whether adherents to intelligent design fit the description. This latter controversy often becomes an exercise in name calling and sheds little light on the subject. I am using the term "creationist" in a wider sense, namely as one who believes that God is the creator. In that sense, all the contributors to this volume are creationists—indeed it is difficult to imagine a Christian who would not be. So, the disagreements between our contributors are not about whether things were created. They are about when things were created and whether current scientific theories are correct descriptions of the process of creation or whether they conflict with biblical affirmations on creation.

Next, there is not complete consensus on the labels I'm using here. Young Earth creationism and Intelligent Design are widely used and accurate descriptors, so we'll stick with them here. Old Earth creationism is sometimes called "progressive creationism" because its adherents typically maintain that God created different kinds or species supernaturally in a progression throughout the long time span of Earth's history rather than all at once (or over the period of six days). Evolutionary creationism has perhaps more often been called "theistic evolution," but I don't think that is a helpful term for a couple of reasons. First, there is a wide variety of theological positions that have been associated with theistic evolution. The label "evolutionary creation" has increasingly been used to refer to those theistic evolutionists who hold to the traditional Christian creeds that the creator God is a personal being. And beyond this, it is strange to modify the scientific position with "theistic" when we don't do that for any other scientific theories (do theists hold to "theistic photosynthesis"?!).

At the risk of some oversimplification, I'll characterize the first three positions in relation to their views on contemporary scientific claims. There is a very broad consensus among professionals in the physical sciences (physics, chemistry, geology, and astronomy) that the universe is 13.8 billion years old and Earth is 4.5 billion years old. There is very broad consensus among professionals in the life sciences (biology and medicine) that life on Earth has evolved from common ancestors. Of course, there are lots of disagreements in the details of theories in both the physical and life sciences, but the overwhelming majority of scientists accept that science has shown beyond a reasonable doubt that the earth is very old and that life (including humans) has evolved from common ancestors.[1]

- Evolutionary creationists accept these central conclusions from both physical sciences and life sciences.
- Old-earth creationists accept the conclusions of the physical sciences on the age of Earth and the universe, but they do not accept the central claim of the life sciences that all life has evolved through common ancestors.
- Young-earth creationists do not accept these central conclusions of either the physical sciences or the life sciences.

Intelligent Design (ID) does not fit into this pattern of characterization since it has adherents spanning all three of these previous categories. Instead, the theory might be described by its central claim that scientific evidence can be used to demonstrate the agency of a designer, which is identified by Christians as the God of the Bible.

Again, within these positions there are plenty of disagreements. For example, young-earth creationists disagree on whether to invoke the appearance of age; old-earth creationists disagree on whether each day in the Genesis 1 account was a longer period of time; evolutionary creationists disagree on the historicity of Adam and Eve; ID theorists disagree on common ancestry. We have not asked the contributors to this volume to speak for everyone in their camps but to present their own views on origins. Undoubtedly the arguments and conclusions would be different if we used different representatives for the general positions.

---

1. See for example the Pew surveys of scientists' beliefs here: http://www.pewinternet.org/2015/07/23/an-elaboration-of-aaas-scientists-views/.

Contributors and Their Organizations

When Zondervan approached me about editing a new version of the book, I proposed using leaders from the most prominent science and faith organizations in America affiliated with the four views. We were very pleased when our first choice for each of the positions accepted our invitation to contribute.

Ken Ham was a high school science teacher in Queensland, Australia before resigning in 1979 to form a young-earth creationist apologetics ministry. In 1987 he moved to the United States and worked with another young-earth organization, the Institute for Creation Research. He founded Creation Science Ministries in 1994, which changed its name to Answers in Genesis in 1997. Ham continues to serve as the president of AiG. The organization develops and distributes resources in support of Young Earth creationism and runs the Creation Museum and Ark Encounter tourist attractions in northern Kentucky (see more at answersingenesis.org).

Hugh Ross earned a PhD in astronomy from the University of Toronto and researched quasars and galaxies at the California Institute of Technology. During college he became a Christian and decided to test the scientific and historical accuracy of the holy books of different religious traditions. He was persuaded that only the Bible passed the test. Ross founded Reasons to Believe in 1986 as an apologetics organization, attempting to demonstrate the truth of Christianity by showing the Bible to be scientifically accurate. Ross is still the president of the Los Angeles-based organization (see more at reasons.org).

Deborah B. Haarsma earned a PhD in physics from MIT in 1997 and taught physics and astronomy for fourteen years at Calvin College. She became president of BioLogos in 2013. BioLogos was founded by Francis Collins in 2007 after his book, *The Language of God*, sparked many questions among people wondering how a world-class scientist could be a committed Christian. The BioLogos website launched in 2009 and continues to provide resources aimed at showing the harmony between evolutionary science and biblical Christianity (see more at biologos.org).

Stephen C. Meyer began his career working in earth science and then did graduate work in the history and philosophy of science, earning a PhD in the field from the University of Cambridge in 1991. He taught at two different Christian colleges and then helped to found the Center for Science and Culture at the Discovery Institute. The center, for which Meyer remains the program director, aims to counteract the claim that human beings and nature are the result of blind purposeless processes but instead are the result of intelligent design (see more at discovery.org).

It might be noticed that none of these contributors is professionally trained in theology. The topics involved in the origins discussion are necessarily interdisciplinary, and it is consistent with the broader academic field of science and religion that many of the leading voices are scientists who have acquired fluency in the theological topics. All of the contributors in this volume are experienced at explaining both scientific and theological facets of the origins debate to general audiences.

What to Look for in This Book

The format of this book is consistent with other recent volumes in the Counterpoint series with four contributors. There are four parts to the book, corresponding to the four views of the contributors. Each part consists of an original essay by the contributor representing that view, responses by the other three contributors, and a rejoinder by the author representing the position.

Each of the contributors was asked to write their essays with the following questions in mind:

- What is your position on origins—understood broadly to include the physical universe, life, and human beings in particular?
- What do you take to be the most persuasive arguments in defense of your position? What are the biggest challenges for your view?
- How do you demarcate, correlate, and use evidence about origins from current science and from divine revelation?
- What hinges on having the correct view of origins?

My Own View

It doesn't take much digging to find that I myself have a fairly settled view on the topic of origins. I have worked for BioLogos for several years and generally subscribe to the position of evolutionary creation.

Of course, that raises questions of partiality or bias, but I hope readers will see that each position has been presented fairly and charitably.

My primary goal for this book has been for it to be an accurate snapshot of the origins conversation in America right now. As such, it was my role as editor to enable the contributors to represent their positions as well as possible. I suggested edits to all of them that I thought helped to make their points stronger or clearer, but it remained entirely up to the individual contributors whether to accept those suggestions. They retained full and final authority over the words in their sections.

Beyond the scholarly goal of showing the state of the debate, I hope this book facilitates gracious dialogue between Christians with different viewpoints. We need not let the passion and conviction with which we hold our own beliefs undermine what is supposed to be a central aspect of our Christian witness to the rest of the world: Jesus prayed in John 17 that his disciples would be one so the world might believe in Jesus. Insofar as we consider ourselves to be Christ's disciples, we must pursue that unity. I don't think that means we will come to agree completely on even very important issues. But perhaps as we hold each other accountable for faithfully interpreting Scripture and the created world, we might come to understand and respect that our views flow out of genuine differences about the best interpretations and not out of some nefarious motives.

I hope that readers of this book will see the leaders of these organizations interacting civilly and with integrity. Perhaps that will help to change the tone of the debate about origins in our generation. And beyond that, wouldn't it be amazing if people outside the church would witness this conversation and remark like Tertullian reported a pagan official to have done: Look at how they love each other! Origins is an important topic. But we must remember that Jesus didn't say, "By this everyone will know that you are my disciples, if you have the same view on origins" or even ". . . if you have the correct view on origins." Even if no one reading this book changes their minds, some good will come out of it if we increasingly understand, respect, and even love each other more.

Without further ado, I am pleased to present these four views on origins.

YOUNG-EARTH CREATIONISM

KEN HAM

America, like the rest of the formerly "Christian West," is experiencing a breath-taking and accelerating moral and spiritual meltdown that few would have predicted even ten years ago. Sexual liberty (probably never on the minds of the framers of the US Constitution) is threatening to destroy the religious liberty guaranteed in the First Amendment of the Constitution. Postmodern relativism, which is really another name for atheism, rules the culture: There is no absolute truth and no absolute morality.

Furthermore, the "nones" (those who profess no supposed religious affiliation) now approach 25 percent of the population.[1] Sixty to eighty percent of young people raised in Bible-believing homes and churches are leaving the church, and many are abandoning the faith, before or when they graduate from high school.[2] The Bible and Christianity have largely been thrown out of the government-run schools and universities. Christians are facing increasing persecution (loss of jobs, destruction of businesses, etc.) for not submitting to the LGBTQ revolution.

How has this happened in a nation whose founding and culture (until well into the twentieth century) were profoundly influenced by biblical Christianity like no other nation in history? I believe the answer is related to Psalm 11:3: "When the foundations are being destroyed, what can the righteous do?"

---

1. Robert P. Jones et al., *Exodus: Why Americans are Leaving Religion and Why They're Unlikely to Come Back* (Washington, DC: Public Religion Research Institute, 2016), 2.

2. Ken Ham and Britt Beemer, *Already Gone: Why Your Kids Will Quit Church and What You Can Do About It* (Green Forest, AR: Master Books, 2009).

The clear teaching and the most natural reading of Genesis 1–11, indeed the whole Bible, is that (1) God created the universe in six literal, approximately twenty-four-hour days about six thousand years ago; (2) He cursed the whole originally "very good" creation after and in response to Adam's rebellion; (3) He destroyed the world with a year-long, global, catastrophic flood at the time of Noah; and (4) He judged mankind at the Tower of Babel, supernaturally dividing the people into different languages and thereby into different people groups. That is what the church almost universally believed for the first eighteen hundred years until the early nineteenth century, when most of the church accepted the idea of millions of years that was developing in geology which was then followed by Darwin's theory in 1859.

Since *The Genesis Flood* (1961) by John Whitcomb and Henry Morris, a growing number of Christians, including PhD scientists, all over the world again believe this young-earth view to be biblically required and scientifically sound.[3] But that biblical creation view has been under attack by secular scientists (and sadly, subtly by many professing Christian scientists) for over two hundred years. Genesis 1–11 is the foundation of the whole rest of the Bible. All major and minor doctrines—and the gospel itself—are founded directly or indirectly on those first eleven chapters. In the minds of many in the church, both young and old, the foundations have been destroyed.

For decades, most parents and churches have not taught general biblical or creation apologetics. Neither have most seminaries. If they teach apologetics, they generally ignore the question of origins. Churches have not given adults and children reasons for why they believe the Bible and the gospel so they could defend their faith in the face of skeptical challenges. Many kids raised within a young-earth creationist worldview were not taught how to defend that view biblically and scientifically and so were easily influenced by seemingly overwhelming scientific evidence presented by evolutionists in the schools, universities, and through the media. Through a national survey by America's Research Group, we have documented that a major reason for the mass exodus of young people from the church is that the church had no answers to the claims of evolutionists, so young people concluded that the Bible

---

3. See a list of some of those modern and historical creation scientists with a PhD in science at https://answersingenesis.org/creation-scientists/.

is not trustworthy.[4] In contrast, I have found as I have spoken in many churches, Christian schools, colleges, and in many nations over the past thirty-five plus years that kids who have been well taught in creationist apologetics have generally stood strong in that conviction.

For young-earth creationists that apologetic task begins with Scripture, for it is the inspired, inerrant Word of God. God teaches us to build our thinking on the solid rock of His Word (Matt 7:24–27). We are not to turn from it to the right or the left (Josh 1:8–9). We are to avoid being taken captive by the traditions and philosophies and speculations of men by clinging to the Word of Christ (2 Cor 10:3–4; Col 2:8). God's creation speaks to us non-verbally about His existence and attributes (Rom 1:18–20; Pss 19:1; 97:6). But Scripture speaks to us verbally and truthfully about so much more. And as we shall see, creation is cursed, whereas Scripture (the written Word) is not. Without the biblical revelation about the cosmos-impacting fall of man, the creation gives a confusing message about the Creator.[5] Therefore, we start our thinking about origins (as in all other areas) with Scripture, God's inerrant, holy Word.

Biblical Evidence for Young-Earth Creation

Genesis 1–11 is history—not poetry, parable, prophetic vision, or mythology. This is seen in the Hebrew verb forms used in Genesis 1 and following, which are characteristic of historical narrative, not poetry.[6] Genesis 1–11 has the same characteristics of historical narrative as Genesis 12–50, most of Exodus, much of Numbers, Joshua, 1 and 2 Kings, etc. The early chapters of Genesis name real people, describe real places, and discuss real events in real time. Also, the other biblical authors and Jesus treat Genesis 1–11 (using specific names like

---

4. See Ham and Beemer, *Already Gone*.

5. This is clearly seen in many atheist responses to intelligent-design arguments that are divorced from Scripture and advocated by those who accept the millions of years of death. The atheists give examples of natural evil, such as mosquitos carrying malaria or hurricanes ravaging the land and ask, "How intelligent is that? What kind of a God would make a world like that?"

6. See Steven Boyd, "The Genre of Genesis 1:1–2:3: What Means This Text?" in *Coming to Grips with Genesis*, eds. Terry Mortenson and Thane H. Ury, (Green Forest, AR: Master Books, 2008), 163–92. "A layman's summary of Boyd's research" is in Donald DeYoung, *Thousands, Not Billions: Challenging an Icon of Evolution* (Green Forest, AR: Master Books, 2005), 157–72.

Adam, Eve, Noah) as literal history.[7] Even many old-earth proponents recognize that Genesis 1–11 is historical narrative (i.e., describing in a straightforward manner real events in time-space history[8]), not poetry, myth, or some other kind of figurative kind of literature.[9] What does that history teach us? Many Christians say, "Genesis 1 tells us *that* and *why* God created, not *how* and *when* He created." Actually, the chapter does not tell us why God created but certainly does tell us a significant amount about when and how, as the following arguments demonstrate.

The Creation Days Were Literal

Young-earth creationists contend that the Bible is very clear that the days of the creation week in Genesis 1:1–2:3 are literal, twenty-four-hour days, just like our days today. Several lines of evidence support this conclusion. In my experience and reading, many Christians who say that it is not clear how long the days of creation were in Genesis 1 have overlooked some or much of this biblical evidence.

"Day" Is Defined Literally

The Hebrew word for day (*yom*) is defined in its two literal, normal senses the very first time it is used in the Bible (Gen 1:5): (1) the light portion of the dark-light cycle contrasted with night (*laylah*) and (2) the whole dark-light cycle. The days are numbered (first, second, third, etc.), and each is preceded by the refrain "and there was evening (*'ereb*), and there was morning (*boqer*)." Every other place in the Old Testament where *yom* is modified by a number it always means a literal twenty-four-hour day.[10] And every other use of *laylah*, *'ereb*, and *boqer* refers to a

---

7. Mortenson and Ury, eds., *Coming to Grips with Genesis*, 315–72.

8. We must not make the mistake of thinking that an account is not accurate history if there were no human eyewitnesses (e.g., the account of the first five days of creation week), for then we would have to draw the unbiblical and historically inaccurate conclusion that Jesus was not conceived by the Holy Spirit working in Mary or that Jesus was not raised from the dead (no human saw either event). God can and did move men to write accurate history about many events that neither they nor any other human ever personally saw.

9. See, for example, the arguments in Walter Kaiser, *The Old Testament Documents: Are They Reliable and Relevant?* (Downers Grove, IL: IVP, 2001), 53–83.

10. Only two verses are ever cited by old-earth proponents as an objection to this claim: Zechariah 14:7 and Hosea 6:2. But in the first case, the context of verses 14:1, 4, and 6 shows that they are referring to the same unique day (in Hebrew *yom ehad*, just as at the end of Gen 1:5), the day the Lord returns at the end of the age. The Messiah Jesus is not going to return over long ages, but suddenly, in an instant ("in the twinkling of an eye:" 1 Cor 15:52 and 1 Thess 4:13ff). In Hosea, the prophet calls the people to repentance and gives a promise

literal night or literal evening or literal morning, respectively, of a literal day. Also, Genesis 1:14 says that the heavenly bodies were created for man to measure literal years, literal seasons, and literal days (*yamim*, plural of *yom*).[11] That the days are sequential and non-overlapping is clear from the repeated phrases "and God saw" (7x), "it was so" (6x), and "it was good" (6x). The repetition is emphatic: God finished the work of one day before the next day commenced.

Furthermore, if God created over long ages of time (millions of years), there are various ways in Hebrew that He could have said that.[12] He could have used *dor* (translated as "time," "period," or "generation"). Or He could have used a phrase such as "after a long time" (Josh 23:1), or "thousands upon thousands" of years (cf. Gen 24:60), or "countless thousands" of years (cf. Num. 10:36), or "ages" (Joel 2:2). He could have borrowed a word from a neighboring language, as many languages do today and as God did with the Aramaic words *zeman* or *'iddan* (both translated "time" or "times") in the books of Nehemiah and Daniel.[13] Instead, God chose to use the only Hebrew word (*yom*) that means a literal twenty-four-hour day.

Exodus 20:8-11

This critical passage is God's own commentary on Genesis 1. God tells the Israelites to work six days and rest on the seventh because He created in six days and ceased creating on the seventh. The commandment makes no sense if the days are not literal in verse 11 as they are in verses

---

of spiritual healing and reviving "after two days" and "on the third day." But it is no comfort if it doesn't mean that God will quickly respond mercifully to their returning to the Lord. What would it mean if the promise was that God would revive them two to three hundred (or thousand or million) years after they repent? The promise only makes sense when we take the days literally and take the phrases as meaning "quickly." Neither of these verses shows that *yom* modified by a number can mean something other than a literal day.

11. See also Gerhard F. Hasel, "The 'Days' of Creation in Genesis 1: Literal 'Days' or Figurative 'Periods/Epochs' of Time?" *Origins* 21:1 (1994): 5–38; Andrew E. Steinmann, "אֶחָד As an Ordinal Number and the Meaning of Genesis 1:5," *Journal of the Evangelical Theological Society* 45:4 (2002): 577–84; Robert McCabe, "A Defense of Literal Days in the Creation Week," *Detroit Baptist Seminary Journal* 5 (2000): 97–123.

12. Scripture repeatedly affirms in various ways that it is God-breathed ("inspired," 2 Tim 3:16) and therefore refers to itself as the "Word of God." God is the ultimate author. He moved men to write exactly what He wanted written (2 Pet 1:20–21) while using each one's unique life experience, training, and personality. So what the human author said is what God said.

13. He used *zeman* in Nehemiah 2:6 and Daniel 2:16, 21; 4:33 (Heb 4:36); and 7:25, and *'iddan* in Daniel 4:16, 23, 25, and 32 (Heb 4:13, 20, 22, and 29).

8–10. If God wanted to say "you work six days because I created over six long periods of time," He could have said that in Hebrew, as noted above.

Verse 11 verse stands as an insurmountable brick wall against any attempt to add millions of years into Genesis 1. They can't be inserted into each of the days or between the days or before the days, for the verse says "in six days the LORD made the heavens and the earth, the sea, and *all that is in them*" (emphasis added). That means that the first day begins in Genesis 1:1 (when God created the earth), not in 1:3 (when He created light), and there was no time before verse 1.

The Order of Creation

Not only does the time period of creation in Genesis 1 contradict the time claimed for the evolution of all these things, but the order of creation events in Genesis 1 also contradicts the order of events in the evolutionary story of the universe and of life. For example, in Genesis the earth was created before light and the sun, moon and stars, whereas in evolutionary cosmology most stars were formed before the sun, which gave birth to the earth and moon. A global ocean preceded dry land in Genesis but in evolutionary geology the earth started as a molten ball, cooled and developed a dry crust, and then millions of years later seas formed. In Genesis we are told that all land plants were created before any sea creatures, and birds were created before any land animals, including what we today call dinosaurs (a modern name given to a particular group of land animals), all of which is the opposite order of evolution.[14]

Also, there are logical problems if we put millions of years into the days or between the days. How could plants survive without animals and insects to pollinate them? Why would God make creatures that lived and died, some kinds becoming extinct, for millions of years before He created man, whom He created to rule over all the other creatures He made (Gen 1:26–28)?

God Created Supernaturally

Ten times Genesis 1 records "and God said." God created by His Word. He spoke and it was done. He created the first animate and inanimate

---

14. See further contradictions in order in https://answersingenesis.org/why-does-creation -matter/evolution-vs-creation-the-order-of-events-matters/.

things supernaturally and virtually instantly. On the day that they were created they were fully formed and fully functioning.[15] For example, the first plants, animals, and people were created as mature adult forms (not as seeds or fertilized eggs or infants). The plants immediately had fruit on their branches and the animals and people were immediately ready to obey God's command to be fruitful and multiply. These statements are clearly contrasted with how all the subsequent plants, animals, and people would come into existence: reproduction by natural procreation after their kinds. When God said, "Let there be . . . ," He did not need to wait millions of years for things to come into existence. He spoke, and creatures came into existence immediately. As Psalm 33:6–9 emphasizes, this applies to the heavenly bodies as well as all the creatures on earth. To postulate millions of years between these supernatural acts of creation seems very inconsistent with the wisdom and the power of God. Why would God create the earth and leave it covered with water for millions of years when He says He created it to be inhabited (Isa 45:18)? Why would He create plants and then wait millions of years before creating animals and people who would eat plants for food (Gen 1:29–30)? Why would He create sea creatures and birds and wait millions of years before creating land animals and people?

How God created is revealed in the earthly ministry of the Lord Jesus, who is the creative Word who became flesh (John 1:1–3, 14). He revealed His glory as the Creator in His very first miracle when He instantly and supernaturally turned water into wine (John 2:1–11). All subsequent miracles were likewise instantaneous results from His spoken word or His touch, not the result of natural processes. Genesis 1 records a week of miracles.

The Genesis Genealogies Are Strict Chronologies

Genesis reveals vital information for how long ago the creation week occurred. Genesis 5 and 11 give us the genealogies from Adam to Noah and Noah to Abraham. But unlike all other genealogies in the Bible and in ancient Near Eastern literature, those in Genesis give the age of the patriarch when his son was born and how many years after that birth

---

15. When God said, "Let the earth sprout vegetation" (Gen 1:11 ESV, NASB), it was a supernatural growth to maturity, just as occurred when God made a plant to grow large enough in a few hours or less to provide shade for Jonah (Jonah 4:6).

the patriarch lived. So, these chapters give strong evidence of providing a chronology.

Some young-earth creationists and probably all old-earth creationists think there may be missing names in these Genesis genealogies because the Hebrew words translated "begat" and "son" don't always mean a literal son and because some other biblical genealogies leave out names (e.g., Matt 1). But six of the nineteen genealogical links in Genesis 5 and 11 are demonstrably literal father-son links because of the non-chronological information provided. Even if there are some missing names (which I think there are good reasons to doubt), there can be no missing years because the age of the father is given when the son is born. So, it doesn't matter if, for example, Enoch is the grandson or great-grandson of Jared; Enoch was born when Jared was 162 years old.

So, Adam was created about 2000 years before Abraham, who according to most scholars was born a little before 2000 BC. Since Adam was created on the sixth literal day of history that places the creation of the universe a little more than six thousand years ago. Even if Adam was created 10,000–12,000 years ago, as some young-earth creationists suggest, this is still irreconcilable with the evolutionary timescale, which dates the first *Homo sapiens* to two hundred thousand years ago or earlier.[16]

No Death Before the Fall

A critical issue that most Christians overlook in regard to the age of the creation is when death and suffering came into the world. In my experience and that of other AiG speakers talking to Christian audiences in many countries and reading old-earth Christian literature for many years, it is clear that most Christians, including most Bible scholars and theologians, have overlooked this issue or have treated it in a shallow way that reveals they have not seriously considered, much less refuted, young-earth creationist arguments.

---

16. Evolutionists don't agree on exactly what is a human being. So dates for the first human range from two hundred thousand to four hundred years ago or more. See, for example, https://en.wikipedia.org/wiki/Timeline_of_human_evolution and https://en.wikipedia.org/wiki/Neanderthal. For arguments in favor of the conclusion that the Genesis 5 and 11 genealogies are gapless chronologies, see chapter 5, "When Was Adam Created?" in *Searching for Adam: Genesis and the Truth about Man's Origin*, ed. Terry Mortenson (Green Forest, AR: Master Books, 2016); also at https://answersingenesis.org/bible-characters/adam-and-eve/when-was-adam-created/.

The Pre-Fall Creation

Six times in Genesis 1 God says the creation was "good" and at the end of the sixth day He declared everything "very good." This included the fact that both man and the animals and birds were vegetarian (Gen 1:29–30). To give us some understanding of what "very good" means we should note that the only thing declared "not good" before the fall was that Adam was alone for a few hours while naming animals before God created Eve.

The Fall and Curse

When Adam and Eve sinned they immediately died spiritually, evidenced by their hiding from God (Gen 3:8).[17] Then God pronounced judgment. He cursed the serpent who deceived Eve (v. 14). Whether God changed the anatomy or just the behavior of the serpent, it was a physical judgment. The verse says God cursed the serpent more than (or above) all cattle and beasts of the field, which implies that all animals were cursed. Eve and all women after her would have increased pain in childbirth—a physical judgment (v. 16). The ground was cursed (v. 17) and as a result thorns and thistles would grow, making future farming toilsome (v. 18–19). This was the ground outside the garden, for Adam and Eve were expelled from it (v. 23). Contrary to what some have said, this curse on the ground was not what man would do in misusing the environment. Genesis 5:29 makes it clear, using the same Hebrew words for "curse" and "ground," that it was the Lord, not man, who cursed the ground. The final aspect of God's judgment at the fall is that physical death entered the human race (v. 19), a fact confirmed by Romans 5:12 and 1 Corinthians 15:21–22, both of which speak of physical, not just spiritual, death.

Genesis 3 teaches that God judged the non-human creation because of Adam's sin. But we see the same reality in subsequent history. In the flood, God destroyed not only sinful humanity except for Noah's family but also all the land animals and birds not in the ark and the surface of the earth. God described the flood as a curse on creation

---

17. For an in-depth discussion of the issue of no death before the fall, see https://answers ingenesis.org/theory-of-evolution/millions-of-years/the-fall-and-the-problem-of-millions-of -years-of-natural-evil/.

(Gen 8:21). In Deuteronomy 28 God's blessings and curses in response to Israel's obedience or disobedience affect their children, their crops, and their livestock. The curses even affected the weather. And when God threatened Nineveh with judgment because of its wickedness, He said that judgment would have fallen on their animals too (Jonah 4:11).

This curse on the whole creation is further described in Romans 8:19–23. Paul tells us that the non-human creation was subjected to futility and put into slavery to corruption. The "whole creation" is groaning and suffering (v. 22), waiting eagerly to be set free from all this when Jesus comes again and gives believers their resurrection bodies. In the history of the church the vast majority of pastors and theologians who have commented on this passage have said that this subjection to futility and slavery to corruption happened in Genesis 3.[18] If the creation was subject to futility and corruption right from the first moment, it is inconceivable that God would call it "very good."

The Future Redemptive Work of Christ

Jesus Christ did not complete His redemptive work in His death and resurrection. He's coming again to put an end to sin but also the consequences of sin in the non-human creation. Acts 3:21 speaks of the future restoration of all things. Colossians 1:15–20 teaches that Christ is the Creator of all things, and, in addition to reconciling sinners to God, His atoning work on the cross will reconcile all things on earth and in heaven to Himself. When Christ returns, there will be no more suffering and death caused by life in this fallen world because the curse of Genesis 3 will be removed (Rev 21:3–5; 22:3).

Summary of the Biblical Testimony

So the big picture of history, according to God's Word, is creation, fall, redemption, and restoration. But the evolutionary story contradicts this. In that view the world did not start out good and then fall. Rather there has been steady progress from simple to complex life forms. And as long

---

18. See Henry B. Smith, Jr., "Cosmic and Universal Death from Adam's Fall: An Exegesis of Romans 8:19–23a," *Journal of Creation* 21:1 (2007): 75–85; http://creation.com/cosmic-and-universal-death-from-adams-fall-an-exegesis-of-romans-819–23a. For a briefer discussion, see Douglas Moo, *The Epistle to the Romans* (Grand Rapids: Eerdmans, 1996), 513–14; Thomas Schreiner, *Romans* (Grand Rapids: Baker, 1998), 435; and John Murray, *The Epistle to the Romans* (Grand Rapids: Eerdmans, 1993), 301–02.

as there has been life, there have been death and disease and carnivorous behavior along with natural disasters like hurricanes, tsunamis, and asteroid impacts, which have been one of the driving forces of evolutionary change. Most significantly, evolutionists say that the fossil record (supposedly formed over millions of years before man) gives evidence of five major extinction events when 60–90 percent of the species living at the time went extinct. We find cancer, arthritis, and brain tumors in dinosaur bones supposedly millions of years old. There are fossil thorns and thistles in rock layers that evolutionists date to be 300–400 million years old.

Non-Christians see this contradiction to which most Christians seem blind. Ronald Numbers is a prominent historian of science and an agnostic. He put it this way.

For creationists, history is based on the Bible and the belief that God created the world 6,000–10,000 years ago. . . . We humans were perfect because we were created in the image of God. And then there was the fall. Death appears and the whole account [in the Bible] becomes one of deterioration and degeneration. So we then have Jesus in the New Testament, who promises redemption. Evolution completely flips that. With evolution, you don't start out with anything perfect, you start with primitive little wiggly things, which evolve into apes and, finally, humans. There's no perfect state from which to fall. This makes the whole plan of salvation silly because there never was a fall. What you have then is a theory of progress from single-celled animals to humans and a very, very different take on history, and not just human history.[19]

So, to accept millions of years of animal death, disease, and extinction as well as earthquakes, hurricanes, tornadoes, and tsunamis requires a conscious or unconscious rejection or ignoring of (or superficial attention to or failure to apply one's orthodox belief in) the Bible's clear teaching about the "very good" pre-fall creation, the cosmic impact of the fall on the whole creation (not just mankind), and Christ's full redemptive work in the cosmos.

---

19. Ronald Numbers, quoted in Gwen Evans, "Reason or Faith? Darwin Expert Reflects," http://www.news.wisc.edu/16176, 3 Feb. 2009.

Noah's Flood: Global Catastrophe That Radically Rearranged the Earth

Noah's flood is critical to the question of the history and age of the earth. But in my reading and experience of speaking to Christian audiences in many countries for over three decades I find that most Christians ignore that event when considering the age of the earth or they deny that it was a global catastrophic flood.

It Was Historical

I've already argued that Genesis 1–11 is history. The rest of Scripture attests that the flood really happened. Ezekiel 14:14–20 and Isaiah 54:9 refer to Noah as historical. Luke lists Noah as part of the historical genealogy linking Jesus to Adam (Luke 3:23–38). Peter affirms that eight people were saved from the flood, which was just as historical as the judgment of Sodom and which happened as surely as Jesus will come again (1 Pet 3:20; 2 Pet 2:4–6; and 3:3–7). Jesus Himself affirmed the historicity of the flood as a warning of the judgment to come (Matt 24:37–39). People who reject the historicity of the flood have difficulty finding plausible interpretations of these verses.

It Was Global

The flood was not a localized flood in the Mesopotamian Valley of the Tigris and Euphrates Rivers, as many Christians suppose. Scripture could hardly be clearer. The purpose of the flood was to destroy not only sinful human beings but all the land animals and birds not in the ark and on the surface of the earth itself (Gen 6:7, 13). Only a global flood would accomplish that. The purpose of the ark was to save animals and birds to repopulate the earth after the flood (Gen 7:1–3). But if the flood were localized, it would not bother any animals and birds outside the flood zone, so there would be no need for the ark. The water covered all the pre-flood mountains "under the entire heavens" (Gen 7:19–20), and the ark landed on top of a mountain with no other mountains in view for seventy-four days (Gen 8:4–5)—only a global flood could do that. There were 371 days from the beginning of the flood till the ground was dry enough to disembark from the ark. No local flood could last that long. In Genesis 9:10–17 God promises to Noah and his descendants, the animals and birds and their offspring, and to the earth itself that He will never again destroy the world with a flood. If the flood was local, God lied, for since the time of Noah many local floods have destroyed some people, animals, and parts of the earth. Note also that Peter linked the formation of the earth out of water during creation and the destruction of the earth by water during the flood to the global and universal impact of the coming judgment (2 Pet 3).

It Was Catastrophic

The flood would have had to be catastrophic to accomplish its purpose of destroying the earth. Genesis 7:11 indicates there were two sources of water: subterranean waters and rain. It rained globally non-stop for forty days and nights (7:12), but it continued to rain till the 150th day (8:2). That alone would be catastrophic, causing massive erosion and mudslides.

But the rain apparently wasn't the primary source of water since the fountains or springs of the great deep are mentioned first both in 7:11 at the beginning of the flood and in 8:2 at the beginning of the receding of the floodwaters. The Hebrew word translated "burst forth" or "burst open" in 7:11 is used elsewhere to refer to the breaking of rock (Judg 15:19), an earthquake (Num 16:31), and the splitting of a mountain to create a huge valley (Zech 14:4). Such tectonic activity on the ocean floor all over the earth for months would produce devastating tsunamis to assault the pre-flood landmasses, causing destruction beyond comprehension.

Now what would we expect to find from this flood? As I often say, billions of dead things, buried in rock layers, laid down by water, all over the earth. All the continents are covered with sedimentary rock layers containing billions of fossils, and we find marine creatures on the top of our highest mountains, including Mt. Everest.

The Views of Jesus, the Apostles, and Isaiah

Several passages show that Jesus believed that Adam and Eve were created at the beginning of creation, not billions of years after the beginning (as all old-earth views imply), which confirms the young-earth creationist view (Mark 10:6; 13:19; Luke 11:50–51).[20] On a four-thousand-year time

---

20. I am not saying that the age of the earth was the focus of these verses. Rather, they reflect the young-earth creationist worldview of Jesus. For a thorough discussion of Jesus' words and old-earth attempts to reinterpret them, including evidence that the phrase

scale the sixth day was at the beginning of creation in non-technical language that Jesus was using.

Paul also made it clear that he was a young-earth creationist. In Romans 1:20 he says that God's existence and at least some of His attributes have been clearly understood by people "since the creation of the world"[21] so that they are without excuse for not honoring Him as God. Surely this great student of Scripture would have had in mind what David said a thousand years earlier (Ps 19:1; cf. Ps 97:6) and what Job said a thousand years before that (Job 12:7–10). The creation has always revealed the Creator to humans from the beginning of creation.

Similarly, Isaiah 40:21 implies that the prophet was a young-earth creationist. The parallelism of the verse shows that "from the beginning" and "from the foundations of the earth" (KJV) refer to the same point in time. What the people of Isaiah's day knew about God is what people (Adam and Eve, Cain and Abel, etc.) knew right at the foundation of the earth (the beginning of creation), which is also what all idolaters in Paul's day knew and what atheists throughout history and today have known. He is a fool who says there is no Creator, for His glory is seen in His creation (Pss 14:1; 19:1).

If the evolutionary view of 13.8 billion years is true, then Jesus, Paul, and Isaiah were badly mistaken and cannot be completely trusted in other things they teach.

For these reasons and more, I and many other Christians believe that God's Word clearly teaches young-earth creation. God was the eyewitness to all the events of Genesis 1–11, and it is His inspired, inerrant record. Also, humans were eyewitnesses to many of these events.[22]

"creation of the world" refers to the whole creation week and not just the first act of creation in Genesis 1:1, see Terry Mortenson, "Jesus, Evangelical Scholars and the Age of the Earth," in *Coming to Grips with Genesis*, 315–46. For a short, layman's discussion, see Terry Mortenson, "But from the Beginning of . . . the Institution of Marriage?"; www.answersingenesis.org/docs2004/1101ankerberg_response.asp, a response to a web article by John Ankerberg and Norman Geisler on Mark 10:6.

21. So read the NASB, ESV, NKJV, NIV, NLT, and NRSV. The KJV, KJ21, and HCSB render *apo ktiseos kosmou* as "from the creation of the world." But *apo* ("from") here surely means "since." For reasons behind this conclusion, see Ron Minton, "Apostolic Witness to Genesis Creation and the Flood," in *Coming to Grips with Genesis*, 351–54.

22. Of course Adam, Noah, and Shem were human eyewitnesses to many of the events of Genesis 1–11 during their lifetimes. The reference to the "book of the generations of Adam" (Gen 5:1) and the clearly implied intelligence of Cain (in building a city) and others in Genesis 4 (in developing mining, metallurgy and musical instruments) and Noah and family (in building the ark), strongly suggests that man had the ability to write from the very beginning. The

Therefore, Scripture must control our interpretation of the scientific evidence and our critique of evolutionary, naturalistic interpretations.

Scientific Evidence Confirming Genesis

The scientific evidence confirming the literal truth of Genesis 1–11 is overwhelming and increasing with time as a result of the research of both evolutionists and creationists. But before discussing some of that evidence, we need to distinguish two kinds of science in order to think carefully about the origins controversy. I like to call them experimental (or observational) science and historical science.

Experimental science is what most people think of when they hear the word science. It uses the method of *repeatable, observable experiments* to determine how the creation *operates* or functions *in the present* so that we can manipulate it to develop new technologies, find cures for disease, or put a man on the moon. Most of biology, chemistry, and physics, and all of engineering and medical research are in the realm of experimental/observational science. Like everyone else, creationists love this kind of science and the benefits resulting from its research. But this kind of science can't answer the question, how did the Grand Canyon or Saturn form? Or how did the first plants, animals, and people come into existence? Those are historical events that cannot be repeated in the lab.

In contrast, historical science includes historical geology, paleontology, archaeology, and cosmology. Criminal investigation is a form of historical science too. These sciences use reliable eyewitness testimony (if any is available) and observable evidence in the present to determine or reconstruct the *past, unobservable, unrepeatable* event(s) that produced the evidence we see in the present. Creationists and evolutionists are looking at the same observable evidence. But young-earth creationists trust the eyewitness testimony of the Creator, and secular evolutionists reject that testimony out of a sinful, rebellious heart.

From my and other AiG speakers' reading and interaction with evolutionists, most of them (whether lay people, students, or scientists) implicitly or explicitly deny this critical distinction between these two kinds of science, and many Christians fail to recognize the distinction. Many

---

eleven *toledot* ("these are the generations of") distributed through Genesis may indicate, among other things, that in inspiring Genesis God guided Moses in the use of preexisting documents or oral tradition passed on by the patriarchs.

examples could be cited. I'll mention just two. In 2013 Zack Kopplin was a 19-year-old student studying history at Rice University. As an outspoken atheist he was committed to keeping any scientific criticisms of evolution and any discussion of scientific evidence for creation out of the public schools of his home state of Louisiana. A news report quoted him saying,

> Creationism confuses students about the nature of science. If students don't understand the scientific method, and are taught that creationism is science, they will not be prepared to do work in genuine fields, especially not the biological sciences. We are hurting the chances of our students having jobs in science, and making discoveries that will change the world.

The reporter added about Kopplin,

> He worries that, if Louisiana (and Tennessee, which also has a similar law) insists on teaching students creationism,[23] students will not be the ones to discover the cure to AIDS or cancer. "We won't be the ones to repair our own damaged wetlands and protect ourselves from more hurricanes like Katrina," he says.[24]

Or consider these comments by Bill Nye the Science Guy on a *Larry King Now* program.

> *Nye*: My concern has always been, you can't use tax dollars intended for science education to teach something akin to the earth is ten thousand years old. Because that's just wrong. It's very much analogous to saying the earth is flat. You can show that the earth is not flat. You can show that the earth is not ten thousand years old. That's it. We're not teaching that in schools.
>
> *King*: So why do they [creationists] continue to believe it?

23. Creationists do not insist or advocate this at all, and neither did the laws in these two states, so this is a distortion. What we insist is that students should be allowed to hear scientific criticisms of evolution in the public schools. See the discussion in my article in the next footnote.

24. George Dvorsky, "How 19-year-old Activist Zack Kopplin Is Making Life Hell for Louisiana's Creationists," http://io9.com/5976112/how-19+year+old-activist-zack-kopplin-is-making-life-hell-for-louisianas-creationists, Jan 2013. For a careful analysis of Kopplin's views, see Ken Ham and Steve Golden, "The Legacy of Brainwashing," http://www.answers ingenesis.org/articles/2013/01/21/legacy-of-brainwashing.

Nye: So apparently people with these deeply held religious beliefs, they embrace that whole literal interpretation of the Bible as written in English as a worldview. At the same time they accept aspirin, antibiotic drugs, airplanes, but they're able to hold these two worldviews. And this is a mystery. The Bible is full of history, but it's not a science textbook.[25]

But this is no mystery, if Nye would stop implicitly denying the difference between experimental science and historical science. Nye is right that the Bible is full of history, but that historical record begins in Genesis 1:1. While Genesis 1–11 is not a science text (regarding experimental science), it is inerrant history by the eyewitness Creator, whose existence and attributes are revealed in what He made and the book He inspired, the truth of which Nye suppresses in unrighteousness.

The famous Harvard zoologist, evolutionist, and atheist Ernst Mayr saw the difference between these two kinds of science when he wrote:

Evolution is a historical process that cannot be proven by the same arguments and methods by which purely physical or functional phenomena can be documented. Evolution as a whole, and the explanation of particular evolutionary events, must be inferred from observations.[26]

However, the inferences of the evolutionists are made on the basis of the assumptions of a naturalistic (i.e., atheistic) worldview. In their thinking and interpretation of the observable evidence they assume that (1) nature or matter is all that exists and (2) everything can and must be explained by time, chance, and the laws of nature working on matter.[27] Biblical creationists reject those assumptions, not only in the fields of biology and anthropology, but also in geology and astronomy, for they are contrary to the Word of the Creator, which provides His eyewitness testimony that we need in order to correctly interpret the physical evidence to reconstruct the past.

---

25. "Larry King Now," April 1, 2013, http://www.hulu.com/watch/473418.

26. Ernst Mayr, *What Evolution is* (New York: Basic Books, 2001), 13.

27. Not all scientists believe this. Many do believe in God (however defined), but most do their scientific work as if the naturalistic worldview is true.

The controversy over evolution and the age of the creation is not in the realm of experimental science but in the realm of historical science. And the latter is heavily influenced by worldview *assumptions* that scientists use to *interpret* the evidence we see in the present to reconstruct the past history of the creation, including its origin.

The difference between young-earth creationists and all our Christian and non-Christian opponents is that we accept God's eyewitness testimony in Scripture and use it to interpret the physical evidence that we see in the present. Our opponents either reject the Word of God or ignore many of the details of the Word and use the secular world's naturalistic assumptions and interpretations of physical evidence to reinterpret God's Word to make it fit with some parts, or all, of the evolutionary story about the past. Thus, I contend, regardless of any sincere intentions to the contrary, they are undermining the authority of the Word of God. And in reality, the issue of the age of the earth for Christians comes down to one of authority. Who is the ultimate authority, God or man, or what is the final authority, God's Word or man's word?

Historical Roots of the Idea of Millions of Years and Evolution

Naturalism's control of science did not begin with Darwin's ideas of evolution but over fifty years earlier with the idea of millions of years in geology. In the late eighteenth and early nineteenth centuries deist and atheist and many professing Christian scientists attempted to unravel the history of the rocks and fossils by explicitly or implicitly rejecting the truth of Genesis 1–11 and using (knowingly or unknowingly) the assumptions of naturalism.[28] One of the most influential men was James Hutton in Scotland, considered by many to be the father of modern geology.[29] He wrote,

> The past history of our globe must be explained by what can be seen to be happening now. . . . No powers are to be employed that are not natural to the globe, no action to be admitted except those of which we know the principle.[30]

28. See Terry Mortenson, *The Great Turning Point: The Church's Catastrophic Mistake on Geology—Before Darwin* (Green Forest, AR: Master Books, 2004).

29. See for example, Jack Repcheck, *The Man Who Found Time: James Hutton and the Discovery of the Earth's Antiquity* (Cambridge: Perseus Publishing, 2003).

30. Quoted in A. Holmes, *Principles of Physical Geology*, 2nd ed. (Edinburgh, Scotland: Nelson, 1965), 43–44.

By insisting on this "rule" of geological reasoning, he ruled out creation and the flood before he ever looked at the geological evidence. Neither the events of the creation week (Gen 1) nor the flood (Gen 6–8) were happening when he wrote those words. But also, the creation week was a series of supernatural, divine acts, and the flood was initiated and attended by supernatural acts of God.[31] So Hutton was ruling out the supernatural from his theory of earth history, not because of scientific evidence but because of his anti-biblical (deistic or atheistic—historians aren't sure) worldview. Elsewhere Hutton wrote, "But, surely, general deluges form no part of the theory of the earth; for, the purpose of this earth is evidently to maintain vegetable and animal life, and not to destroy them."[32] He ruled out the global flood and insisted on slow, gradual erosion and sedimentation to explain the rock record because he was reasoning that the present is the key to the past. This is a fundamental error, for the totally trustworthy eyewitness testimony of the Creator in His Word is the key to understanding both the past and the present.

The Oxford-trained, lawyer-turned-geologist Charles Lyell built on the anti-biblical, uniformitarian, naturalistic foundation of Hutton's ideas in his highly influential, three-volume *Principles of Geology* (1830–1833). Lyell remarked,

> I have always been strongly impressed with the weight of an observation of an excellent writer and skillful geologist who said that "for the sake of revelation as well as of science—of truth in every form—the physical part of Geological inquiry ought to be conducted as if the Scriptures were not in existence."[33]

To a fellow uniformitarian geologist, he wrote in a private letter that he wanted to "free the science [of geology] from Moses."[34] In other words, he wanted to silence God's eyewitness testimony about origins.

---

31. God's supernatural activity in the flood account is clearly seen at least in God bring the animals to Noah in the Ark (Gen 7:8–9), the initiation of the unleashing of the waters on the same day (Gen 7:11), and the beginning of the receding of the floodwaters by stopping those same sources of waters (Gen 8:2).

32. James Hutton, *Theory of the Earth* (Edinburgh, Scotland: William Creech, 1795), 1:273.

33. Charles Lyell, Lecture II at King's College London on May 4, 1832, quoted in Martin J. S. Rudwick, "Charles Lyell Speaks in the Lecture Theatre," *The British Journal for the History of Science*, vol. IX, pt. 2, no. 32 (July 1976): 150.

34. Charles Lyell, quoted in Katherine Lyell, *Life, Letters and Journals of Sir Charles Lyell, Bart* (London: John Murray, 1881), 1:268.

To develop their anti-biblical view of earth history, Lyell and Hutton used the naturalistic assumptions described above and also the uniformitarian assumption that all the processes of geological change (erosion, sedimentation, volcanoes, earthquakes, etc.) have always happened in the past at the same *rate*, *frequency*, and *power* as we observe today on average per year. Creation and the flood were rejected for philosophical and religious reasons, not because of anything they saw in the rocks and fossils. The highly regarded historian of geology, Martin Rudwick, has observed,

> Traditionally, non-biblical sources, whether natural or historical, had received their true meaning by being fitted into the unitary narrative of the Bible. This relationship now began to be reversed: the biblical narrative, it was now claimed, received its true meaning by being fitted, on the authority of self-styled experts, into a framework of non-biblical knowledge. In this way the cognitive plausibility and religious meaning of the biblical narrative could only be maintained in a form that was constrained increasingly by non-biblical considerations. . . . At least in Europe, if not in America, those geologists who regarded themselves as Christians generally accepted the new biblical criticism and therefore felt the age of the earth to be irrelevant to their religious beliefs.[35]

The great Harvard geologist Stephen Jay Gould added,

> Charles Lyell was a lawyer by profession, and his book [*Principles of Geology*] is one of the most brilliant briefs ever published by an advocate . . . Lyell relied upon true bits of cunning to establish his uniformitarian views as the only true geology. First, he set up a straw man to demolish . . . In fact, the catastrophists were much more empirically minded than Lyell. The geologic record does seem to require catastrophes: rocks are fractured and contorted; whole faunas are wiped out. To circumvent this literal

---

35. Martin, J. S. Rudwick, "The Shape and Meaning of Earth History," in *God and Nature*, eds. David C. Lindberg and Ronald L. Numbers (Berkley, CA: University of California Press, 1986), 306, 311.

appearance, Lyell imposed his imagination upon the evidence. The geologic record, he argued, is extremely imperfect and we must interpolate into it what we can reasonably infer but cannot see. The catastrophists were the hard-nosed empiricists of their day, not the blinded theological apologists.[36]

Actually, the old-earth catastrophists of the early nineteenth century (some of whom were professing Christians) were not the really hard-nosed empiricists of their day; rather it was the geologically competent scriptural geologists who were not only hard-nosed by the geological evidence but hard-nosed by God's eyewitness testimony, as Mortenson has documented.[37]

Commenting on gradualism (another name for uniformitarian naturalism), Gould and fellow evolutionist Niles Eldredge candidly admit, "The general preference that so many of us hold for gradualism is a metaphysical stance embedded in the modern history of Western cultures: it is not a high-order empirical observation, induced from the objective study of nature."[38] The development of the idea of millions of years of earth history was not, as the scientific majority wants us to believe, the result of the unbiased, objective pursuit of truth and interpretation of the empirical evidence. Anti-biblical worldview assumptions were massively influential.

Darwin applied the same principles to biology: slow, gradual, natural processes will explain the origin of living creatures, including man. In fact, he wrote,

He who can read Sir Charles Lyell's grand work on the *Principles of Geology*, which the future historian will recognize as having produced a revolution in natural science, yet does not admit how incomprehensibly vast have been the past periods of time, may at once close this volume.[39]

36. Stephen Jay Gould, "Catastrophes and Steady-State Earth," *Natural History* (Feb. 1975): 15–17.

37. Mortenson, *The Great Turning Point*.

38. Stephen Jay Gould and Niles Eldredge, "Punctuated Equilibria: The Tempo and Mode of Evolution Reconsidered," *Paleobiology* 3 (1977): 145.

39. Charles Darwin, *The Origin of Species*, repr. of 1859 1st ed. (London: Penguin Books, 1985), 293.

Furthermore, he admitted,

> I always feel as if my books came half out of Lyell's brains and that I never acknowledge this sufficiently, nor do I know how I can, without saying so in so many words—for I have always thought that the great merit of the *Principles* [*of Geology*], was that it altered the whole tone of one's mind & therefore that when seeing a thing never seen by Lyell, one yet saw it partially through his eyes.[40]

Astronomers have applied the same assumptions in their hypotheses about the evolution of stars, galaxies, and the solar system. Science has been controlled by an anti-biblical philosophical/religious worldview for almost two hundred years.[41]

Geological Evidence for Global Flood and Young Earth

Davis Young is professor emeritus of geology at Calvin College. He has greatly influenced many Christians, including seminary professors and pastors, to accept millions of years of evolution. Regarding the Grand Canyon and geology, he says,

> If rocks are historical documents, we are driven to the related conclusion that the available evidence is overwhelmingly opposed to the notion that the Noahic flood deposited rocks of the Colorado Plateau only a few thousand years ago. . . . The Christian who believes that the idea of an ancient earth is unbiblical would do better to deny the validity of any kind of historical geology and insist that the rocks must be the product of pure miracle rather than try to explain them in terms of the flood. An examination of the earth apart from ideological presuppositions is bound to lead to the conclusion that it is ancient.[42]

---

40. Charles Darwin, *The Correspondence of Charles Darwin, Vol. 3* (Cambridge: Cambridge University Press, 1987), 55.

41. For more on these historical developments see Mortenson, *The Great Turning Point*, and his article, https://answersingenesis.org/age-of-the-earth/are-philosophical-naturalism-and-age-of-the-earth-related/.

42. Davis A. Young, "The Discovery of Terrestrial History," in *Portraits of Creation*, Howard J. Van Till, Robert E. Snow, John H. Stek, and Davis A. Young (Grand Rapids: Eerdmans, 1990), 80–81.

But there is no such thing as "an examination of the earth apart from ideological presuppositions." Every scientist has a worldview, which affects the observations and the interpretation of the evidence. Creation geologists don't invoke a miracle to explain how the flood caused the layers of the Grand Canyon. Rather, they reject the presuppositions that Young and secular geologists use to interpret the evidence. The evidence for the flood has been there all along, but most scientists don't see it because of their anti-biblical assumptions.

Derek Ager, a prominent twentieth-century evolutionary geologist, commented on the influence of Lyell on geology and sheds light on this point:

> Just as politicians rewrite human history, so geologists rewrite earth history. For a century and a half the geological world has been dominated, one might even say brainwashed, by the gradualistic uniformitarianism of Charles Lyell. Any suggestion of "catastrophic" events has been rejected as old-fashioned, unscientific and even laughable.[43]

He added,

> Perhaps I am becoming a cynic in my old age, but I cannot help thinking that people find things that they expect to find. As Sir Edward Bailey (1953) said, "to find a thing you have to believe it to be possible."[44]

Having visited over fifty countries, studying geological formations, Ager saw plenty of evidence for major catastrophes. But because of his rejection of the truth of Genesis 1–11 and disbelief in Noah's flood, he never saw the evidence for the unique, catastrophic, yearlong, earth-altering, global flood. Most geologists before and after Ager (including most Christian geologists) have missed the evidence for the flood for the very same reason.

The evidence is all over the earth. It includes marine fossils on the tops

---

43. Derek Ager, *The New Catastrophism* (Cambridge: Cambridge University Press, 1993), xi.
44. Ibid., 190–91.

of our mountain ranges and massive lava deposits on a scale far greater than we see today. We observe the absence of evidence of slow chemical and physical erosion at the boundaries between sedimentary layers (as we would expect if millions of years passed between the deposition of one layer and the deposition of the next layer). The lateral extent of many thick layers is continental or even sometimes intercontinental in scale.

Fossilized plants and animals (many in exquisite detail and some with no hard parts, such as worms or jelly fish) must have been buried and fossilized quickly (dead animals along a highway don't become fossilized because they are eaten by scavengers and subjected to other decay processes). This means that the rock layers that entomb these fossils had to be deposited rapidly. All over the world, often in association with coal deposits, there are upright fossil trees that cut through many layers of rock showing that the layers were deposited rapidly before the trees could rot. There is also soft tissue found in dinosaur fossils and blood in the abdomens of fossilized mosquitos.[45]

We see multiple rock layers bent like a stack of pancakes that slid off the side of a plate. In the Grand Canyon the whole mile-thick sequence of sandstones, shales, and limestones, which are claimed by evolutionists to represent 300 million years, are bent the same way with no evidence of the type of expected breaking or metamorphism, indicating that the layers were still relatively soft and wet when the earthquake occurred that bent the layers. Hard rock can be bent without breaking under great heat and pressure, but when this happens the rock is metamorphosed at the bend. Instead, creation geologists note that the many examples of folded rock layers show no evidence of major cracking or metamorphism.[46]

All of this and more is powerful geological and paleontological evidence of the reality of the flood of Noah's day described in Genesis 6–8 and affirmed as literally true by Jesus (Matt 24:37–39) and the apostle Peter (1 Pet 3:20, 2 Pet 5–6, 2 Pet 3:3–7).

---

45. Kevin Anderson, *Echoes of the Jurassic* (Chino Valley, AZ: CRS Books, 2016).

46. This and other evidences are explained and illustrated by Andrew Snelling in the DVDs available from Answers in Genesis: https://answersingenesis.org/store/product/geology-set/?sku=90-7-791. For more depth, see Snelling's two-volume, 1128-page *Earth's Catastrophic Past*. Dr. Snelling has a PhD in geology from the University of Sydney in Australia, and has done geological research in the Grand Canyon and on four continents. He is Director of Research at Answers in Genesis.

We are told that radiometric dating methods have proven that the igneous and sedimentary rock layers (like we see exposed in the Grand Canyon but are on every continent) are millions of years old. However, there are many good scientific (as well as biblical) reasons not to believe those dates. They are based on the same naturalistic uniformitarian assumptions controlling the rest of science, and there are many published examples of rocks of known age giving dates of hundreds of thousands or millions of years that human eyewitnesses saw form only decades or centuries ago.[47]

Created Kinds, Not Microbe-to-Microbiologist Evolution

Concerning the creation of animal and plant kinds, Genesis says God created distinct "kinds" (Hebrew *min*) of plants and animals. Creation scientists think, based on published evidence of successful breeding, that the created kinds are primarily equivalent to the *family* (not *species* or *genus*) in the modern classification system. Darwin didn't have the supposed evidence of one kind changing into another. It is true that new species can be seen to form—but only within each kind. Speciation is not evolution in the molecules-to-man sense—no new information is added into the genome of the type needed to change one kind of creature into another kind, i.e., to prove microbe-to-microbiologist evolution.[48]

Scientific Challenges

Although many other questions (e.g., about ape-men, the big bang, etc.) can be answered in detail, young-earth creation scientists don't have all the answers to their questions. But God's Word gives us the key truths

47. See the four-part online free video lecture by Andrew Snelling: https://answersin genesis.org/media/video/age-of-the-earth/radiocarbon-dating/. Also, see Andrew Snelling, "Radiometric Dating: Problems with the Assumptions," https://answersingenesis.org/geology/radiometric-dating/radiometric-dating-problems-with-the-assumptions/; Snelling, "Radioisotope Dating of Rocks in the Grand Canyon," https://answersingenesis.org/geology/radiometric-dating/radioisotope-dating-of-rocks-in-the-grand-canyon/; and Snelling, "Significance of Highly Discordant Radioisotope Dates for Precambrian Amphibolites in Grand Canyon, USA," https://answersingenesis.org/geology/grand-canyon-facts/radioisotope-dates-for -precambrian-amphibolites-in-grand-canyon/, originally published in the 2008 *Proceedings of the Sixth International Conference on Creationism*, 407–24, and the resources in the previous footnote.

48. For more on this point see Georgia Purdom, "Evidence of New Genetic Information?" https://answersingenesis.org/genetics/mutations/evidence-of-new-genetic-information/; "Nylon-eating Bacteria Again," https://answersingenesis.org/blogs/georgia-purdom/2012/03/01/nylon-eating-bacteria-again/; and "Bacteria Evolve 'Key Innovation' or Not?" https://answersin genesis.org/blogs/georgia-purdom/2012/11/08/bacteria-evolve-key-innovation-or-not/.

they need to pursue those answers as they do ongoing scientific research. Two of the most challenging questions are these. One, how can we see the light from stars and galaxies that are millions of light-years away, if the universe is only a little more than six thousand years old? Creation physicists and astrophysicists are working on a number of models to deal with this question within a young-earth biblical framework, but none of them have been (and perhaps ever can be) shown to be demonstrably correct. But these creation scientists point out that the evolutionists[49] also have an equally difficult and unresolved light travel-time problem. Called the "horizon problem," it is that even given 13.8 billion years for the age of the universe there has not been enough time for the light to get equally distributed to produce the uniform background radiation temperature (2.7 degrees Kelvin) that is observed everywhere astronomers look.[50] Second, creation scientists are doing more research to discover what radioactive isotopes are telling us since they are not giving us the true age of rocks. AiG geologist Dr. Andrew Snelling is working on research on this topic.[51] There are plenty of other questions in biol-

49. Some readers may object that light travel-time doesn't have anything to do with evolution. But as an examination of even just the covers and contents of many secular astronomy and geology textbooks will show, astrophysicists speak of "stellar evolution," "galactic evolution," and geologists speak of the "evolution of the earth." Like biological evolution, these other stories about the past are based on the assumption that everything can be explained by time, chance, and the laws of nature working on matter. The big bang theory is an evolutionary story about the origin of the universe.

50. Jason Lisle, "Does Distant Starlight Prove the Universe Is Old?" in *The New Answers Book 1*, ed. Ken Ham (Green Forest, AR: Master Books, 2006), 245–54.

51. This series of technical papers demonstrates from the conventional literature that the decay rates of all these radioactive isotopes used conventionally to date rocks as millions and billions of years old have actually been all calibrated (or adjusted) so the ages derived from them agree with the ^{238}U decay (U-Pb) ages. See "Determination of the Radioisotope Decay Constants and Half-Lives: Rubidium-87 (^{87}Rb)," *Answers Research Journal* 7 (2014): 311–22, https://answersingenesis.org/geology/radiometric-dating/determination-radioisotope-decay-constants-and-half-lives-rubidium-87–87rb/; "Determination of the Radioisotope Decay Constants and Half-Lives: Lutetium-176 (^{176}Lu)," *ARJ* 7 (2014): 483–97, https://answersingenesis.org/geology/radiometric-dating/determination-radioisotope-decay-constants-and-half-lives-lutetium-176/; "Determination of the Radioisotope Decay Constants and Half-Lives: Rhenium-187 (^{187}Re)," *ARJ* 8 (2015): 93–111, https://answersingenesis.org/geology/radiometric-dating/determination-radioisotope-decay-constants-and-half-lives-rhenium-187/; "Determination of the Radioisotope Decay Constants and Half-Lives: Samarium-147 (^{147}Sm)," *ARJ* 8 (2015): 305–21, https://answersingenesis.org/geology/radiometric-dating/determination-radioisotope-decay-constants-and-half-lives-samarium-147/; "Determination of the Radioisotope Decay Constants and Half-lives: Potassium-40 (^{40}K)," *ARJ* 9 (2016): 171–96, https://answersingenesis.org/geology/radiometric-dating/determination-radioisotope-decay-constants-half-lives-potassium-40/; "Determination of the Radioisotope Decay Constants and Half-lives: Uranium-238 (^{238}U) and Uranium-235 (^{235}U)," *ARJ* (in preparation).

ogy, geology, and astronomy to explore as well within the interpretative framework of the eyewitness testimony of the Creator.

Why Genesis Matters

A Gospel Issue

The Bible calls death an "enemy" (1 Cor 15:26). When God clothed Adam and Eve with coats of skins (Gen 3:21), a good case can be made that this was the first death—the death and bloodshed of an animal. Elsewhere in Scripture we learn that without the shedding of blood there is no remission of sins (Heb 9:22), and the life of the flesh is in the blood (Lev 17:11). Because Adam sinned, a payment for sin was needed. Because death was the penalty for sin, death and bloodshed were needed to atone for sin. So, Genesis 3:21 would describe the first blood sacrifice as a penalty for sin—looking forward to the one who would be the Lamb of God (John 1:29) to die "once for all" (Heb 10:10–14) so that everyone who trusts in Him would be forgiven and receive eternal life.

The Israelites sacrificed animals over and over again as a ceremonial covering for sin. But Hebrews 10:4 tells us that the blood of bulls and goats cannot take away our sin—we are not physically related to animals. We needed a perfect human sacrifice. So, all this animal sacrifice was looking forward to the one called the Messiah (Jesus Christ).

Now if there were millions of years of death and bloodshed of innocent animals before Adam's fall, then how could substitutionary animal death be a covering for sin after the fall? If all that supposed death before the fall was declared by God to be "very good," how can animal sacrifice after the fall be associated with forgiveness of sin? Any old-earth scenario makes nonsense of the doctrine of atonement. Also, if there were death, disease, bloodshed, and suffering before sin, then all that natural evil would be God's fault—not our fault! Why would God require death as a sacrifice for sin if He were the one responsible for death and bloodshed, having created the world with these bad things in place?

Whether they realize it or not, all old-earth proponents in the church have a view of death and natural evil that is irreconcilable with the Bible's teaching about the pre-fall creation, the curse on the creation at the fall, and the future removal of that curse at the second coming of

Jesus Christ (Rev 22:3). Put simply, all old-earth views put death before man. The Bible has man before death.

One of today's most-asked questions is how Christians can believe in a loving God with so much death and suffering in the world. The correct answer is that God's just curse because of Adam's sin resulted in this death and suffering in both the human and non-human creation. We are to blame. God is not an unloving or incompetent Creator of a "very bad" world. He is an absolutely good God who made a "very good" world, which He justly cursed because of man's rebellion. God had a loving plan from eternity to rescue people from sin and its consequence of eternal separation from God in hell and to restore and redeem the whole creation ruined by sin (Acts 3:21; Col 1:15–20).

So, to believe in millions of years is a gospel issue. This belief ultimately impugns the character of the Creator and Savior and undermines the foundation of the soul-saving gospel.

A Salvation Issue?

But the age of the creation is not a salvation issue. Many Christians do believe in millions of years and are truly born again. Their belief in millions of years doesn't affect their own salvation and may not affect their daily Christian life. But it does affect *other* people, such as their children or people they teach in church or unbelieving friends, neighbors, and work associates whom they attempt to evangelize. When a Christian doesn't believe Genesis but accepts what the scientific majority says about the age of the creation, it sends a message to others that you can pick and choose which parts of the Bible to believe. The old-earth Christian's example becomes a stumbling block to others. For instance, telling young people they can reinterpret Genesis to fit in millions of years sets a deadly example: Rather than interpreting Scripture in context and by comparing Scripture with Scripture, they can start outside Scripture with some human authority (e.g., the majority view among scientists or theologians, or their favorite Christian leader) and use their views to add ideas into Scripture.

Over time such people can (and many do) get the idea that the Bible is not God's infallible Word. This creates doubt in God's Word—and doubt often leads to unbelief. Eventually they can reject Scripture altogether. Since the gospel comes from a book they don't trust or believe is true, they can easily reject the gospel itself.

What the great nineteenth-century evolutionist, T. H. Huxley, who coined the term "agnostic" to describe his view, said in 1893 has been repeated by other unbelievers in briefer words ever since:

I am fairly at a loss to comprehend how any one, for a moment, can doubt that Christian theology must stand or fall with the historical trustworthiness of the Jewish Scriptures. The very conception of the Messiah, or Christ, is inextricably interwoven with Jewish history; the identification of Jesus of Nazareth with that Messiah rests upon the interpretation of the passages of the Hebrew Scriptures which have no evidential value unless they possess the historical character assigned to them. If the covenant with Abraham was not made; if circumcision and sacrifices were not ordained by Jahveh; if the "ten words" [i.e., Ten Commandments] were not written by God's hand on the stone tables; if Abraham is more or less a mythical hero, such as Theseus; the Story of the Deluge a fiction; that of the fall a legend; and that of the creation the dream of a seer; if all these definite and detailed narratives of apparently real events have no more value as history than have the stories of the regal period of Rome—what is to be said about the Messianic doctrine, which is so much less clearly enunciated: And what about the authority of the writers of the books of the New Testament, who, on this theory, have not merely accepted flimsy fictions for solid truths, but have built the very foundations of Christian dogma upon legendary quicksands?[52]

So, the age of the earth and universe is not a salvation issue per se—somebody can be saved even without believing what the Bible says on this issue. But it is a salvation issue indirectly. Christians who compromise with evolution and/or millions of years are, contrary to their intentions, encouraging others toward unbelief concerning God's Word and the gospel.

---

52. Thomas H. Huxley, *Science and Hebrew Tradition* (New York: D. Appleton, 1893), 207–08. See http://infidels.org/library/modern/mathew/sn-huxley.html for Huxley's explanation of his view and the invention of the word "agnostic."

Conclusion

The Bible clearly teaches young-earth creation and that was the almost-universal belief of the church until the beginning of the nineteenth century. It is historic Christian orthodoxy[53] and all old-earth creationist and theistic evolutionist views are relatively recent novelties. And a small but growing number of PhD scientists in biology, genetics, geology, and astronomy/physics (many of whom were once evolutionists or didn't believe Genesis regarding the global flood and the age of the creation) believe that the scientific evidence overwhelmingly confirms the literal truth of Genesis 1–11.[54]

Over the last two hundred years most Christians have tried one of various ways to harmonize the Bible with evolution and/or millions of years. During that time the once Christian West (Western Europe, Great Britain, and North America) has not become more Christian or more open to the gospel but has become increasingly morally and spiritually wicked and opposed to the gospel. Also, much of the church in the West has become spiritually and doctrinally corrupt as the cultures have become controlled by an atheistic, naturalistic worldview. And as I and other AiG speakers know from lecturing in over forty countries on every continent and from AiG's website being visited by people in over one hundred countries, cosmological, geological, and biological evolution have become a major impediment to the gospel in all other countries of the world as well. People reason that if the opening chapters of Genesis

---

53. Someone might object that Christian orthodoxy is reflected in the ecumenical creeds (e.g., Apostles' Creed, Nicene Creed, and Athanasian Creed) and none of them say anything about the how and when of creation or the extent, nature, and duration of Noah's flood. So, it is contended, this is not part of Christian orthodoxy. But this is a mistaken view for these creeds, which, though an important witness to some truths of orthodox Christianity, were written to address specific issues at those times and they do not summarize all the truths that orthodox Christians believed and that are important. For example, none of them mention the miracles that Jesus did, nor do they refer to the church's universal belief that the Bible is the inspired Word of God. Similarly, they do not mention belief in a young earth and global flood, for the simple fact that this was not a point of disagreement among Bible-believing Christians until the nineteenth century. See Mortenson, *The Great Turning Point*, 40–44. See also the comment of the old-earth geologist Davis Young, "It cannot be denied, in spite of frequent interpretations of Genesis 1 that departed from the rigidly literal, that the almost universal view of the Christian world until the eighteenth century was that the earth was only a few thousand years old." Davis A. Young, *Christianity and the Age of the Earth* (Thousand Oaks, CA: Artisan Sales, 1988), 25, with similar statements on pp. 13, 20, 22, and 39.

54. For a partial list of modern and historical creation scientists see https://answersin genesis.org/creation-scientists/.

are not truly historical (as many non-believers think the biblical author clearly intended to be understood), then why trust the rest of the Bible, including its morality, the gospel, and its teachings about the end of the world?

By contrast, where creationist apologetics (both biblical and scientific) have been taught well in families and churches, adults and children have been strengthened in their faith in and submission to God's Word and emboldened in their witness. And many lost people have come to faith in Jesus Christ after seeing that the scientific evidence actually confirms the literal historical truth of Genesis 1–11. They conclude that the gospel is true because the historical foundations of the gospel are true.

Soon after Darwin's *The Descent of Man* (1871), many in the church were not only accepting evolution as the explanation for the origin of plants and animals, but many also began to reject the supernatural creation of Adam from dust and Eve from his rib. By the 1880s the then editor of a Christian journal estimated that "perhaps a quarter, perhaps a half of the educated ministers in our leading Evangelical denominations" believed "that the story of the creation and fall of man, told in Genesis, is no more the record of actual occurrences than is the parable of the Prodigal Son."[55]

So here is the progression of compromise over the past two hundred years. First, the church accepted that the earth is millions of years old but insisted that plants and animals were supernaturally created (not evolved) and that Adam was created supernaturally by God about six thousand years ago. Then came the view that the earth is old and animals and plants evolved over millions of years but that God created Adam and Eve about six thousand years ago. Later, many Christians insisted that Adam was supernaturally created but long before six thousand years ago. Others said that Adam's body evolved from some lower animal, which changed into a human by the infusion of the divine image. Now we have professing evangelicals who claim to believe in inerrancy and yet believe that Adam never existed as an individual but rather mankind evolved spiritually and physically from some ape-like creatures over the course of tens of thousands of years.

---

55. Quoted in Ronald Numbers, *The Creationists* (New York: Alfred A. Knopf, 1992), 3.

The church's compromise with millions of years opened the door to further compromise of biblical truth over the next two centuries, including the current growing denial of a literal Adam and a literal fall. Once the slippery slide started on the age of the earth, there was no stopping the theological compromise, except with those who returned to the supreme authority of Scripture and believed God rather than the majority of scientists. The claim of millions of years is the foundation of this current battle about Adam and also of the controversy in our culture over marriage, gender, and sex. We cannot with any exegetical or hermeneutical consistency argue that there are only two genders (male and female) assigned by God as a gift at conception and that marriage is one man and one woman for life and that sex is only for within marriage, if there was no literal Adam and Eve, whose creation is described in Genesis 1–2. But we can't just contend for a literal Adam, critical as that is. We must also contend for a young earth because the same Word of God that teaches a literal Adam and literal fall also teaches that the whole creation is only a little more than six thousand years old.[56]

---

56. https://answersingenesis.org/who-is-god/god-is-good/the-god-of-an-old-earth/.

HUGH ROSS

I agree with much of what Ham has written. I'm utterly convinced, as he is, that the Bible is "God's infallible [and inerrant] Word." I uphold "the supreme authority of Scripture." I believe Genesis 1–11 communicates "literal historical truth," and "scientific evidence overwhelmingly confirms the literal truth of Genesis 1–11." Genesis 1, as I see it, clearly describes a chronology of supernatural events that occurred in history. I agree the creation days are "sequential and non-overlapping," and that Genesis 1 tells us "how and when He [God] created."

Ham and I also share the view that presenting scientific evidence for the historical accuracy of Genesis 1–11 is an effective way to bring people to faith in Christ. Both of us would say that "to believe in inerrancy and yet believe Adam never existed as an individual" (p. 48) seems contradictory. Like Ham, I'm convinced that Noah's flood inundated more than just Mesopotamia and, indeed, wiped out all humans except those on the ark.

Nevertheless, my literal interpretation of the Bible's inerrant creation texts differs from Ham's on multiple points. In this limited space, I can only offer some examples:

1. I see the surface of Earth's waters (Gen 1:2) as the frame of reference for the six creation days' narrative.
2. Unlike Ham, I believe Hebrew poetry and imagery convey explicit truths about creation history. For example, Job 38:8–9 says God "wrapped it [the sea] in thick darkness," making "the clouds its garment." Job affirms, here, an opaque primordial atmosphere, not the sun's nonexistence, caused darkness "over the surface of the deep."

3. An integration of Genesis, Job, and Psalms leads me to believe that Earth's atmosphere was opaque before day one, became translucent on day one, and then became transparent, at least occasionally, from day four onward, not that the sun was created on day four. This sequence aligns with life's needs. Earth's first life needs light for photosynthesis. The animals created after day four need lights in the sky as "signs" to regulate their complex biological clocks. The text reaffirms that God made the sun, moon, and stars.

4. I concur with Hebrew scholar Jack Collins[1] that Genesis 1:1–2's sentence structure implies time passed between the initial creation event and the "formless and void" Earth, and between the primordial earth and the first creation day.

5. While Ham asserts, "the creation gives a confusing message about the Creator" (p. 19), I disagree, citing Romans 1:20: "God's invisible qualities—his eternal power and divine nature—have been clearly seen, being understood from what has been made."

6. Ham says "creation is cursed" and by itself cannot be trusted to reveal truth. This assertion contradicts Romans 1, Psalm 19, and many other passages. When sin entered the world through Adam, humanity's sinfulness became the scourge of Earth. As Genesis 3:17 states, "Cursed is the ground because of you." Humanity changed, not the physical laws God established in the beginning. The laws of nature were designed from the outset to serve God's redemptive purpose and plan, put into effect before the beginning of time.

7. Ham views Exodus 20:11 as an "insurmountable brick wall" for old-earth creationism, perhaps because the English text says, "For in six days . . ." However, the Hebrew says, "For six days . . ." and uses the verb 'asah ("made, fashioned"), not bara' ("create"). God is portrayed as a divine craftsman. Exodus 20:11 is stating that God fashions the universe, Earth, and life throughout their histories.

8. Ham wonders why God would wait millions of years between his creation acts. I believe Job and Psalms provide an answer.

---

1. C. John Collins, *Genesis 1–4: A Linguistic, Literary, and Theological Commentary* (Phillipsburg, NJ: P&R, 2006), 51.

God's plan was to pack Earth with as much life as possible, as diverse as possible, for as long as possible, given unchanging physical laws, so we humans would have the resources (biodeposits) necessary to fulfill the Great Commission in a relatively brief time window.

9. I agree with Ham that God's creation miracles occurred instantaneously, but I disagree they occurred nearly simultaneously. From the text and nature's record, a picture emerges of countless (instantaneous) miracles across billions of years.

10. Ham's insistence on the completeness of the Genesis 5 and 11 genealogies contradicts the research of many conservative biblical scholars.[2] A careful reading of the original Hebrew text reveals that neither genealogy is exhaustive.

11. To equate "the beginning of creation" in Mark 10:6 and "the beginning of the world" in Luke 11:50–51 with the cosmic creation event is to misidentify the context of those verses. In Mark, Jesus referred to the creation of the first human pair, and in Luke, to humanity's story from Abel onward.

12. Ham asserts that if God created over long ages, he would have inspired Moses to use Hebrew words other than *yom*. However, none of the words Ham suggests refers to a specific, finite epoch of time.

On the one hand, Ham claims "humans were eyewitnesses to many of these [creation] events," but on the other he claims they're "unobservable" (p. 31). Adam and Eve were created at the end of the sixth day. They could not have been eyewitnesses to prior creation events. I would add that because the velocity of light is finite and constant, astronomers today actually can witness past events. By observing distant reaches of space, astronomers directly witness the preparatory work God did long before Earth and Adam existed.

Ham's core message is this: "The issue of the age of the earth for Christians comes down to one of authority [of God's Word]" (p. 34). He implies that disagreement with his view denies biblical authority. In making such a statement, he (inadvertently) equates his particular

---

2. Walter C. Kaiser Jr., *Hard Sayings of the Bible* (Downers Grove, IL: InterVarsity Press, 1996), 48–50, 102–104.

interpretation of Genesis with "God's Word." While the text is inerrant, no mere reader of the text can be. Let me add that I, too, fully embrace the authority of God's Word.

The "historical roots of the idea of millions of years" as presented by Ham represents a serious distortion of history. Ancient Christian writings previous to Isaac Newton (who, long before James Hutton and Charles Lyell, explicitly expressed his old-earth interpretation of Genesis 1 in a letter to the king's chaplain in 1681[3]) show that early biblical scholars viewed Earth's age as doctrinally insignificant. Among more than two thousand pages of ancient Christian commentary on Genesis 1, only about two pages address creation's timescale. Some scholars say those two pages endorse a young-earth belief, others an old-earth belief. We can most fairly say they showed tentativeness. The most important point to notice is that the early church fathers remained charitable toward those who held differing views on creation's timescale.

Ham dismisses radiometric dating because certain radiometric dating claims have proven erroneous. Of course, radiometric dates will be inaccurate if misapplied. For accurate dates, samples must fall within an appropriate range: no younger than one-sixth and no older than six times the particular radioisotope's half-life. A large sample size and sample purity are also essential for discerning accurate radiometric dates.

Many young-earth creationist scientists have conceded that if radioisotope half-lives are invariant, the universe and Earth must, in fact, be billions of years old.[4] I believe the Bible itself declares the invariance of physics, and the observable spectra of distant stars and galaxies attest to past constancy. On Earth, physicists measure xenon isotope ratios showing that plutonium was present on the early earth, decaying at the same rate as it does today in nuclear reactors. A natural (now spent) nuclear reactor in Gabon dates back to a time when uranium-235 had not yet decayed to its current low level.

Radiometric dating represents only one of many indicators of Earth's

3. Isaac Newton, "Newton to Burnet," letter 247 in *The Correspondence of Isaac Newton*, ed. H. W. Turnbull, vol. 2, 1676–1687 (Cambridge: Cambridge University Press, 1960), 333; Hugh Ross, *A Matter of Days: Resolving a Creation Controversy*, 2nd ed. (Covina, CA: RTB Press, 2015), 51.

4. Larry Vardiman, Andrew A. Snelling, and Eugene F. Chaffin, eds., *Radioisotopes and the Age of the Earth* (El Cajon, CA: Institute for Creation Research, 2000), 42–44, 306–07, 312–13, 316–18, 334–37, 374, http://www.icr.org/i/pdf/research/rate-all.pdf.

age.[5] The Dome C Antarctic ice core shows us eight hundred thousand annual layers, confirmed to be annual by the dust signatures of volcanic eruptions with known historical dates. The cores reveal eight cycles of the one-hundred-thousand-year variation in the eccentricity of Earth's orbit. Sediment cores provide a continuous record of Earth's orbital cycles over the past 3.9 million years. The sheer quantity of Earth's biodeposits indicates life has existed on Earth at near maximum possible abundance for at least several hundred million years.

I am encouraged by Ham's acknowledgment of the problem of distant galaxy light. However, he's mistaken in claiming old-earth creationists lack a solution to "the horizon problem." Cosmic inflation solves it. Cosmic inflation is an expected outcome of the symmetry breaking that occurs when (due to cosmic cooling) the strong-electroweak force separates into the strong nuclear force and the electroweak force. An unmistakable signature of cosmic inflation is the scalar spectral index of radiation left over from the creation event. The most accurate measurement to date leaves no reasonable doubt that a cosmic inflation event occurred.[6]

Ham wonders why marine fossils exist on Mount Everest if Noah's flood was not global. The answer is the Himalayas were once sea floor crumpled by the tectonic collision between the Indian subcontinent and Asia.

Ham thinks a world with "death, disease, bloodshed, and suffering before sin" is "a very bad world," a world God would never call "very good" (p. 44). God certainly could have created a world with no death, disease, or pain. However, that would be a world where humans either lack free will (with no possibility for love) or continually face the awful risk of rebellion. God's goal was to give humans a realm in which love is real, and by his loving intervention sin and evil could be permanently conquered and eliminated while keeping free will intact. The new creation (Rev 21)—where free will is safe because it's already been tested by the strongest possible temptation—is his ultimate plan.

Animal predation, as awful as it may seem, serves a beneficial purpose. Studies show, for example, that herbivore herds thrive in the

---

5. For documentation of the following evidences and many more see my book, *A Matter of Days: Resolving a Creation Controversy*, 2nd ed. (Covina, CA: RTB Press, 2015).

6. A. T. Crites et al., "Measurements of E-Mode Polarization and Temperature-E-Mode Correlation in the Cosmic Microwave Background from 100 Square Degrees of SPTpol Data," *Astrophysical Journal* 805 (May 2015): id. 36, doi:10.1088/0004-637X/805/1/36.

presence of carnivores and deteriorate without them. We haven't yet entered the new creation.

As I explain in my book *Why the Universe Is the Way It Is*, God has good reasons for creating gravity, electromagnetism, the nuclear forces, and thermodynamics. Yes, these physical laws result in death and decay, but they critically serve his ultimate plan to conquer and eliminate sin and evil. Similarly, what we often refer to as natural "evils" actually prove beneficial to humanity. Earthquakes, hurricanes, and wildfires, for example, all serve good purposes where God designed the number and intensity of these events to maximize the good outcomes.

Suffering, too, which no one tends to welcome, also serves God's good purposes, assisting our growth and the advance of his kingdom. His people are not immune to the pain and heartache nonbelievers face, but his grace allows us to glorify him in the midst of suffering—a compelling witness. The trials we experience as our character is molded into greater Christlikeness can even bring us "pure joy," according to James 1:2.

I find most ironic Ham's claim that old-earth creationism "creates doubt in God's Word" (p. 45). Throughout my forty-three years as a pastor and evangelist, I've seen the opposite. My own story and countless others contradict this claim. The more closely I studied the world of nature, the more reasons I found for complete confidence in the truth of his Word.

DEBORAH B. HAARSMA

I'm grateful for this first opportunity to interact directly with Ken Ham and the views of Answers in Genesis (AiG) on Young Earth creationism (YEC). Not all young-earth creationists share all the views of AiG, and I will indicate my responses accordingly.

YEC and EC agree on the core of the Christian faith.

Evolutionary creationism (EC) joins with YEC in believing that the God of the Bible is the creator of the entire universe and that Jesus Christ is the only path to salvation. Often Ham has labeled evolutionary creationists as "compromised Christians," so it was good to see Ham affirm here that "the age of the creation is not a salvation issue. Many Christians do believe in millions of years and are truly born again" (p. 44) and that evolutionary creationists have "sincere intentions" (p. 34).

American society is facing serious problems, but evolutionary science is not the cause.

The causes of sin and injustice are serious and complex, arising from worldviews dominated by selfishness, pride, and relativism, as well as atheistic scientism. Some atheists falsely cite science to justify immoral behavior or rejection of God, and such claims need to be soundly rejected by all Christians. However, science itself does not make these worldview claims, and evolutionary science, like other science areas, can be seen from a thoroughly Christian perspective. Evolution*ism* must be rejected, but evolutionary science does not destroy the foundations of Christian faith; no scientific discovery can.

Answers in Genesis falsely portrays the views and practices of scientists.

Sadly, Ham and AiG repeat falsehoods on important points. It is simply false to claim that "the scientific evidence confirming the literal

55

truth of Genesis 1–11 is overwhelming and increasing with time" (p. 31). In fact, the scientific evidence is overwhelmingly and increasingly against the young-earth creation view. While Ham claims that evolution and an old earth are the result of "anti-biblical" worldviews among scientists (p. 35), the fact is that scientists of many cultures and worldviews have reviewed and accepted this evidence on its merits.[1] Ham's discussion of the early geologists fails to mention early Christian geologists who went into the field with no anti-Christian bias, even seeking a young earth and global flood, and were convinced otherwise by the evidence in God's creation.[2] Jesus commands us to love our scientist neighbors and share the gospel with them, which is hard to square with misrepresenting their work and accusing them of unprofessional bias. Other young-earth creationists avoid such blanket falsehoods about science and the scientific community while still arguing for a young earth.[3]

Historical science is reliable and integrally tied to experimental and observational science.

AiG believes that historical science is fundamentally different and less reliable than experimental science. But historical and experimental sciences are closely tied together. For example, astronomical observations of gasses in galaxies, the light of which originated millions of years ago, are regularly compared to lab experiments on similar gasses today. Genetic methods that have proven reliable in studying today's cancer are the same methods used to measure genetic changes in evolution.[4]

Theological concerns about death and suffering have better answers than rejecting established science.

See my initial essay and references therein for more on this important point.

---

1. Ninety-nine percent of biologists accept that humans evolved. Pew Research Center, "An Elaboration of AAAS Scientists' Views," July 23, 2015, http://www.pewinternet.org/2015/07/23/an-elaboration-of-aaas-scientists-views/.

2. See Davis Young and Ralph Stearley, *The Bible, Rocks, and Time* (Downer's Grove, IL: InterVarsity Press 2008).

3. Including two whom I have joined for on-stage dialogues and panel discussions: biologist Todd Wood of the Core Academy of Science and biblical scholar Roy Gane of Andrews University.

4. See S. Joshua Swamidass "Cancer and Evolution," BioLogos blog post, January 11, 2017, http://biologos.org/blogs/guest/cancer-and-evolution.

The YEC interpretation of Genesis ignores the original context and distracts from the original intent.

EC takes the Bible seriously as inspired by God, and thus holy, trustworthy, and authoritative for our lives.[5] Evolutionary creationists emphasize that Scripture was revealed in a pre-scientific context, in which God accommodated his message to the understanding of the people of the time. The Bible is God's revelation *for* people of all times, but it was God's word *to* them before it comes to us. That context is essential. The "most natural reading of Scripture" (p. 18) is not a simple universal meaning—a "natural" reading depends on the culture and mindset that a reader brings to it.

Ham asks, "Who is the ultimate authority, God or man, or what is the final authority, God's Word or man's word?" (p. 34). Of course, all Christians agree that God is the ultimate authority. But Ham's argument sets up a false choice. It equates the young-earth interpretation of Scripture with Scripture itself, forgetting that our human interpretations may be in error and do *not* carry God's authority. The argument also forgets that science, while indeed performed by fallible and fallen men and women, is investigating God's creation itself and thus worth taking seriously. God has revealed himself in both Scripture *and* nature, and both carry his authority (Ps 19). The choice before us is not humans vs. God, nor science vs. the Bible, but human science vs. human biblical interpretation.

Many Old Testament scholars, including evangelicals, do not see the text of Genesis 1 as *requiring* a literal six-day, twenty-four-hour creation.[6] Hebrew scholars find that Genesis 1–11 is a different genre than other Old Testament passages; while these chapters may refer to historical events, they do so in a very different mindset than a modern historical account. God accommodated his message to this ancient mindset by using imagery and metaphors common in the ancient Near East in order to teach fundamentally new truths. Note that these

---

5. Some evolutionary creationists also claim the term "inerrant" for Scripture, viewing the Bible as inerrant in what it intends to teach. An example would be B. B. Warfield, the conservative Presbyterian who originated the modern concept of inerrancy and also accepted the evidence for evolution. Other evolutionary creationists do not use the term inerrant, finding it unhelpful or divisive, but uphold the inspiration and authority of Scripture.

6. E.g., Johnny V. Miller and John M. Soden of Lancaster Bible College in *In the Beginning We Misunderstood: Genesis 1 in Its Original Context* (Grand Rapids: Kregel, 2012).

chapters do not have the genre of "God's eyewitness testimony," and that such an interpretation would require a dictation view of inspiration. Other biblical passages refer back to Genesis in the same spirit of accommodation (e.g., creation in one week in the Ten Commandments, accommodating to the seven-day pattern common in the ancient world).

EC does not use science to drive the interpretation of Scripture, nor does science teach us to "pick and choose which parts of the Bible to believe" (p. 45). As I explain in my essay, science can sometimes prompt a closer look at a passage (e.g., Galileo's observations of the solar system prompted a new look at Ps 93:1), but science simply doesn't have the tools to determine the best interpretation. EC never uses science to throw out a passage but instead looks to good practices of biblical hermeneutics. If good hermeneutics allows multiple possible interpretations, science can inform our choice. For example, evangelicals are currently discussing many views of Adam and Eve: Genetics rules out Adam and Eve as sole progenitors but is consistent with both historical and non-historical views. Many evolutionary creationists see Adam and Eve as real historical people, leaders of the early human population.

Many YEC arguments have serious scientific errors.

Evolutionary creationists believe that God could have created any way he wanted. God is powerful enough to create through an instantaneous supernatural act and powerful enough to design natural processes that lead to the same result over billions of years. The evidence embedded in God's creation shows us which method God chose to use, and EC accepts the evidence for the latter.

Ham mentions several scientific arguments with little detail on each (p. 40). Here are responses:[7]

- Marine fossils on tops of mountains. Yes these exist, but they do not require a global flood. Rather, the rock formed from sediment

---

7. For more responses to YEC arguments, see Stephen Mosier et al., "Flood Geology and the Grand Canyon: What Does the Evidence Really Say?" BioLogos blog post, June 29, 2016, http://biologos.org/blogs/archive/flood-geology-and-the-grand-canyon-what-does-the-evidence-really-say; Carol Hill, Gregg Davidson, Tim Helbel, and Wayne Ranney, eds., *The Grand Canyon: Monument to an Ancient Earth* (Grand Rapids: Kregel, 2016); and Davis A. Young and Ralph F. Stearley, *The Bible, Rocks, and Time* (Downer's Grove, IL: InterVarsity Press, 2008).

on a continental shelf below sea level, then was elevated to mountain height by the motion of the continental plate.

- Thick rock layers are continental in extent. Yes, but these rocks are not a uniform layer over an entire continent as predicted by the global-flood model. Rather, the rock is found in many overlapping sections, showing it formed in multiple periods as the continental plate rose and fell relative to sea level.
- Billions of dead things are buried in rock. Yes, but the species are not mixed together as expected from the violence of a global flood. Rather, rock formations like the Grand Canyon show discrete layers, each containing only organisms from a particular ecosystem (some only from land, some only from rivers, etc.). Moreover, no mammals, birds, dinosaurs, or flowering plants are found in the Grand Canyon fossils, which is highly inconsistent with the claim of a global flood.
- Erosion between sedimentary layers is absent. No, this erosion is clearly seen in several places at the Grand Canyon and elsewhere when a lower layer shows areas of erosion (river channels, caves, etc.) that were filled in by sediment of the layer above.

Let's reject the way that atheists frame the relationship between science and Christianity.

Ham quotes multiple atheists, not to contradict them so much as to affirm the dichotomy that atheists see between scientific findings and a literal reading of Scripture and between the practice of science and a Christian worldview. The essay concludes that "Science has been controlled by an anti-biblical philosophical/religious worldview for almost two hundred years" (p. 38). EC strongly disagrees with this dichotomy and challenges the atheist framing. EC counters atheists by showing that the best interpretations of Scripture are not in conflict with scientific findings and that the practice of science arises naturally from a Christian worldview. Christians in science through the centuries have affirmed both the Bible and new scientific discoveries, including Harvard University botanist Asa Gray, a devout Christian who was among the first Americans to accept Darwin's theory, and many others.

The AiG approach hinders Christian discipleship and evangelism by tying faith to incorrect science.

AiG and BioLogos each have very serious concerns about the other's approach to discipleship and evangelism. Ham's advice to the church for Christian young people is to teach YEC apologetics as strongly as possible; sadly, this trains young people to use incorrect science as the basis of their faith. At BioLogos, we instead teach Christian young people high-quality science and strong biblical hermeneutics, giving them a solid foundation for their faith. Ham's response to anti-biblical worldviews in the public square is to claim that science confirms a literal six-day creation; sadly, this leads science-minded seekers to doubt the intellectual credibility of the Christian faith. BioLogos instead promotes the voices of top scientists who are devout Christians and shows seekers that mainstream science fits better within a Christian worldview than within atheism.

Other young-earth creationists do not tie evangelism and discipleship so closely to their commitment to a young earth. My own childhood church taught YEC but never as a central tenet of the faith, enabling my faith to hold strong even as I learned the scientific evidence for an old earth. Since AiG says this is not a salvation issue, my hope is that AiG and other young-earth creationists would join BioLogos in encouraging churches to present origins as a secondary issue. We can all encourage churches to present and discuss the multiple views in this book, including EC as an option that *does* uphold God's Word and the gospel. Let's show our young people that our unity in Christ is larger than our disagreements. May the world know we are Christians by our love for one another and for the world.

STEPHEN C. MEYER

In my article making the case for intelligent design (p. 178ff.), and in my response to Hugh Ross, I note that intelligent design is an age-neutral theory that does not take a position on the interpretation of the book of Genesis or the age of the earth. This feature of the theory gives rise to an interesting asymmetry. Though all creationists are proponents of intelligent design, not all proponents of intelligent design are either young-earth or old-earth creationists. Instead, advocates of intelligent design include both young-and old-earth creationists and some theistic evolutionists (in particular, those who believe that God's guidance of the evolutionary process is *detectable* in retrospect against the backdrop of what nature ordinarily does). Since all creationists *are* necessarily proponents of intelligent design, I don't—speaking as a representative of the theory—have much criticism to offer of either Ken Ham or Hugh Ross's positions on the age of the earth. Nevertheless, I can offer a personal response to Ken Ham's article (as I do for Hugh Ross's article).

Though I thought Mr. Ham explained his position clearly, I'm not persuaded by either his biblical or scientific arguments. Like Hugh Ross, I think the Bible writers seem to be assuming much more time in their description of God's creative acts than the young-earth position allows. Moreover, I don't think that a careful (even literal) reading of Genesis 1 supports a young-earth view. In addition to Ross's biblical arguments against a young earth, an additional consideration has proven dispositive for me.

Genesis 1:14 describes how God, on the fourth day of creation, either made or "caused to appear" (depending how one renders the Hebrew verb *hayah*) the sun and the moon. The text also specifically states that these celestial bodies were given to mark the seasons, the days, and the years.[1] As the NIV translates the passage: "Then God said, 'Let there be

---

1. I am grateful to my daughter Bethan K. Meyer for first pointing this out to me.

lights in the vault of the sky to separate the day from the night, and let them serve as signs to mark sacred times, and days and years.'"

The text clearly teaches that the sun and the moon were made to perform a function for human beings, namely, the marking of time, including the period of time associated with a day. Oddly, however, three "days" of creation already preceded the day in which the time-marking celestial bodies were either first created or revealed. That raises an obvious question. If the divinely appointed time markers either did not yet exist or were not yet visible from planet Earth, how was time being marked on Earth during days one, two, and three of creation? Clearly, time was not being marked in the way human beings have long marked time by observing the sun's apparent movement across the ecliptic as the earth rotated on its axis. With the sun not yet in existence or at least not yet visible, its apparent movements would not be marking a solar day of twenty-four hours as we do today.

Thus, it's logical to conclude that in the absence of visible time-marking celestial bodies the first three days of creation were neither solar-marked days nor necessarily twenty-four hour periods. Consequently, many scholars, including the Hebrew philologist and biblical scholar Jack Collins, have insisted that a close reading of the Genesis text implies that days of creation are not typical days as measured by human beings on planet Earth using the apparent movement of the sun.[2] Instead, Collins argues that the days of creation described in Genesis are *God's* days—marking the beginning and end of a definite series of creative acts within an indeterminate period of time as measured from an earth-bound human point of view.

Moreover, since the first usage of a term in the Bible in a particular context typically determines its meaning in all subsequent uses in similar contexts, it is reasonable to assume that the Hebrew word for day (*yom*) used in the Genesis account of subsequent creation days (and in the account of God's ongoing rest on the seventh day) similarly designates one of *God's* days of creation—a day of indeterminate length from a human point of view.

Another related biblical text reinforces this conclusion for me. Psalm 90:4 reminds us that "A thousand years in your [i.e., God's] sight are

___

2. C. John Collins, *Science and Faith, Friend or Foes* (Wheaton, IL: Crossway, 2003), 77–96, 105–10.

like a day . . ." The psalmist here clearly states that God's reckoning of time—indeed, his reckoning of "a day"—is not necessarily the same as ours. Curiously, this psalm is the only psalm attributed to Moses, the traditional author of Genesis and the person Jesus himself identified as such. If we accept the conservative view on the authorship of Psalm 90 and Genesis 1 as advocates of a young earth typically do, then we must conclude that the one psalm in the Bible written by the author of Genesis emphasized that a day viewed from God's perspective may be much longer than twenty-four hours, encompassing many days or years from a human point of view. While the psalm does not specifically offer an interpretation of the Genesis text, it does suggest a reason to doubt that the days of Genesis as described by Moses are necessarily twenty-four-hour periods—particularly when Genesis 1 itself appears to indicate that we ought not interpret those days as solar-denominated periods of time.

Some young-earth advocates have responded to this argument by claiming that God could have used his foreknowledge to know that the apparent motion of the sun all the way around the earth *would* mark a twenty-four-hour period. On this view, he could have used that knowledge of future twenty-four-hour solar days to limit the first three days of creation to twenty-four hours as well. That, of course, is a logical possibility, but one to which the Genesis text does not even allude. Consequently, no one would derive this view from reading the text, still less from a literal reading of it. Other young-earth proponents postulate that God provided some other source of light to mark time before the creation of the sun (even appealing to the perpetual light of day in the New Jerusalem as described in Rev 21:23). Nevertheless, this interpretation doesn't explain how, even in the presence of another source of light, time would have been marked as it is today before the sun appeared. It also offers speculation derived from considerations external to the Genesis text, even as young-earth proponents claim their view is based on a literal reading of it.

Since I doubt that the Genesis text, even read literally, teaches a young earth, I have never felt compelled to interpret the scientific evidence concerning the age of the earth in light of that assumption. Though I hold a high view of the inspiration and authority of Scripture, I think that Scripture itself is telling us that at least the duration of the first three days of creation could not have been measured as we measure time today. Because I also think that it makes most sense to interpret subsequent uses of *yom* in the Genesis 1 creation text as representing periods of similarly indeterminate duration from a human point of view, I doubt that we can date the age of the earth as Bishop Ussher famously tried to do by adding the number of Genesis days to the rest of recorded human history to calculate an absolute age of the earth in several thousands of years.

I've looked instead to the scientific evidence from the "book of nature" to answer questions about the age of the earth. There I find the case for the great age of the earth and universe quite compelling for many of the same scientific reasons that Deborah B. Haarsma and Hugh Ross explained in their essays. (Indeed, despite my profound disagreements with Dr. Haarsma about the status of contemporary evolutionary theory, I do agree with her arguments about the age of the universe and the earth).

Having said all this, I think it's important not to overemphasize the issue of the earth's age or to make it a *casus belli* among Christians. Theologically, it seems far more important to me (speaking again personally as a Christian layman) to know *that* there is a God who created life and the universe than to know exactly how long ago he did his creating.

I realize that some young-earth friends will reply that the authority of Scripture is at stake in debates about the age of the earth. But for the reasons stated above, I disagree. I may be wrong, but I hope my young-earth friends will, upon reading what I've written, recognize that I am seeking to understand the Genesis text on its own terms without imposing on it an externally driven interpretative framework at odds with its clear meaning.

Speaking as a Christian, one of my concerns with theistic evolution is that many theistic evolutionists—though sincere in their Christian beliefs—do precisely that. Indeed, many proponents of theistic evolution openly acknowledge that they presuppose the truth of contemporary evolutionary theory.[3] They then proceed to interpret the biblical text in

---

3. See for example the statement on the BioLogos website: "At BioLogos, we present the Evolutionary Creationism (EC) viewpoint on origins. Like all Christians, we fully affirm that *God is the creator of all life*—including human beings in his image. We fully affirm that

light of that assumption, importing into it evolutionary ideas alien to its plain meaning. For example, most theistic evolutionists insist that God's creative activity is *not* detectable in the observable features of living systems or the natural world. Yet, Romans 1:20 affirms that "God's invisible qualities—his eternal power and divine nature" can be clearly seen and understood "*from what has been made*" (emphasis added).

In my view, it is one thing to look to external sources of scientific, historical, or archeological information to provide context or to help clarify possible meanings of ambiguous scriptural passages. It's quite another to impose an interpretive framework on a passage that flatly contradicts its central meaning, as I fear leading theistic evolutionists are doing in their evolutionary readings of Genesis 1. Nevertheless, I don't think the same charge can be fairly leveled at those who think the biblical text allows for the possibility of an ancient earth. Indeed, because, as I have argued, the Genesis text leaves the exact length of the creation days unspecified, it does no violence to the text to rely on external sources of information from the natural sciences to help answer questions about the age of the earth and universe.

Even so, it's important to recognize that people who hold high views of biblical authority (and similar hermeneutical principles) can honestly disagree about what Genesis teaches about the age of the earth. For this reason, making that issue a touchstone of orthodoxy has been an unnecessarily divisive issue within the church. It has also distracted attention from more important issues and evidence, including the compelling evidence for the existence of an intelligent and transcendent Creator.

Finally, speaking as a proponent of the theory of intelligent design, I want to make clear that scientists of both persuasions on the age issue are welcome within our growing ranks. Proponents of the theory seek to determine what caused different living systems, the universe, and its fine-tuning to arise. We also want to discover more about the nature and intricacies of the design present in both physical and biological systems.

---

the Bible is the inspired and authoritative word of God. *We also accept the science of evolution as the best description for how God brought about the diversity of life on earth.*" (emphasis added); http://biologos.org/common-questions/christianity-and-science/biologos-id-creationism. See also Denis Alexander, *Creation or Evolution: Do We Have To Choose?* 2nd ed. (Oxford and Grand Rapids: Monarch, 2014), 282–304. In this passage Alexander offers several revisionist interpretations or "models" of the Genesis text that all presuppose the truth of contemporary evolutionary theory.

Established methods of design detection allow us to discern the activity of a designing intelligence in past events and in certain features of life and the universe.[4] Though these methods can assist others trying to construct natural historical narratives (as Hugh Ross with his "testable creation models" and young-earth geologists are both attempting to do), the primary purpose of the theory of intelligent design is not to construct a comprehensive natural history. As such, issues of age are peripheral to the main concerns of the theory.

Advocates of the theory are concerned to understand the true cause(s) of the origin of living systems and the universe—whether they originated many thousands, or many millions or billions, of years ago. Any scientist willing to follow the evidence in pursuit of knowledge of those causes, whatever his or her view of the age of the earth, is welcome within our ranks.

4. William A. Dembski, *The Design Inference* (Cambridge: Cambridge University Press: 1998). Stephen C. Meyer, *Signature in the Cell: DNA and the Evidence for Intelligent Design*, (San Francisco: HarperOne: 2009) 324–72.

KEN HAM

Thoughtful readers will realize that I cannot give rebuttals to all the points I disagree with in the arguments of the other contributors to this book. But I will say that all three contributors repeatedly equate "science" with what the scientific majority believes, and they equate "science" or "evidence" or "facts" with what are actually naturalist, uniformitarian assumptions. Meyer and Ross somewhat see those assumptions controlling biology, but they and Haarsma are missing or ignoring those assumptions controlling geology and astronomy.[1] They are also confusing the biblical fact that the creation infallibly reveals the Creator to every person who has ever lived with the false idea that creation infallibly reveals how and when God created.[2] So I urge readers to consider the resources cited in the footnotes of my sections.

But in this conclusion, I want to emphasize a few points. First, truth is not determined by majority vote in either science or theology, and there are very competent PhD scholars on all sides of this debate. We must be like the Berean Jews in Acts 17:11 and test every truth claim by Scripture.

Second, while I do hold to a young-earth creation, it is not "Ken Ham's interpretation." Millions of Christians today around the world hold this view, as did Jesus, the apostles, and virtually all orthodox Christians prior to 1800.[3]

---

1. For example, old-earth arguments from ice cores, tree rings, and lake sediments are based on false assumptions, circular reasoning, and misreading of the technical literature that old-earthers cite. See http://www.icr.org/article/icr-aig-refute-biologos-old-earth-argument/; https://answersingenesis.org/age-of-the-earth/do-varves-tree-rings-radiocarbon-measurements-prove-old-earth/; and http://www.icr.org/article/ice-cores-seafloor-sediments-age-earth.

2. The vague mantra that "all truth is God's truth" is also deceptive because not all truth claims are true and the history of science is littered with abandoned claims once called "established truth."

3. See chapters 1–3 and 11–12 in Terry Mortenson and Thane H. Ury, eds., *Coming to Grips with Genesis* (Green Forest, AR: Master Books, 2008).

Third, while Ross professes belief in inerrancy, Meyer doesn't say explicitly. Haarsma evidently rejects the doctrine of inerrancy and is badly mistaken when she says that B. B. Warfield "originated the modern concept of inerrancy."[4] They all say they believe the Bible is inspired and authoritative. But with respect to the critical Scripture passages below, related to evolution and the age of the earth, clearly the truth claims of the scientific majority is the authority by which they evade or deny what God's Word so clearly teaches.

Exodus 20:8-11

C. John Collins has influenced the thinking of Meyer and Ross (and I suspect Haarsma too). But Collins has completely missed the point in Exodus 20:8–11. The passage does not *contrast* God's work and rest from man's work and rest. Rather it *equates* the length of man's work week with God's creation week. Furthermore, that the days of Genesis 1 are sequential and non-overlapping is clear from Genesis 1, and it is implied in Exodus 20:8–11. Haarsma and Meyer ignore these verses. Ross's bald assertion, based on a misleading comment about *'asah* and *bara'*, about the meaning of Exodus 20:11 in no way supports his old-earth view.[5] So Exodus 20:11 truly stands as a brick wall against any attempt to put millions of years before Adam either in the days, between the days, or before the days of Genesis 1. God's Word clearly teaches that He created "the heavens and the earth, the sea, and *all that is in them*" (emphasis added) in six literal (twenty-four-hour) days.[6]

No Death Before Adam's Fall

Ross, Meyer, and Haarsma provided little or no response to my biblical argument on this point, which is thoroughly defended in the article I footnoted.[7] My chapter (citing Gen 5:29) explains why Ross is wrong about the curse on the ground (Gen 3:17): it is not what man does but what God did to the creation. The idea of millions of years of animal death, disease,

---

4. Inerrancy is the orthodox belief of the church through the centuries. See chapters 12–13 in Norman L. Geisler, *Inerrancy* (Grand Rapids: Zondervan, 1980).

5. https://answersingenesis.org/genesis/did-god-create-bara-or-make-asah-in-genesis-1/.

6. Ross is right that it doesn't say "in" six days in Hebrew. But take it out of the English and the verse still says God created everything during a period of six literal (twenty-four hour) days.

7. See https://answersingenesis.org/theory-of-evolution/millions-of-years/the-fall-and-the-problem-of-millions-of-years-of-natural-evil/.

violence, and extinction is utterly incompatible with the Bible's teaching as well as orthodox Christian teaching for two thousand years.

Noah's Flood

Space prevented me from giving much geological evidence of the flood, but Andrew Snelling's work cited in my chapter (notes 46–47) will. But the real issue is what God's eyewitness testimony in Genesis describes: a global, year-long, catastrophic flood that destroyed all the air-breathing land animals, birds, and people not in the ark and destroyed the surface of the earth. By logical implication it would have buried billions of creatures in sediments that would have become rock layers and fossils. Noah's flood produced most of the geological evidence that evolutionists attribute to millions of years. The writings of old-earth geologists that Haarsma cites in note 7 of her response to me give little or no discussion of Genesis 6–9. Haarsma and Ross deny that the flood was global, and I suspect Meyer does, too. But a local flood is simply not what God's inerrant Word teaches. So, where is their commitment to the authority of Scripture?

The Order of Creation

Haarsma, Meyer, and Ross either deny (explicitly or implicitly) or ignore the order of events on the clearly sequential days of Genesis 1 that flatly contradict the order of events in the old-earth story. So, where is their commitment to the authority of Scripture?

Genesis 5 and 11 Chronogenealogies

Most evangelical Bible scholars in the twentieth century do say that these genealogies do not tell us how old the earth is. But they have been misled by an erroneous 1890 article by William H. Green, which has now been thoroughly refuted.[8]

Conclusion

Genesis 1–11 is foundational to the gospel and the ideas of evolution and millions of years do massive damage to the truth and authority of that

---

8. Jeremy Sexton, "Who Was Born When Enosh Was 90? A Semantic Reevaluation of William Henry Green's Chronological Gaps," *Westminster Theological Journal* 77 (2015): 193–218; http://pastorsexton.com/articles/. See also https://answersingenesis.org/bible-characters/adam-and-eve/when-was-adam-created/.

foundation. In this 500th anniversary year of Martin Luther nailing the *Ninety-five Theses* on the door of the Wittenberg Church, I and my fellow staff at Answers in Genesis stand with Luther in saying our consciences are captive to the Word of God. Unless we are persuaded from the Scriptures that we are wrong, we will not recant our teaching and defense of young-earth creation, which historically is the biblically orthodox faith of the church. Therefore, we at Answers in Genesis are doing everything we can to help call the church back to the Word of God.

OLD EARTH (PROGRESSIVE) CREATIONISM

HUGH ROSS

The Belgic Confession (1561) declares the natural realm a "most elegant book," revealing God's divine nature and power, a book so clear as to remove our excuse for ignorance and rebellion and to expose our hopelessness apart from the Creator's good will toward us. Through special revelation, the sacred Scriptures, God affirms and clarifies his redemptive purpose and the specific plan by which he makes redemption available to all people. Both Scripture's words and creation's works originate from the One who is truth and reveals truth. Both are subject to interpretation and, therefore, to human error. Yet God has sent his Spirit to guide us persistently to truth.

From these foundational beliefs, old-earth creationists anticipate God's "two books" will prove consistent internally, externally, and mutually. One provides more detail on the redemptive story, the other more detail on the creation story, but they speak in perfect harmony. Neither negates or undermines the other.

Scripture and nature's record agree that God transcendently created the universe with its physical laws. He then prepared within it a habitat for humanity where a vast number of people ultimately receive the redemption he offers. Scripture and natural history further reveal that God introduced life and then brought forth a sequence of increasingly diverse and complex life-forms, each playing a vital role in preparing for the existence and redemption of a countless number of humans. The formation of our galaxy cluster, galaxy, planetary system, planet, and variety of life-forms is called *progressive* in that each successive creative act prepares for the next, leading toward more diverse, complex, and advanced life, up to the creation of humans.

Concerning life's progression, old-earth creationists consider mass speciation events as divine interventions, occasions in which God introduces diverse species appropriate for Earth's changing conditions and in optimal ecological relationships. Between these events we see several long periods during which Earth's life experiences microevolutionary changes, adaptations propelled by a combination of environmental conditions, challenges from invasive species, and genetic factors. However, we reject the concept of universal common descent, the notion that all life is part of an uninterrupted genetic continuum from a last universal common ancestor (LUCA). Our observations of the natural world confirm the message we see in Scripture: that "kinds" reproduce according to their kind. Thus, most progressive creationists reject the claim, for example, that Neanderthals and humans share a common ancestor or that birds and dinosaurs share a common ancestor.

Unlike young-earth and evolutionary creationists, old-earth creationists acknowledge no conflict between the Genesis 1 order of creation events and mainstream scientific chronology. This affirmation of congruence (not to be mistaken for fusion, or total overlap) rests on a number of *literal* interpretive options, described below, and differs from mainstream science only in identifying the means by which life progresses, not in the actual historical record.

Old Earth creationism is a big tent. It includes multiple interpretations of the Genesis creation account:

1. creation "days" as revelatory days,
2. twenty-four-hour creation days separated by long eras,
3. creation "days" as a literary framework,
4. twenty-four-hour creation days following a time gap between Genesis 1:1 and 1:3,
5. analogical or time-relative creation days,
6. creation days as ages or long time periods,
7. any combination of the above.

Old-earth creationists refrain from claiming to hold the only valid understanding of Genesis. Because space forbids me from addressing this whole range of views, I will constrain my remarks to the day-age view, the one I regard as most defensibly integrated with established biblical and scientific research.

Day-Age Creationism

The day-age perspective springs, in part, from the Hebrew word for "day" used in Genesis. This word, *yom*, has four distinct literal definitions in Biblical Hebrew:

1. a portion of the daylight hours,
2. all of the daylight hours,
3. one cycle from evening to evening, or morning to morning (one of Earth's rotation periods),
4. a long, yet finite time period.

Day-age creationists see three different literal usages of *yom* appearing in the first Genesis creation account. They view creation day 1 as contrasting night from *day*—the second definition above. Creation day 4 contrasts seasons, *days*, and years—the third definition. In Genesis 2:4 *yom* refers to the entire creation period—the fourth definition. The day-age view considers the creation days as six sequential, non-overlapping, long time periods.

The day-age view upholds *sola Scriptura*, the doctrine that the Bible alone is the authoritative propositional revelation from God. However, this doctrine in no way denies the reliability of God's general revelation, nature's record. Scripture itself declares nature's record reliable. The day-age position acknowledges that Bible authors sometimes use figurative language to convey God's message and meaning, but such language always conveys truth and never contradicts it.

Detectability of Divine Intervention

Day-age creationists believe in the objective reality of a supernatural realm. They hold that nature provides observable, measurable verifications of God's supernatural handiwork. They believe that science has firmly established that the universe began in a transcendent event and unfolds in an utterly improbable way for humanity's benefit, sustained moment by moment in the constancy of nature's laws. Scripture describes three distinct kinds of "miracles," or divine interventions, in nature's record:

> *Transcendent Miracles:* Acts of God that transcend the laws of physics and space-time dimensions of the universe. Examples are the creation of the cosmic space-time dimensions, establishment of the physical laws, and creation of humanity's unique spiritual nature.
>
> *Transformational Miracles:* Acts of God in reconstituting or refashioning some aspect of the created realm. Transformational miracles take place within, not outside, the laws of physics and the cosmic space-time dimensions. Here God interacts with what already exists to produce results far beyond what natural processes alone, given our space and time constraints, could reasonably be expected to generate. An example would be God fashioning the earth and its continents and oceans with the exact features necessary to sustain abundant, diverse, and globally distributed advanced life.[1]
>
> *Sustaining Miracles:* God's continuous action throughout cosmic history to sustain and ensure just-right conditions for human existence and survival. According to Colossians 1:17, "in him [Christ] all things hold together." Day-age creationists anticipate that all the laws and constants of physics as well as all discoverable features of the universe, Earth, and life will manifest exquisite fine-tuning and constancy for the fulfillment of God's stated purposes.

Transcendent miracles are rare and transformational miracles occur less frequently than sustaining miracles. From a biblical perspective, transcendent and transformational creation miracles occurred long ago, "in the beginning," or during the six creation epochs. Genesis says God ceased from his creation work by the end of the sixth day. So, research probing nature and how it functions in the epoch since humanity's appearance would be expected to show only natural-process changes (and sustaining miracles), while research focused on the natural realm *before*

---

1. Hugh Ross, *Improbable Planet: How Earth Became Humanity's Home* (Grand Rapids: Baker, 2016).

human history (during the six creation days) would be expected to yield evidence of God's transcendent and transformational creation miracles.

Constant Physical Laws

One reason nature's record can be counted on to consistently reveal truth is that the laws and constants of physics are changeless. In Jeremiah 33 God compares his immutable character to the changelessness of laws governing the heavens and the earth. Astronomical measurements affirm this biblical statement (a verifiable scientific prediction) to better than fifteen places of the decimal that the physical laws and constants remain invariant throughout space and time.[2]

Some creationists argue that the first humans' defiance of God and perhaps Noah's flood, too, caused major changes in physics—either the introduction of decay or dramatic changes in decay rates. Both biblical texts and scientific data refute such assertions.

Prior to Adam's sin, the second law of thermodynamics was fully operational. According to Romans 8, the entire creation has been "groaning," right up to the present, as a consequence of its "bondage to decay" (vv. 20–22). Since the space-time dimensions cannot be separated from one another, "the entire creation" implies the law of decay applies to the entire spatial and temporal extent of the universe. Genesis 1 and 2 depict starlight, metabolism, and human work, all predating human sin and all requiring entropy. The sun's (and other stars') stable burning, organisms' metabolizing of food, and Adam's (pre-sin) performance of work all require the laws of physics to be in continuous operation at their current values from the beginning of time. Even a tiny variation would have rendered these functions impossible.[3]

Constructive Integration

Day-age creation stands in contrast to both the conflict and complementarity views of the relationship between science and Scripture. "Constructive integration" seems an appropriate label of the day-age

2. Michael R. Wilczynska et al., "A New Analysis of Fine-Structure Constant Measurements and Modelling Errors from Quasar Absorption Lines," *Monthly Notices of the Royal Astronomical Society* 454 (Dec 2015): 3082–93, doi:10.1093/mnras/stv2148.

3. For more on how Adam's fall impacted his physical environment, see my book, *A Matter of Days: Resolving a Creation Controversy*, 2nd ed. (Covina, CA: RTB Press, 2015), 89–104.

model. It anticipates a straightforward, harmonious integration of Scripture's book with nature's record, rather than a nonexistent overlap or minimal overlap. The emergence of the scientific method and scientific revolution from the Reformation era[4] revealed something about the Bible's scientific motivation and content. Constructive integrationists point to the abundance of Scripture passages specifically describing the natural realm and natural history.[5] They also note that science has made huge strides in exploring philosophical questions that were once the private preserve of theologians.

Constructive integrationists consider biblical inspiration to imply that each passage communicates relevant messages to all generations of humanity, not just to the generation of that book's human author. As Peter comments, "It was revealed to them [the prophets] that they were not serving themselves but you" (1 Pet 1:12a). Peter explains that Old Testament prophets and even angels longed to understand what the Holy Spirit was inspiring the prophets to record (1 Pet 1:10–12). The prophets and angels realized that full understanding of the inspired words remained for future generations. In other words, just as Bible writers sometimes predicted—through the Holy Spirit's agency—future events in human history, so, too, they sometimes described natural phenomena far in advance of their own understanding.

Constructive integrationists see evidence for the supernatural inspiration of Scripture in the way ordinary words communicate extraordinary truths that remain relevant to all generations of humanity. Even one short passage may contain multiple layers of meaning that unfold through multiple generations. Such communication exceeds the capability of mere humans. Constructive integrationists argue that only the Holy Spirit's inspiration can explain the depth of content in the Bible's texts addressing creation and the natural realm.

Constructive integration does not imply that conflicts between science and theology will never arise. Indeed, it anticipates that seeming

---

4. Thomas F. Torrance, *Theology in Reconstruction* (Grand Rapids: Eerdmans, 1965); idem, *Reality and Scientific Theology* (Edinburgh: Scottish Academic Press, 1985); idem, "Ultimate and Penultimate Beliefs in Science," in *Facets of Faith and Science, Volume I: Historiography and Modes of Interaction*, ed. Jitse M. van der Meer (New York: University Press of America, 1996), 151–76.

5. For a listing, see my article, "Creation Passages in the Bible," Reasons to Believe, January 1, 2004, http://www.reasons.org/articles/creation-passages-in-the-bible.

contradictions will arise. The scientific enterprise is no more equivalent to nature than biblical theology is to Scripture. Scientists measure and experiment in an effort to understand nature's record. Because of incomplete knowledge, limited technology, and less-than-perfect objectivity, ongoing research still provides incomplete, limited, and less-than-perfect understanding of nature's truths. The same goes for theology. Theologians analyze, compare, and contrast in an effort to understand the Bible's words. Again, due to incomplete knowledge, lack of direct access to the writers, and less-than-perfect objectivity, theological research provides still incomplete, limited, and less-than-perfect understanding of Bible passages.

Day-age creationists align with the findings of the International Council on Biblical Inerrancy, with its affirmations and denials regarding the relationship between Scripture and science.[6] This alignment constitutes a rejection of hard concordism, the notion that all of Scripture connects with *all* the facts of nature. Moderate concordism better describes the day-age view.[7] In this view, the Bible anticipates and depicts *some* of science's major findings, especially discoveries relevant to life's biggest questions and central biblical themes, but not all. To link biblical passages[8] outlining fundamental features of big bang cosmology (creation *ex nihilo*, cosmic expansion from a space-time beginning under constant physical laws, including a pervasive law of decay) with findings of ongoing scientific research seems reasonable and appropriate. Attempts to link particle physics or dinosaur history, for example, with specific biblical texts seem an unreasonable stretch.

Creation-Model Approach to Evangelism

Constructive integrationists seek to show that the more we learn from and understand God's "two books," the more solid our basis becomes for personal faith in Christ. People gain confident hope from seeing

---

6. These statements are posted on Reasons to Believe's website, "International Council on Biblical Inerrancy (ICBI)/The Chicago Statement on Biblical Hermeneutics (Articles 19–21)," Reasons to Believe, January 1, 1997, http://www.reasons.org/articles/international-council -on-biblical-inerrancy-icbi-the-chicago-statement-on-biblical-hermeneutics-articles-19–22.

7. For a fuller description of my concordist theology, see my article, "Defending Concordism: Response to the Lost World of Genesis One," *Today's New Reason to Believe*, Reasons to Believe, June 22, 2012, http://www.reasons.org/articles/defending-concordism-response-to -the-lost-world-of-genesis-one.

8. Hugh Ross, *Big Bang—The Bible Taught It First!* July 1, 2000, http://www.reasons.org/ articles/big-bang-the-bible-taught-it-first.

that both the Bible and nature faithfully testify, without contradiction, of God's attributes, his providential care for his creatures, and his desire for relationship with humanity. In a skeptical age, constructive integration plays an important part in establishing both the plausibility and relevance of Scripture. The more opportunities God gives to show how science in its multiple disciplines integrates with all sixty-six books, the more reasons we can offer people to trust Christ.

Providing a testable, biblical creation model answers the charge that creation and intentional design remain outside science's purview because they're not falsifiable. Also, such a model, unlike most theistic-evolution and evolutionary-creation models, offers clear scientific distinctions from deism, providing multiple scientific evidences—post cosmic creation event—for God's direct involvement in nature. The day-age perspective enables the development of a biblical creation model that is verifiable or falsifiable by achievable scientific discoveries. Such a model provides a measurably more comprehensive and harmonious explanation of nature's record than nontheistic, deistic, and nonbiblical theistic models. It also potentially points toward or predicts future scientific discoveries. A biblical creation model, measurably distinct from nontheistic, deistic, and nonbiblical theistic models, opens doors for discussions of the gospel that otherwise remain shut. It marshals scientific evidence showing that the God of the Bible is our intelligent, intentional designer and that he has intervened repeatedly throughout natural history on our behalf to make himself and his redemptive purpose known.

A creation-model approach also redirects barrier-building focus on the inadequacies of naturalism and/or evolutionism. Neither scientists nor those who respect them will abandon a useful paradigm, no matter how flawed it may be, until they see a viable alternative, one that provides a more consistent and comprehensive explanation of the natural realm and yields greater predictive success. To carry any weight, it must be unambiguous in its core claims, including the identity of the designer, the timing and circumstances surrounding life's origin, Adam's identity, and sin's origin.

Biblical Support for the Day-Age Model

More than half a century ago, British cosmologist Sir Fred Hoyle wrote, "There is a good deal of cosmology in the Bible. . . . It is a remarkable conception."[9] Indeed, the Bible contains far more content on the origin, structure, and history of the universe and life than any other ancient text or holy book. Furthermore, various passages exhort readers to look to nature's record—as people without a written record have always done—for evidence of the Creator's existence and his divine nature, attributes, and redemptive intent.

Because the Bible contains abundant commentary on the natural realm (more than twenty major passages and hundreds of additional verses), it supplies ample material from which to construct a scientifically testable model establishing Christ as Creator, Lord, and Redeemer. Far from being just another ancient Near Eastern creation myth with vague allusions to science, Genesis 1–11, Job 37–39, Psalm 104, and Proverbs 8 provide a detailed, specific, and chronologically accurate account of nature's origins, structure, and history, as well as a foreshadowing of the scientific method.

Contrary to young-earth creationists (among others) who assert day-age creationists trust science more than the plain teaching of Scripture, biblical evidence for a creation history much longer than ten thousand years supports, and I believe should compel, the old-earth interpretation. To defend the authority, inspiration, and inerrancy of Scripture from a young-earth perspective would seem all but impossible in light of the following sampling of insights from various Old and New Testament texts:

1. *Sixth-day Events.* In this final creation period, God introduces three distinct kinds of specialized land mammals and then humans, both male and female. Genesis 2 describes events between God's creation of the man and the woman. God planted a garden, making "all kinds of trees to grow out of the ground" (v. 9). Then God placed the man, Adam, in the garden to tend it. He then had Adam name all the *nephesh* ("soulish" creatures endowed with intelligence, emotion, and volition; v. 19) God brought to him. Apparently, Adam thoroughly examined each creature before naming it. He had sufficient time to discover the joys of interaction with these *nephesh* and to observe his own aloneness. Finally, God caused Adam to sleep deeply, performed "surgery," crafted a woman, and then awakened Adam (vv. 21–22).

9. Fred Hoyle, *The Nature of the Universe* (Oxford: Basil Blackwell, 1952), 109.

Adam's exclamation upon first seeing Eve is recorded in Genesis 2:23—*happa'am*. The expression is found elsewhere in the Hebrew Bible (see Gen 29:34–35; 30:20; 46:30; Judg 15:3) and is similar to the English expression "at last!" Still later on this same day, God taught Adam and Eve about their responsibility to manage Earth's resources for the benefit of all life and about the vital importance of sustaining green plants as the food chain's basis. This instruction likely took considerable time. When examined together, just this latter portion of the sixth day's activities seems to have filled many weeks, months, or years, even without sin's interference.

2. *Seventh Day's Continuation.* To mark off each of the first six creation days Moses wrote, "There was evening, and there was morning—the [numbered] day." The wording suggests each "day" had a start and a finish. However, no such wording is attached to the seventh day, neither in Genesis nor anywhere else in Scripture. Given the parallelism in this account of creation days, the distinct change in reference to the seventh day strongly suggests that while this day clearly began, it has not yet ended.

In Psalm 95, John 5, and below, in Hebrews 4, we read that God's rest day continues:

> Somewhere he [God] has spoken about the seventh day in these words: "On the seventh day God rested from all his works." . . . it still remains for some to enter that rest . . . There remains, then, a Sabbath-rest for the people of God; for anyone who enters God's rest also rests from their works, just as God did from his. Let us, therefore, make every effort to enter that rest. (Heb 4:4–11)

From such passages, we ascertain the seventh day extends for a minimum of several thousand years and remains open-ended (though finite). It seems plausible, then, that the first six days also were extended time periods.

3. *Different Timeframes.* Psalm 90:4 declares, "A thousand years in your sight are like a day that has just gone by, or like a watch [four hours] in the night." Moses' words, also quoted in 2 Peter 3:8,

remind us that God's days are not our days. Recognizing God existed before he created cosmic time, this difference in time perspective seems obvious.

4. *God's Eternality Compared.* Figures of speech used in Psalm 90:2–6, Proverbs 8:22–31, Ecclesiastes 1:3–11, and Micah 6:2 all depict the immeasurability of God's ancientness, comparing it to the longevity of Earth's mountains and foundations. Compared to three billion years, a three-thousand-year terrestrial history (at the time these words were written) seems an inadequate or inappropriate metaphor for God's eternality.

5. *Statements about Earth's Antiquity.* Habakkuk 3:6 declares that the mountains are "ancient" and the hills are "age-old." In 2 Peter 3:5, the heavens are said to have existed "long ago." Such adjectives would carry little impact if the universe and Earth's hills were only a few days older than humankind.

6. *Numbered Days, Not Twenty-four-hour Days.* Although *yom* attached to an ordinal or cardinal number often refers to a day of human activity, no grammatical rule requires that a numbered *yom*, especially in reference to divine activity, be a twenty-four-hour period of time. Even for human activity there is a biblical exception. Hosea 6:2 reads, "After two days he [God] will revive us [Israel]; on the third day he will restore us." For centuries Bible expositors have noted that "days" referred to in this passage (where both cardinal and ordinal numbers are connected with *yom*) represent years, perhaps as many as a thousand or more.

7. *Sabbath Analogies to God's "Work Week."* Exodus 20:10–11 is often cited as proof the Genesis days are twenty-four-hour periods: "For in six days the LORD made the heavens and the earth . . . but he rested on the seventh day." (The preposition *in* does not appear in Hebrew manuscripts.) However, this deduction is akin to saying the eight-day Feast of Tabernacles celebration proves the wilderness wanderings in Sinai lasted only eight days.

Sometimes the Sabbath refers to a year (Lev 25:4). While human well-being is best served by one twenty-four-hour day's rest in every seven days, the land's well-being in yielding crops needs one year's rest in every seven years to be optimal. Given that God has no biological limitations, his rest period is completely flexible. Exodus 20 focuses more closely on the pattern of work and rest, a ratio of six to one.

8. *Bloodshed and the Atonement Doctrine.* The Bible teaches the shedding of Christ's blood is the one and only acceptable atoning sacrifice for sin. Hebrews 10:1–4 explains that the blood of animal sacrifices *could not*—and *did not*—take away sin. Thus, in no way does the atonement doctrine demand a creation scenario in which none of God's creatures bled or died before Adam sinned.

9. *"Evening and Morning" Statements as Transitions.* Some creationists cite the Hebrew words *'ereb* and *boqer*, translated "evening" and "morning," as conclusive indicators the creation days must be twenty-four-hour periods. However, *'ereb* also means "sunset," "night," "at evening," "at the turn of the evening," or "between evenings,"[10] and *boqer*, "the dawn," "end of darkness," "the coming of dawn," or "beginning of day."[11] So *'ereb* and *boqer* in Genesis 1 may well refer to the ending of one time period and the beginning of another, regardless of the length of that period.

Some argue a twenty-four-hour period is implied because, as they say, everywhere else in the Old Testament where "evening(s)" and "morning(s)" appear, the context indicates a twenty-four-hour day. However, in none of these passages does "day" (*yom*) even appear. In none does the Genesis 1 phraseology ("and there was evening, and there was morning") appear, and in each case the context is a period of human activity, not God's.

Many more biblical arguments for long creation days exist, as documented in my book *A Matter of Days* (2nd exp. ed., 2015). Long creation days make the defense of biblical authority, inspiration, and inerrancy a relatively straightforward task. They permit a literal and consistent interpretation of *all* biblical creation texts.

---

10. Francis Brown, S. R. Driver, and Charles A. Briggs, *A Hebrew and English Lexicon of the Old Testament* (Oxford: Clarendon, 1962), 787–88; R. Laird Harris, Gleason L. Archer Jr., and Bruce K. Waltke, eds. *Theological Wordbook of the Old Testament*, 2 vols. (Chicago: Moody, 1980), 2:694; H. W. F. Gesenius, *Gesenius' Hebrew-Chaldee Lexicon to the Old Testament*, trans. Samuel Prideaux Tregelles (Grand Rapids: Baker, 1979), 652.

11. Brown, Driver, and Briggs, *Hebrew and English Lexicon*, 133–34; Harris, Archer, and Waltke, *Theological Wordbook of the Old Testament*, 1:125; Gesenius, *Hebrew-Chaldee Lexicon*, 137.

Creation Acts Chronology

A century ago Bible scholar Friedrich Delitzsch wrote, "All attempts to harmonize our biblical story of the creation of the world with the results of natural science have been useless *and must always be so*"[12] (emphasis added). Such a view remains prevalent to this day. Some Bible interpreters say the Bible got the story right and scientists got it all wrong. Others say science tells the true story and the biblical story is merely poetic, or essentially silent with respect to natural history.

The day-age view delivers Christians from such defeatist perspectives. It acknowledges Genesis as an elegant literary masterpiece that also provides a chronological account of God's miraculous acts in preparing Earth for human life. It gives an accurate account of Earth's transformation from lifeless orb to home for a vast number of humans able to receive God's offer of eternal life. If the creation days in Genesis 1 are six consecutive long time periods and the reference frame for the six-day account is Earth's early water-covered surface (Gen 1:2; Job 38:8–9), the passage yields a creation narrative in perfect accord—both descriptively and chronologically—with the established scientific record.[13]

Genesis 1 also demonstrates what scientists might refer to as the Bible's predictive power. Here's an example. The text states vegetation (on land) proliferated prior to animal life in the oceans. Until recently, research seemed to indicate the reverse, and some skeptics enjoyed pointing out this apparent error. However, discoveries made in 2009 and 2011 verify that vegetation predated the Avalon and Cambrian explosions of animals in the oceans by hundreds of millions of years.[14] Likewise, the scientific record shows that the advanced land mammals most critical for launching human civilization appeared after birds and sea mammals, as Genesis 1:20–25 (and Job 38–39) indicates.

---

12. Friedrich Delitzsch, *Babel and Bible*, trans. Thomas J. McCormack and W. H. Garuth (Chicago: Open Court, 1903), 45.

13. I describe and document this accord in *Navigating Genesis: A Scientist's Journey Through Genesis 1–11* (Covina, CA: RTB Press, 2014).

14. L. Paul Knauth and Martin J. Kennedy, "The Late Precambrian Greening of the Earth," *Nature* 460 (Aug 2009): 728–32, doi:10.1038/nature08213; Paul K. Strother et al., "Earth's Earliest Non-Marine Eukaryotes," *Nature* 473 (May 2011): 505–09, doi:10.1038/nature09943.

Answer to Fossil Record Enigma

One of the great natural history mysteries lies in the dearth of speciation once humans appeared on the terrestrial scene. Prior to the human era, an enormous number and frequency of new species, new genera, new families, new orders, and even new phyla of life appeared. During the human era, a drastic decline has occurred, especially for higher taxa. For example, of the eight thousand mammal species present at humanity's origin, only about four thousand remain,[15] none of which is indisputably new. The decline for all taxa goes far beyond humans' negative environmental impact.

Genesis 1–2 offers an answer. During six long eras, God systematically introduced new life-forms as changing conditions permitted or even required. During the seventh—the human era—God ceased from his work of creating new life-forms.

One of the beauties of the biblical creation account is that it provides opportunities to test competing creation/evolution models. If Genesis accurately outlines life's history, scientists should be able to detect a marked difference between current biological history and pre-human biological history. If the biblical narrative is true, long-term evolution experiments performed in real time under real-world conditions should reveal that the limits of naturalistic evolution fall far short of what's needed to explain the record of pre-human life. Current evidence suggests that natural processes more often lead to extinction than speciation and, where speciation does occur, it yields only minor changes.

An ongoing long-term evolution experiment at Michigan State University on *E. coli* bacteria has shown that replaying the evolutionary process rarely, if ever, produces identical morphological outcomes, even under strictly controlled laboratory conditions designed to force these outcomes. This result is problematic for models in which God never intervenes or only subtly intervenes to direct evolution, given that hundreds of pairs of species distant from one another on evolutionary phylogenetic trees share many identical morphological structures.[16]

---

15. Ross, *Navigating Genesis*, 252–253, endnote 38.

16. I briefly describe this challenge to evolutionary creation models in my book, *More Than a Theory: Resolving a Testable Model for Creation* (Grand Rapids: Baker, 2009), 169–70. My colleague Fazale Rana has written numerous articles on our website, http://reasons.org, on the problem of repeated evolutionary outcomes (i.e., repeated design outcomes) for models of biological evolution.

I view these hundreds of pairs as repeated optimal designs miraculously inserted by a masterful Designer.

Noah's Flood[17]

Young-earth creationists, in a rejection of the scientific record, teach that Noah's flood was global in extent and it accounts for all Earth's major geologic features. Evolutionary creationists, on the other hand, reject a literal reading of the flood story because, as they see it, such an interpretation contradicts established science. These interpretations reflect a failure to integrate all the biblical texts pertaining to the flood.

According to Genesis 6–8, God caused a great flood to wipe out the entire human population and all the *nephesh* (higher animals) associated with humanity—all but the people and animals on board Noah's ark. Peter clarifies this deluge was worldwide with respect to people and the animals associated with them, which is *not* to say global. Humanity was not yet globally dispersed (Gen 10–11). In 2 Peter 2:5 we read that "the world of the ungodly" was flooded. Second Peter 3:6 says "the world of that time" (*tote kosmos* in Greek) was flooded. These are references to people rather than land. The flood's extent was determined by how far people had spread. Genesis 11 gives us a clue when it reveals the unwillingness of humans—even long after the flood—to spread out and fill the earth. When Bible writers made reference to "the world," their focus most often was on people, not the planet. Today's global citizens immediately assume "planet" without thinking.

Limitation of the flood's extent is confirmed in other texts beyond Genesis that elaborate on creation day 3. For example, the creation psalm (Ps 104) tells us that when God separated the dry land from the sea, he "set a boundary they [the waters] cannot cross; *never again* will they cover the earth" (emphasis added). Likewise, Job 38:8–10 and Proverbs 8:29 indicate that the continents formed *permanent* boundaries for the oceans.

In Genesis 8 we read that the floodwaters took seven to ten months to recede. Recession of that time length suggests a large quantity of water, primarily melting snow and ice, indicating Noah's flood likely occurred sometime during the last Ice Age. Such a date would be consistent with

---

17. For a thorough biblical and scientific defense of this flood model see my book, *Navigating Genesis*, 139–95.

a reasonable calibration of the Genesis 11 genealogy,[18] an era when easy migrations across Arabia's empty quarter would have been possible.[19] This timing also aligns with mitochondrial DNA dates for migration of large human populations from the Middle East and Africa into Europe, East Asia, Australia, and North and South America.[20] Noah's flood may well have occurred at a time when most of the Persian Gulf and Red Sea area was dry land. The topography of that time would have allowed for a flood of sufficient extent to affect the entire human population.

One of the added features of this flood perspective, in addition to providing biblically and scientifically viable interpretation of the text, is that it answers the question of how the four rivers mentioned in Genesis 2 could have come together in the garden of Eden.[21] They did converge during the last Ice Age in what is now the southeastern part of the Persian Gulf. This flood view also explains why virtually every ethnic group on the planet tells a story about an ancient devastating flood.

Perspective on Death

Most young-earth creationists portray death as cruel and evil in every context. They conclude that death on the scale with which it appears in the fossil record could not have existed prior to Adam's sin and cite Romans 5:12 in support of this conclusion. But does it? Romans 5:12 says, "Sin entered the world through one man, and death through sin, and in this way death came to all people." By two qualifications, "death through sin" (which only humans can commit) and "death . . . to all people," Paul clarifies that Adam's sin inaugurated death among humans. Neither here nor anywhere else in Scripture does God's word say that Adam's offense brought death to all *life*.

Physical death, though grievous, yields valuable redemptive benefits. Death of nonhuman life blessed humanity with a treasure chest of more than seventy-six quadrillion tons of biodeposits[22] (e.g., coal, oil, natural

---

18. Ross, *Navigating Genesis*, 75.

19. Hugh Ross, "Did Arabia Provide a Migration Route for Early Humans?" *Today's New Reason to Believe*, Reasons to Believe, May 28, 2015, http://www.reasons.org/articles/did-arabia-provide-a-migration-route-for-early-humans.

20. Fazale Rana with Hugh Ross, *Who Was Adam? A Creation Model Approach to the Origin of Humanity*, 2nd ed. (Covina, CA: RTB Press, 2015), 127–41, 268–70, 363–65.

21. Ross, *Navigating Genesis*, 97–100.

22. Ibid., 166–69.

gas, clathrates, limestone) from which to build a global civilization and facilitate the fulfillment of the Great Commission in mere thousands, rather than millions, of years. Christ's crucifixion and resurrection demonstrate, water baptism illustrates, and Paul repeatedly writes that only through death can we truly live, both now and forever.

Two-Creation Reality

Death and decay's temporary necessity aligns with the day-age vision of the future creation, the new heavens and new earth, which Scripture describes as perfect in every way. While the creation in which humanity now resides is "very good," God promises an eternal home that is unimaginably better. The current creation serves its purpose as the best possible realm in which God efficiently, rapidly, and permanently conquers evil and suffering while allowing free-will humans to participate in his redemptive process and plan. Every galaxy, star, and life-form that has ever existed in this 13.8-billion-year-old universe facilitates fulfillment of God's redemptive plan.

Once the full number of humans comprising God's kingdom has been granted and received citizenship, evil and suffering will be permanently removed, the universe will have fulfilled its purpose, and we'll be ushered by God into an entirely new and different realm (Isa 65:16–17; Rev 21–22). God and his people and the angelic hosts will finally live together, face to face, experiencing unbroken fellowship and perfect love. Death, decay, pain, and darkness (physical and spiritual) will be forever banished. This new creation, as Bible writers struggled to describe, will be more than merely Eden restored. It will be radically different—framed by different dimensions and governed by different laws.[23]

Nephesh Uniqueness

Evolutionary creationists point to common features humans share with birds and mammals—social behaviors and aspects of the intellect, will, and emotion—as indicators of common descent. Yet Genesis 1 seems to single out the *nephesh*, that is, the soulish animals, for their distinction from previously existing creatures.

The use of the Hebrew verb *'asah* ("to make") implies that something

---

23. I contrast the purposes and distinct features of the present creation and the new creation in my book, *Why the Universe Is the Way It Is* (Grand Rapids: Baker, 2008), 27–206.

about the *nephesh* is not entirely new and unique, whereas the use of the verb *bara'* ("to create") in this same context suggests that something about the *nephesh* is truly new and exceptional. That these animals possessed physical bodies was not new. However, their relational capacity showed a step-function advance. Looking back, we see that these creatures were uniquely and optimally capable of interacting and bonding with members not only of their own species but also with a species that did not yet exist when they appeared—the human species. In the context of special creation, as opposed to common descent, one would expect these *nephesh* to possess capacities for social interaction with humans, features of intelligence, and emotion that facilitate bonding with, serving, and pleasing human beings.[24]

Human Exceptionalism[25]

One of the more striking differences between old-earth creationists and other creationists arises in regard to humanity's origin and identity. Young-earth creationists consider Neanderthals and hominids such as *Homo erectus* as fully human descendants of Adam, while evolutionary creationists consider Neanderthals and humans as descendants of an earlier, nonhuman common ancestor and Adam one descendant from among many early humans. However, day-age creationists view humans as separate and distinct from Neanderthals and other hominid species, and all three as creatures specially created by God's design and intervention. We view all humans as the descendants of two historical persons, Adam and Eve, specially created by God and uniquely bearing his image (Gen 3:20; Acts 17:26; Rom 5:13–19).

Just as Genesis 1 uses two verbs to describe God's introduction of *nephesh*, it uses two verbs (the same two) to describe the creation of humans. This usage implies we humans share certain characteristics with these animals but also possess features utterly unique. We humans alone are spiritual beings endowed with the capacity to form relationships not only with our own and other species but also with a higher being—the highest Being.

---

24. I deal with *nephesh* exceptionalism and human exceptionalism in-depth in *Hidden Treasures in the Book of Job: How the Oldest Book in the Bible Answers Today's Scientific Questions* (Grand Rapids: Baker, 2011), 105–85.

25. For a book-length defense of a day-age human origins model, see *Who Was Adam?*

Day-age creationists point to a wealth of scientific evidence showing that humans alone, as distinct from Neanderthals, *Homo erectus*, and other species, possess the capacity for symbolic recognition, for complex language, art, and music, and for spiritual and philosophical engagement. Humans alone manifest awareness of God, sin, moral judgment, and life beyond death. Humans alone demonstrate technological advancement, including the development of agriculture and civilization. New evidence shows that even during episodes of extreme environmental instability, humans were able to maintain small mixed farms (with multiple species of crops and livestock) and to manufacture flour and clothing.[26]

Engaged Creator

The day-age creation perspective envisions far more divine engagement and far less natural processes than either the young-earth or evolutionary creation views. In the young-earth model, herbivores evolved rapidly into carnivores, undergoing radical alteration of their livers and gastrointestinal tracts at the time of Adam's fall. This model further requires the up to several thousand animal species rescued from the flood in Noah's ark to rapidly evolve into millions of species shortly thereafter. While young-earth creationists prefer to call this evolution "diversification," they nonetheless invoke rates of natural-process genetic and morphological change many times more rapid and efficient than even the most optimistic atheistic Darwinist would propose. Philip Kitcher, philosopher of science at Columbia University observes, "The rates of speciation 'creation-science' would require . . . are truly breathtaking, orders of magnitude greater than any that have been dreamed of in evolutionary theory."[27]

Evolutionary creationists believe life progresses from Earth's first life-form all the way to humans through the continuous process of common descent. Most would agree that God somehow directed the mechanisms of natural selection, mutation, and gene exchange. However, their model(s) propose no tangible means for distinguishing between directed and *undirected* biological evolution. As for life's origin,

---

26. I describe this evidence in "The First Humans Developed Food-Processing Technology," *Today's New Reason to Believe*, Reasons to Believe, October 5, 2015, http://www.reasons.org/articles/the-first-humans-developed-food-processing-technology.

27. Philip Kitcher, "Born-Again Creationism" in *Intelligent Design Creationism and Its Critics*, ed. Robert Pennock (Cambridge, MA: MIT Press, 2001), 259.

evolutionary creationists acknowledge that no naturalistic explanation currently exists, but most express confidence that such an explanation is possibly forthcoming.

Day-age creationists interpret the Bible as declaring that God miraculously intervened to create Earth's first life. They also agree that decades of research have eliminated all reasonable naturalistic explanations for life's origin on Earth.[28] The Bible's use of the Hebrew word *min*, for "kind," suggests that for the higher animals (Lev 11:13–18; Deut 14:12–18), natural-process evolution is limited to the species level, and for lower animals (Lev 11:22) to the genus level. Affirmation of these limitations emerges from long-term evolution experiments and from studies in conservation biology. These findings speak of a Creator who actively and often miraculously engaged in shaping and introducing new forms of life throughout Earth's history.

Mass Extinction and Mass Speciation Events

The fossil record testifies of many mass extinction events, episodes when 40–95 percent of all Earth's species were suddenly driven to extinction, followed by times when mass speciation brought thousands to millions of new species into existence. Psalm 104 offers what seems an apt description of this pattern: "When you [God] take away their breath, they die and return to the dust. When you send your Spirit, they are created, and you renew the face of the ground" (vv. 29b–30).

Research shows that mass extinction and speciation events occur with a semi-regular period of about thirty million years, timing that correlates with the up-and-down movement of the solar system relative to the galactic plane.[29] This periodicity and these transitions in Earth's kinds of life appear to have played a role in compensating for the sun's changing luminosity. Throughout life's history, the sun has progressively

---

28. For a book-length treatment of a day-age model for life's origin, see Fazale Rana and Hugh Ross, *Origins of Life, Biblical and Evolutionary Models Face Off*, 2nd ed. (Covina, CA: RTB Press, 2014).

29. John J. Matese et al., "Why We Study the Geological Record for Evidence of the Solar Oscillation about the Galactic Midplane," *Earth, Moon, and Planets* 72 (Feb 1996): 7–12, doi:10.1007/BF00117495; Adrian L. Melott and Richard K. Bambach, "Do Periodicities in Extinction—With Possible Astronomical Connections—Survive a Revision of the Geological Timescale?" *Astrophysical Journal* 773 (Aug 2013): id. 6, doi:10.1088/0004–637X/773/1/6; W. M. Napier, "Evidence for Cometary Bombardment Episodes," *Monthly Notices of the Royal Astronomical Society* 366 (March 2006): 977–82, doi:10.1111/j.1365–2966.2005.09851.x.

brightened by 20–25 percent (see Figure 1).[30] Nevertheless, Earth's surface temperature has remained optimal for life. Why? Primarily because
the life-forms that replaced the extinct life-forms more efficiently
removed greenhouse gases from the atmosphere.

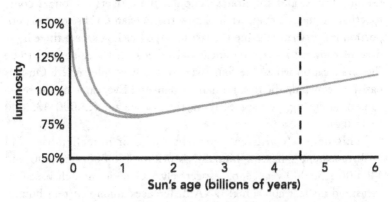

Figure 1: Sun's Luminosity History

The top curve reveals the sun's luminosity history relative to its
current luminosity, presuming the sun's initial mass was 1.3 times its
current mass. The bottom curve shows the sun's luminosity history if the
sun were 1.15 times its current mass. The zero point for the sun's age is
that time when the sun completed its mass accretion from the solar disk.

This ongoing balancing act of compensation for the sun's increasing
brightness defies a natural or subtle evolutionary creationist explanation. Nothing less than active, repeated interventions by a supernatural
Creator could ensure that just-right kinds of life at just-right population
levels living in just-right habitats would replace the extinct species at
just-right times to keep Earth's atmospheric chemistry and surface
temperatures optimal for life throughout the past 3.8 billion years.
(That's in addition to positioning the solar system in the just-right orbit
in the Milky Way Galaxy with the just-right comet and asteroid belts.)
Without God's direct, miraculous interventions throughout the solar
system's history, Earth's geophysics, geochemistry, and biochemistry

---

30. For an up-to-date review of the faint-sun paradox, see Hugh Ross, *Improbable Planet*,
143–64.

would become out of sync with solar and planetary changes, causing Earth to become permanently sterile.

Human Origins Timing[31]

We find a biblical clue for humanity's origin date in Genesis 2. The text mentions four known rivers that originally converged in Eden: Pishon, Gihon, Tigris, and Euphrates. Though these rivers no longer come together on today's map, what is now the Persian Gulf's southeastern portion was dry land during the last Ice Age (sea levels were three hundred feet lower). By tracing ancient riverbeds, that area appears to be the one location where the four rivers would have intersected. On this basis, we conclude the first humans, Adam and Eve, came on the scene sometime during, perhaps early in, the last ice age (12,000–135,000 years ago).

This date is consistent with the range of mitochondrial and Y-chromosome dates for humanity's origin: 150,000 ± 50,000 and 140,000 ± 50,000 years ago, respectively.[32] Genetics models based on measured nuclear autosomal DNA differences among current human populations, as well as estimated (or assumed) natural mutation rates, contradict what seems a clear biblical claim that all humanity descended from one man and one woman. Although evolutionists conclude that humanity descended from a much larger ancestral population, the population size estimates emerging from advancing genetics studies have consistently declined over the past four decades. The initial estimate of hundreds of thousands of individuals has now shrunk to numbers as low as hundreds of individuals.[33] Thus, it seems reasonable to anticipate a continuation of this trend line down to two. Furthermore, current models' estimates conflict with findings from field studies of sheep, horses, and orangutans. The genetic diversity of these creatures proved much greater than current genetics models predicted based on their known

---

31. Ross, *Hidden Treasures*, 105–85.

32. Phillip Endicott et al., "Evaluating the Mitochondrial Timescale of Human Evolution," *Trends in Ecology and Evolution* 24 (2009): 515–521; Qiaomei Fu et al., "A Revised Timescale for Human Evolution Based on Ancient Mitochondrial Genomes," *Current Biology* 23 (2013): 553–59; Fluvial Cruciani et al., "A Revised Root for the Human Y Chromosomal Phylogenetic Tree," *American Journal of Human Genetics* 88 (2011): 814–18; Wei Wei et al., "A Calibrated Human Y-Chromosomal Phylogeny Based on Resequencing," *Genome Research* 23 (2013): 388–95.

33. Lev A. Zhivotovsky et al., "Human Population Expansion and Microsatellite Variation," *Molecular Biology and Evolution* 17 (2000): 757–67.

ancestral populations. Thus, no scientifically verified challenge to the notion of humanity's one ancestral pair yet exists.

God's Redemptive Purpose

Day-age creationists interpret passages such as Ephesians 1:4–5, 2 Timothy 1:9, and Titus 1:2 as saying God initiated redemption before he created the universe. If we consider that in first-century Greek mathematics numbers extended to a billion, Revelation 7:9 seems to imply that God will redeem at least several billion humans, an "uncountable" number.

Romans 8:18–23 and Revelation 21 portray a future home for humanity in God's manifest presence that operates by a radically different set of laws and space-time dimensions, or their equivalent, a realm beyond what we can fully imagine. This home will be ours the moment the full number of humans that will be redeemed finally has been redeemed. This message implies God created the universe and all it contains for the express purpose of providing for the eternal redemption of billions of humans. Consequently, day-age creationists interpret all the Bible's creation content in the context of God's salvific goal. We also interpret science in the context of this goal. We see every component of the universe, Earth, and life as a contributor to making possible the salvation of billions of humans.

This focus on God's redemptive purpose provides a useful framework for integrating biblical texts with scientific findings. We should aim for interpretations most consistent with God's revealed intention to establish an eternal kingdom with billions of humans who received access to it through Jesus Christ, our Creator, Lord, and Savior.

Rich Endowment

Given that God intends to redeem billions of humans within just several thousands of years (estimated duration of appropriate conditions for high-population human civilization[34]), Earth must be endowed with the resources not only to sustain billions of humans but also to support the technology required for Christ's followers to make disciples, relatively quickly, from among all the world's people groups.

For a large, technologically advanced civilization to become possible,

---

34. I explain and document the limits in chapter 15 of my book *Improbable Planet*.

an enormous diversity of minerals and a huge endowment of biodeposits must be present in Earth's crust. Indeed, Earth is richly endowed. The biodeposits list includes limestone, marble, gypsum, coal, natural gas, oil, kerogens, and clathrates. Isotope studies show the vast majority of these resources are of biological origin, and the total quantity of these biologically derived resources adds up to at least seventy-six quadrillion tons.[35] This quantity means that Earth was packed with life at close to its theoretical maximum carrying capacity for many millions of years. Nothing less than the orchestration of a supernatural Maestro would suffice to ensure humans have at their disposal all the biodeposits needed to fulfill the Great Commission in just thousands rather than millions of years.

A civilization fully resourced to fulfill the Great Commission also requires the availability of several thousand different minerals. Before life's origin, Earth possessed only 250 distinct mineral species. Today, thanks to a 3.8-billion-year history of life, Earth's crust possesses 4,300 known mineral species. Again, this quantity and diversity of minerals reflects God's carefully planned and orchestrated supernatural interventions.

Vital Poisons

Primordial salting of Earth with heavy elements produced globally distributed deposits of arsenic, boron, chlorine, chromium, cobalt, copper, fluorine, iodine, iron, manganese, molybdenum, nickel, phosphorous, potassium, selenium, sulfur, tin, vanadium, and zinc—all are among life's vital "poisons."[36] Though advanced life requires minimum concentration levels of these elements in the environment in soluble forms, too much of any one of them proves deadly.

Sulfate-reducing bacteria removes toxic concentrations of these elements from water. For example, some bacterial species consume water-soluble zinc and from that zinc they manufacture pure sphalerite (ZnS).[37] This sphalerite is insoluble and, therefore, nontoxic for advanced life. Plus, when sufficiently large, dense populations of these bacteria die

---

35. I document this in *Navigating Genesis*, 166–69.

36. John Emsley, *The Elements*, 3rd ed. (Oxford: Clarendon, 1998), 24, 40, 56, 58, 60, 62, 78, 102, 106, 122, 130, 138, 152, 160, 188, 198, 214, 222, 230.

37. Matthias Labrenz et al., "Formation of Sphalerite (ZnS) Deposits in Natural Biofilms of Sulfate-Reducing Bacteria," *Science* 290 (Dec 2000): 1744–47, doi:10.1126/science.290.5497.1744.

and settle onto ocean and lake bottoms, they precipitate highly economic ZnS ore deposits.

Researchers now recognize that sulfate-reducing bacteria supplied much, if not all, of the concentrated ore deposits of iron, magnesium, zinc, and lead available to humans. Valuable ores of trace metals such as silver, arsenic, selenium, and other vital poisons may similarly owe their concentrations to sulfate-reducing bacteria.

The dominance of sulfate-reducing bacteria for a billion years or more, early in life's history, paved the way for advanced life—not in a random way but rather in an apparently purposeful, carefully time-managed manner. From 2.9 billion years ago to the present, the abundance and diversity of sulfate-reducing bacteria declined to just-right levels to maintain the delicate balance needed to nourish advanced life but not harm it. Today the release of soluble vital poisons into the environment through erosion is perfectly balanced by the removal of soluble vital poisons by sulfate-reducing bacteria. In addition, concentrated ore deposits resulting from sulfate-reducing bacteria has equipped humanity to form a technologically advanced civilization. The exacting precision of the quantities, diversity, timing, and locations of sulfate-reducing bacteria throughout the past three billion years testifies to a God who supernaturally intervened to ensure humans could thrive and be equipped with all the necessary resources to fulfill the purposes for which they were created.

Avalon and Cambrian Explosions

From 3.8 billion years ago until 575 million years ago Earth was packed with life, but all that life was either unicellular or colonies of unicellular life. This history is not surprising, since not until 575 million years ago did atmospheric oxygen levels increase from 1–2 percent to about 8 percent (see Figure 2).

As soon as atmospheric oxygen jumped from 1 to 8 percent, large-bodied animals up to two meters in length suddenly appeared. The surprise is how immediately these "architecturally" complex organisms appeared. In a geologic moment, after oxygen reached the minimum level for their survival, they were here.[38]

---

38. Don E. Canfield, Simon W. Poulton, and Guy M. Narbonne, "Late-Neoproterozoic Deep-Ocean Oxygenation and the Rise of Animal Life," *Science* 315 (Jan 2007): 92–95,

Figure 2: Oxygenation History of Earth's Atmosphere

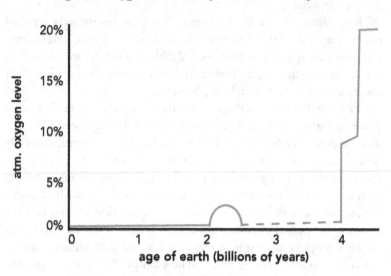

The dotted line is when the oxygen level was roughly a constant 1 percent or it jumped up and down by 0-2 percent.

So sudden and profound was this transition from microbes to large-bodied creatures that paleontologists call it the Avalon explosion. The body size, diversity, and morphological complexity of the Avalon creatures took maximal advantage of oxygen levels, food supplies, and nutrients newly available after this oxygenation event.

Then, between 544 and 543 million years ago, Avalon creatures suffered a mass extinction event. So catastrophic was this event that the number of Avalon species surviving into the subsequent era "can be counted on the fingers of one hand."[39] A short-lived global marine anoxia (lack of oxygen) event offers the most probable, though still debated, explanation.[40]

doi:10.1126/science.1135013; Guy M. Narbonne and James G. Gehling, "Life after Snowball: The Oldest Complex Ediacaran Fossils," *Geology* 31 (Jan 2003): 27–30, doi:10.1130/0091 –7613(2003)031<0027:LASTOC>2.0.CO;2.

39. Guy M. Narbonne, "The Ediacara Biota: Neoproterozoic Origin of Animals and Their Ecosystems," *Annual Review of Earth and Planetary Sciences* 33 (May 2005): 436, doi:10.1146/annurev.earth.33.092203.122519.

40. Hiroto Kimura and Yoshio Watanabe, "Oceanic Anoxia at the Precambrian-Cambrian Boundary," *Geology* 29 (Nov 2001): 995–98, doi:10.1130/0091–7613(2001)029<0 995:OAATPC>2.0.CO;2.

Less than a million years following this mass extinction, the first animals manifesting bilateral symmetry and hard body parts appeared. These first skeletal animals arrived not in just one or two phyla (body plans). Fossils reveal that 50–80 percent of the animal phyla known to exist at any time in Earth's history appeared within no more than a few million years of one another. Of the 182 skeletal designs theoretically permitted by the laws of physics, 146 appear in the Cambrian explosion fossils.[41] The earliest of these fossils include both vertebrates and invertebrates. Nearly every eye design existing today has been found in Cambrian organisms—compound eyes with numerous hexagonal facets, freely moveable eyes on top of both short and long stalks, and inset eyes.[42]

A sea chemistry change, the Great Unconformity, combined with an atmospheric oxygen rise up to 10 percent made possible creatures with skeletons, complex internal organs, and cardiovascular and neural systems. As with the Avalon explosion, no measurable delay can be seen between the emergence of conditions permitting the existence of these animals and their widespread appearance.

Evolutionary models predicted that bottom dwellers appeared long before open-ocean swimmers, creatures that need appropriate bio-mechanics for buoyancy, locomotion, and exploitation of open-water nutrients. Yet both bottom dwellers and open-ocean animals appeared early and simultaneously. Optimized ecological relationships throughout the Cambrian era also surprised evolutionists.[43] Many researchers have commented on the degree to which the Cambrian explosion challenges evolutionary models. Here are three such comments:

- The Cambrian "explosion" of body plans is perhaps the single most striking feature of the metazoan fossil record. The rapidity with which phyla and classes appeared during the early Paleozoic

41. R. D. K. Thomas, Rebecca M. Shearman, and Graham W. Stewart, "Evolutionary Exploitation of Design Options by the First Animals with Hard Skeletons," *Science* 288 (May 2000): 1239–42, doi:10.1126/science.288.5469.1239.

42. Xi-guang Zhang and Brian R. Pratt, "The First Stalk-Eyed Phosphatocopine Crustacean from the Lower Cambrian of China," *Current Biology* 22 (Nov 2012): 2149–54, doi:10.1016/j.cub.2012.09.027; Christopher Castellani et al., "Exceptionally Well-Preserved Isolated Eyes from Cambrian 'Orsten' Fossil Assemblages of Sweden," *Paleontology* 55 (May 2012): 553–66, doi:10.1111/j.1475–4983.2012.01153.x.

43. Simon Conway Morris, "The Community Structure of the Middle Cambrian Phyllopod Bed (Burgess Shale)," *Paleontology* 29 (Sept 1986): 423–67.

coupled with much lower rates of appearance for higher taxa since, poses an outstanding problem for macroevolution.[44]

• Elucidating the materialistic basis of the Cambrian explosion has become more elusive, not less, the more we know about the event itself.[45]

• No single environmental or biological explanation for the Cambrian explosion satisfactorily explains the apparent sudden appearance of much of the diversity of bilaterian animal life.[46]

Currently, no naturalistic evolutionary explanation consistent with available data has been offered for either the Avalon or Cambrian explosions.[47]

Challenges

Biblical Challenges

Young-earth creationist leaders disagree with the day-age view that all the Bible's books are equally authoritative with reference to creation and nature's realm. They say, for example, that narrative passages describing creation and nature's characteristics hold priority over poetic passages.[48] They also deny that Job 37–39, Psalm 104, and Proverbs 8 are any more than trivially relevant to creation theology.[49] However, even limiting virtually all of the Bible's creation content to Genesis, a strong biblical case for an old-earth and a worldwide (though not global) flood can be made. The case is simply more compelling when one includes all one thousand plus Bible passages about creation and the state of the natural realm.

44. Gregory A. Wray, "Rates of Evolution in Developmental Processes," *American Zoologist* 32 (Feb 1992): 131, doi:10.1093/icb/32.1.123.

45. Kevin J. Peterson, Michael R. Dietrich, and Mark A. McPeek, "MicroRNAs and Metazoan Macroevolution: Insights into Canalization, Complexity, and the Cambrian Explosion," *BioEssays* 31 (July 2009): 737, doi:10.1002/bies.200900033.

46. Jeffrey S. Levinton, "The Cambrian Explosion: How Do We Use the Evidence?" *BioScience* 58 (Oct 2008): 855, doi:10.1641/B580912.

47. I provide an extensive review of current Avalon and Cambrian explosion research and its philosophical implications in *Improbable Planet*, 172–78.

48. Tim Chaffey, "Parallelism in Hebrew Poetry Demonstrates a Major Error in the Hermeneutic of Many Old-Earth Creationists," *Answers Research Journal* 5 (July 2012): 115–23, https://answersingenesis.org/hermeneutics/parallelism-in-hebrew-poetry-reveals-major-hermaneutic-error.

49. Elizabeth Mitchell, "Creating Confusion in Genesis with Hugh Ross," *News to Know*, *Answers in Genesis*, September 27, 2014, https://answersingenesis.org/creationism/old-earth/creating-confusion-genesis-hugh-ross/.

Evolutionary creationist leaders challenge the day-age proponents' definition of biblical inerrancy as well as the lexical definitions cited for certain biblical words in the creation passages. A more liberal definition of biblical inerrancy whereby, for example, Genesis 1 and 2 are viewed as non-historical accounts incorporating mistaken features of ancient cosmological myths contrasts sharply with a day-age view. Provable errors here or in other biblical descriptions of nature, creation, or history would certainly be damaging to our model.

Both evolutionary creationists and young-earth creationists challenge our interpretation of Job as a book rich with descriptions of nature and creation. Much of this debate centers on whether the content recorded in Job is the oldest biblical material. If it is, we would expect it to be rich in creation commentary, and we would expect Moses, in writing Genesis 1, to summarize or even omit important pieces of creation history expounded in Job. If it is not, however, then some of our attempts to integrate and augment Genesis' creation content with those found in Job may be suspect.

Scientific Challenges

The two main scientific challenges to our day-age model are apparent evidence for these: (1) imperfect or functionless designs in nature; and (2) limits, rates, and degrees of biological evolution. If God intimately and directly participated in shaping creation history, we would expect the natural realm to be free of inferior or clumsy designs. However, if God used only a smoothly continuous evolutionary process or only subtle discontinuities to achieve his ends, we would expect numerous clumsy or functionless features to accumulate. This accumulation will be especially prevalent for late-appearing species such as our own.

To date, the track record of presumed "bad designs" seems less than stellar. As scientists deepen and widen their investigation, many of these features have been shown optimal. For example, the presumed vestigial appendix, which serves no function in digestion, now proves important to our immune response system. Similarly, the ENCODE project revealed that the human genome, once presumed to be 98 percent functionless, is at least 80 percent functional,[50] with more functionality

---

50. ENCODE Project Consortium, "An Integrated Encyclopedia of DNA Elements in the Human Genome," *Nature* 489 (2012): 57–74.

yet to be explored. If this trend were to reverse, however, showing that seemingly good designs and useful functions are actually useless leftovers, our model would need significant revision.

One important caveat emerges from our view that God has ceased from his creation work. This cessation means entropy is generating decay proportional to an organism's degree of complexity. This decay from entropy should also be proportional to the time since God last intervened on behalf of a particular species.

Both evolutionary and young-earth creationists view diversification of species as occurring with greater efficiency and speed than day-age creationists would acknowledge. Therefore, if real-time and long-term evolution experiments conducted under conditions closely similar to the natural world and without human intervention were to show efficient and productive macroevolution (macrodiversification), such results would seriously challenge day-age creation models.

As for scientific challenges to a billions-of-years-old universe and Earth, these now spring only from what is unknown or unknowable. As the frontiers of scientific knowledge are pushed back, the evidence for and precision in measuring Earth's age consistently increases.[51]

Finally, differing views on creation and evolution result in different approaches to resolving the problem of evil. These differences offer a potentially fruitful arena for evaluating the four perspectives represented here, but space prohibits. My distinct approach to the problem of evil, from both a scientific and biblical perspective, is described in two full-length books.[52] To summarize, God designed the universe with physical laws and dimensions such that evil is restrained. Such laws and dimensions will be replaced in the new creation.

51. Ross, *A Matter of Days*, 145–233.

52. Ross, *Why the Universe*; Hugh Ross, *Beyond the Cosmos: The Extra-Dimensionality of God; What Recent Discoveries in Astronomy and Physics Reveal about the Nature of God*, 2nd ed. (Colorado Springs: NavPress, 1999).

KEN HAM

I agree with Dr. Ross that God has revealed truth through both His Word (special revelation) and His creation (general revelation). But he makes the same serious mistake that Haarsma and so many others make in talking about God's "two books." Scripture clearly teaches that creation infallibly reveals the *Creator* to *all* people in *all* places and times (not just scientifically trained modern people). It does *not* teach that nature reveals how and when God created. And general revelation is *not* equivalent to the consensus view of modern scientists. So, the story of the big bang and a 4.5 billion-year-old earth is *not* general revelation. Mayhue has critiqued Ross's claim elsewhere[1] that nature is the "67th book of the Bible."[2]

I agree that the Cambrian explosion in the fossil record is a massive problem for evolution. I agree with Ross that the Bible has a lot to say about cosmology. But, as astronomer Dr. Danny Faulkner thoroughly discusses, it cannot be harmonized with the evolutionary big bang story.[3] I agree that the Bible is inspired and inerrant. But the helpful International Council on Biblical Inerrancy, we think, had a serious little defect in its statements on inerrancy and on hermeneutics that opens the door to the acceptance of millions of years.[4]

I agree with Ross that the second law of thermodynamics (entropy) did not start at the fall. Henry Morris and other young-earthers once taught that, but by 1981 Henry Morris had changed or clarified his meaning, and most young-earth creationist leaders don't hold that older

---

1. Hugh Ross, *Creation and Time* (Colorado Springs: NavPress, 1994), 56.

2. See footnote 1 in my response to Haarsma.

3. Danny Faulkner, *The Created Cosmos: What the Bible Reveals about Astronomy* (Green Forest, AR: Master Books, 2016).

4. See Terry Mortenson, "Inerrancy and Biblical Authority: How Old-Earth Inerrantists Are Undermining Inerrancy," https://answersingenesis.org/is-the-bible-true/inerrancy-and-biblical-authority/.

view.[5] Jeremiah 31:35–36 and 33:20–26 speak of the movements of the sun and moon at the time of Jeremiah. But these are not blanket statements about the fixity of all physical laws and *rates* of physical processes since the first moment of creation in Genesis 1:1. The laws about the movement of the sun, moon, planets, and stars were not instituted until day 4 of creation week. Ross does not have an orthodox view of the fall or Romans 8:19–23, and he dismisses the young-earth view of no animal death and other natural evil before the fall by saying that Romans 5:12 doesn't support that view. But I used that verse only with respect to human death, and he does not deal with any of the verses I used regarding no animal death before the fall. Most evangelical theologians and Bible scholars (including old-earth proponents) have taught that Romans 8 refers to God's curse on the whole creation at the fall,[6] though these old-earthers don't see that this truth contradicts their old-earth views.[7] Scripture does not support Ross's claim that "the creation in which humanity now resides is 'very good.'" The Bible teaches the opposite, and this fact is fatal for his and all other old-earth views.

On Biblical Teaching

Ross confusingly labels God's providential sustaining control of creation as "sustaining miracles." He also uses "literal" in a very confusing way that is contrary to dictionary definitions.[8] His definition of *yom* as "a long, yet finite time period" is not a literal definition and is misleading. *Yom* is used occasionally to refer to an indefinite period longer than a literal day, but only context can tell us how much longer (and we can't just arbitrarily assume it could be millions of years long). Genesis 2:4 is not an example of a literal, but rather figurative, use of *yom*.[9] Ross's day-age view of each creation day representing millions or billions of years is not a

---

5. See https://answersingenesis.org/creationism/arguments-to-avoid/the-second-law-of -thermodynamics-began-at-the-fall/ and https://answersingenesis.org/physics/the-second -law-of-thermodynamics-and-the-curse/.

6. See notes 17 and 18 in my chapter.

7. See Terry Mortenson's exposure of this inconsistency in his "Systematic Theology Texts and the Age of the Earth: A Response to the Views of Erickson, Grudem, and Lewis and Demarest," https://answersingenesis.org/age-of-the-earth/systematic-theology-texts-and -the-age-of-the-earth/.

8. See http://www.grammar-monster.com/glossary/literal_meaning.htm and http:// grammar.about.com/il/g/literalangterm.htm.

9. In Genesis 2:4 we do not find *yom* modified by a number (as in Gen 1) but *beyom* (translated "when" or "in the day that"). The same *beyom* is used in Numbers 7:10 and 84 to

literal interpretation, and no biblical context supports equating *yom* with millions of years. Nor is it a biblically defensible interpretation, as will be clear from my responses here to his "biblical" arguments for his view.

The *poetic* passages of Job 38–39, Psalm 104, and Proverbs 8 are not creation accounts to be used to interpret the literal *historical narrative* account of God's acts of creation in Genesis 1. Ross falsely accuses AiG writers of treating these passages as not equally authoritative with Genesis 1 and as "trivially" irrelevant to this topic. However, what we reject is the erroneous interpretation of these equally authoritative texts. Only Job 38:4–7 and Psalm 104:5, 19–20 refer to the creation week. Job 38:8–11 and Psalm 104:6–9 refer to Noah's flood: the last verse in each passage echoes the promise of Genesis 9:11 (cf. Isa 54:9), but no such promise is made in Genesis 1. The rest of Psalm 104 and Job 38–39 clearly refer to the world at the times when Job and the psalmist lived since those chapters describe things that did not exist in Genesis 1 (e.g., rain, war, cities, threshing floors, weapons, trumpets, wine, ships, Lebanon, sinners, etc.), and the order of mention in these chapters has no explicit chronology and contradicts the order of creation events in Genesis 1. Proverbs 8:29 tells us that from day 3 the seas would not transgress God's commanded boundaries. But at Noah's flood, God's command about those boundaries changed so as to judge the world with a global flood.

Ross claims that too much happened on day 6 to occur in twenty-four hours. But God's work (creating the garden, Adam, and Eve; commanding Adam; putting Adam to sleep) was supernatural and took minutes at most. God brought the animals to man to name so he didn't need to look for them. Ross imagines that Adam "apparently thoroughly examined" each creature before naming it, but Scripture doesn't even suggest this (e.g., it took mere seconds to name his wife "woman" and "Eve"; Gen 2:24; 3:20). If he named one "beast of the field" kind or bird kind every ten seconds, Adam could have effortlessly named 3,600 animal kinds in ten hours,[10] and in far less than ten hours he would have

---

refer figuratively to the whole period of twelve numbered literal days (*yom*) of sacrifice (Num 7:11–83).

10. At AiG we don't think he named that many because he named "beasts of the field" (which was a subset of "beasts of the earth" on the land) along with birds, and given the tenfold reference to *kinds* in Genesis 1, he certainly named kinds. There are good reasons to think that he named far less than the approximately fourteen hundred *kinds* of land animals and birds that went on the ark. See https://answersingenesis.org/creation-science/baraminology/which-animals-were-on-the-ark-with-noah/.

recognized his aloneness. Seeing Eve for the first time was instant joy. Far less than twenty-four hours was needed for the events on day 6.

Psalm 95 and Hebrews 4 do not say that the seventh *day* (Gen 2:1–3) continues but that God's *rest* from creation work continues, which also means that the natural processes scientists study are not the processes by which God created in Genesis 1. John 5:17 refers to God's continuing providential and redemption work, not His creation work.

In context Psalm 90:4 and 2 Peter 3:8 are referring to the nature of God, not the length of the creation days. Compared to God's eternality both three billion years and three thousand years are equally nothing. But the age of the mountains compared to a man's lifespan is an appropriate metaphor. Furthermore, the words "ancient" and "age-old" are indefinite: How old or ancient is determined by context. The Hebrew and Greek words translated thus are associated with mountains and hills but also with the time of the creation of the heavens, the time of Noah, the times of Terah and Abraham, and the time of the founding of Israel. "Ancient" also are the times of Egyptian pharaohs, of Moses, and of David and Asaph. Human property lines are even called "ancient."[11] There is no biblical basis for associating "ancient" or "age-old" with millions or billions of years. And as I showed in my chapter, footnote 10, Hosea 6:2 cannot be used to argue for the day-age interpretation of Genesis 1. Ross's use of the Feast of Tabernacles to dismiss the young-earth argument from Exodus 20:8–11 fails because Leviticus 23:33–43 does not connect the length of the feast to the length of time in the wilderness but rather links the booth-dwelling during the feast with the tent-dwelling in the wilderness.

Ross rejects the global flood because that literal interpretation contradicts "established science." However, Ross rejects the authority of Scripture, not because of "established science" but because most modern scientists say the global flood never happened. Genesis 6–9, however, simply does not describe a local flood in the Middle East.

Ross says that his day-age view "permits a literal and consistent interpretation of all biblical creation texts." But besides his misleading

---

11. The Hebrew *qedem* is used in Deut 33:15; Neh 12:46; Ps 68:33; and Isa 19:11. The Hebrew *'olam* is used in Josh 24:2; 1 Sam 27:8; Ps 24:7; Prov 22:28; Isa 44:7; and 58:12. The Greek *archaios* is used in Acts 15:21 and 2 Pet 2:5. Habakkuk 3:6 uses the Hebrew *'ad* for ancient mountains. Second Peter 3:5 (like 2:3) uses the Greek *ekpalai*.

use of "literal" again, when you look at his list of "The Major Biblical Creation Texts/Creation Accounts" on his web site,[12] you find more misleading confusion because in the list is Genesis 6–9, Job 34–38 and 39–42, Psalm 104, Romans 1–8, 1 Corinthians 15, and Hebrew 4, etc., none of which is a creation account. There are indeed many passages that refer to the creation week, but there is only one *historical account* of creation week in the Bible (Gen 1–2), and none of the other passages provide any grounds for rejecting the literal interpretation of Genesis 1–2.

On Science

Ross confusingly uses the word "science," erroneously equating it with general revelation, with "nature's record," with "natural history," and with what most modern scientists believe.

Because of imprecise use of "species," "evolution," and "macroevolution," Ross falsely accuses young-earth creationists of believing in evolution. He ignores our biblical and scientific evidence that the original created "kinds" were not equal to the modern classification of "species" and that within each created kind was the genetic information for rapid variation and even speciation, which is categorically different from microbe-to-microbiologist evolution.[13] He also falsely accuses us of believing that "herbivores evolved rapidly into carnivores."

He appears to see that the philosophy of naturalism controls biological sciences. But he fails to see or acknowledge that naturalism is the ruling paradigm by which geologists and astronomers interpret the universe and earth to be billions of years old.[14]

His section on "Human Origin Timing" contradicts his confusing and ever-changing dates for Adam in his other writings.[15]

He cites a lot of highly technical literature in the footnotes, which

---

12. http://www.reasons.org/articles/the-major-biblical-creation-texts-creation-accounts.

13. This semi-technical article explains how rapid variation can arise *within* a created kind, in this case a lizard population: http://www.answersingenesis.org/articles/aid/v3/n1/life-designed-to-adapt. See also this three-minute video, http://www.answersingenesis.org/articles/am/v3/n4/rapid-speciation.

14. See Terry Mortenson, "Philosophical Naturalism and the Age of the Earth: Are They Related?" https://answersingenesis.org/age-of-the-earth/are-philosophical-naturalism-and-age-of-the-earth-related/.

15. See Mortenson's illuminating documented analysis of Ross's dates in chapter 5, "When Was Adam Created?" in *Searching for Adam*, ed. Terry Mortenson, also at https://answersingenesis.org/bible-characters/adam-and-eve/when-was-adam-created/.

most readers would never be able to understand to check if the cited source supports Ross's claim. But I did have AiG's Dr. Danny Faulkner (Professor Emeritus of Astronomy, University of South Carolina Lancaster) check the reference in footnote 2 and it simply doesn't support Ross's claim (including being off by 10 decimal points), though of course all young-earth creationists agree that the universe clearly is well designed for life.

Another example that raises serious doubts about his cited scientific evidence for his day-age view is footnote 12. The two highly technical papers do not even remotely support Ross's claim. In the abstract of the first, the authors tell us that they studied "the 13C/12C ratio of oceanic bicarbonate" from which they "*infer* an explosion of photosythesizing communities on late Precambrian land surfaces" which they "*interpreted*" to "facilitate a rise in O2 necessary for the expansion of multicellular life" (emphasis added). In the second article the authors "report the recovery of large populations of diverse organic-walled microfossils," some of which approached "one millimetre in diameter." "They offer direct evidence of eukaryotes living in freshwater aquatic and subaeri-ally exposed habitats" indicating that "eukaryotic evolution on land *may have commenced* far earlier than previously thought" (emphasis added). These technical articles most definitely do *not* say that land plants of all kinds, including fruit trees bearing fruit, existed before sea creatures of all kinds were made, as Genesis 1 teaches. This is indeed one of many contradictions between the order of creation in Genesis and the order of first appearance in the evolutionary story, as I discussed in my chapter. To be sure, as Ross said, "old-earth creationists acknowledge no conflict" on this point. But they obviously don't acknowledge it because it is a barrier to convincing Christians that their old-earth view is per-fectly compatible with Genesis. Still, the contradictions are there and fatal to Ross's view.

For thorough refutations of Dr. Ross's views here and elsewhere, see Sarfati's work.[16] But the most important reasons I reject his day-age progressive creation view is that it simply cannot be harmonized with Scripture without ignoring or twisting many relevant verses. And that is not the way to treat the inspired, inerrant, authoritative Word of God.

---

16. Jonathan Sarfati, *Refuting Compromise: A Biblical and Scientific Refutation of "Progressive Creationism" (Billions of Years), as Popularized by Astronomer Hugh Ross*, 2nd ed. (Atlanta, GA: Creation Book, 2011).

RESPONSE FROM EVOLUTIONARY CREATION

DEBORAH B. HAARSMA

I'm grateful for the opportunity to continue the many years of conversation between Hugh Ross and me and between Reasons to Believe (RTB) and BioLogos (BL). Not all old-earth creationists share all the views of RTB as Ross notes and I will indicate my responses accordingly.

Old Earth Creation (OEC) and Evolutionary Creation (EC) agree on important points of science and Christian faith.

EC joins OEC in believing that the God of the Bible is the Creator of the entire universe and Jesus Christ is the only path to salvation for humankind. Both Ross and I see nature and Scripture as two books of God's revelation, where "both Scripture's words and creation's works originate from the One who is truth and reveals truth. Both are subject to interpretation and, therefore, to human error. Yet God has sent his Spirit to guide us persistently to truth" (p. 71). We also agree on some theological points, such as that animal death is not the result of human sin and that the new creation will be more than a restoration of the original creation.

Scientifically, OEC and EC both accept the evidence that the universe is ancient and that life appeared gradually over billions of years. Ross and I both emphasize that a biblical worldview gives a strong foundation for doing science and that historical science can give reliable answers about the past. We also agree on some particular scientific points, such as that the basic laws of physics did not change at the time of the fall or the flood, that geological evidence shows a flood never covered the whole planet, and that the first humans lived roughly 150–200 thousand years ago.

EC does not seek scientific predictions in Scripture.

Although both BioLogos and RTB love the "two books" metaphor, we apply it in rather different ways. Both groups uphold the authority and inspiration of Scripture, but RTB sees that authority as requiring a commitment to inerrancy on science as well.[1] Although Ross allows for some figurative language in the Bible, his emphasis is on a literal interpretation, describing it as the most "straightforward" and "consistent approach," making "the defense of biblical authority, inspiration, and inerrancy a relatively straightforward task" (p. 82). As Ross notes, this approach to Scripture is in contrast to both YEC and EC approaches. EC argues that the authority of Scripture does not require a literal, scientific interpretation in order to be true and trustworthy.

Ross follows a concordist approach to Scripture, including a day-age interpretation of Genesis 1 and reading many biblical passages as pointing to modern scientific discoveries, forming a "testable creation model." For example, scientific arguments are framed as, "If Genesis accurately outlines life's history, scientists should be able to detect . . ." (p. 84), which directly links biblical passages to ongoing scientific tests. While Ross may not use the strongest concordism possible, other old-earth creationists would certainly take a milder approach, calling some links an "unreasonable stretch" that Ross calls "reasonable and appropriate" (p. 77). For example, most old-earth creationists and even many concordists would not point to speciation rates after the arrival of humans as a prediction of Genesis 1 or use biblical passages to calculate the dimensions and physical laws of the new creation. The concordist approach is especially problematic when tied to incorrect or changeable science (see below).

Yet evolutionary creationists have more fundamental concerns with Ross's approach, both scripturally and scientifically. Regarding Scripture, we do not see the Bible as making scientific predictions, since the inspired human author and original audience lived in a pre-scientific era and simply didn't think in those terms. While the Old Testament anticipated the coming of Christ and some events in human history, we do not see the purpose of Scripture extending to modern scientific discoveries. Regarding science, we do not see science as an appropriate tool for establishing the authority and truth of Scripture. The concordist approach expects science to do something for which it is not equipped. Many atheist scientists elevate science as the best kind of knowledge, and the concordist approach tacitly accepts this premise. Rather than telling atheists that science validates particular Scripture passages,

---

1. For BioLogos's views of inerrancy, see my response to the YEC essay in this volume.

EC emphasizes the gospel message and explains the central purposes of Scripture.

A curious feature of Ross's approach is the emphasis on design as human-centric. This framing implies that humanity's physical welfare and spiritual salvation are the primary purposes behind things like animal death, the second law of thermodynamics, and animal capabilities. Yes, God designed the universe with us in mind, but surely he also created out of his abundance and for his own pleasure, apart from us.

Some OEC arguments have serious scientific errors.

Ross's essay contains a lot of science content, and a fair amount of it is correct. Unfortunately, though, several scientific statements are incorrect or misleading about the state of the current scientific consensus. In the private dialogues between RTB and BioLogos, we have explained our scientific concerns on several points; RTB scholars have modified their arguments in some areas but not others. Space does not permit a discussion of all of the scientific arguments in the essay; here are responses to a few.

- Creation-acts chronology. It is simply not true that Genesis 1 "yields a creation narrative in perfect accord—both descriptively and chronologically—with the established scientific record." Abundant fossil and genetic evidence shows that birds (day 5 in the Genesis 1 account) appeared hundreds of millions of years after land animals (day 6). Seed and fruit-bearing plants (day 3) appeared hundreds of millions of years after sea creatures (day 5). When an atheist points out these discrepancies of chronology, RTB only reasserts that it does match; EC instead grants the chronological discrepancy and explains the ancient context and non-scientific intent of the text.

- Cambrian explosion. Ross is correct that many body plans appeared suddenly in the fossil record in the Cambrian era, including bilateral symmetry and precursors to vertebrates. But Ross goes on to say, "Many researchers have commented on the degree to which the Cambrian explosion challenges evolutionary models" and concludes, "Currently, no naturalistic evolutionary explanation consistent with available data has been offered." This portrayal of the field is incorrect. First, the quotes from leading evolutionary biologists Morris and Wray are over twenty-five years old rather than current scientific assessments. Second, the quote from Levinton is too brief to convey his views. Levinton's article also describes several potential natural explanations for the Cambrian explosion, reviews molecular clock evidence that the new body plans arose 100 to 400 million years before the Cambrian rather than suddenly, and discusses the possibility that these life forms don't appear as fossils earlier because the rock types before the Cambrian era were inappropriate for preserving fossils. Christian paleontologists make similar points.[2] The Cambrian explosion is not completely lacking in explanation, nor a show-stopper challenge to evolutionary models.

- Convergent evolution. Ross points to "hundreds of pairs of species distant from one another on evolutionary phylogenetic trees [that] share many identical morphological structures" as "problematic for models in which God never intervenes or only subtly intervenes to direct evolution." Actually, the opposite is true. The process of evolution naturally leads organisms from different genetic branches to have similar body plans as they adapt to similar ecosystems. Consider the body shapes of sharks and dolphins; they descended from very different lines (fish vs. mammals), but the ocean environment favors body plans with similar features. Such commonalties are not at all problematic in the evolutionary creation picture but are just what is expected from the evolutionary process that God crafted and sustains.

- Size of the first human population. The genetic evidence is strong and growing that the earliest humans numbered several thousand, not just two. This is shown by multiple lines of evidence;[3] for example, the genetic variation in the human population today simply requires more genetic diversity at the beginning than two individuals could provide. This discovery has jump-started a new evangelical conversation on Adam and Eve, and evolutionary creationists are

2. For a full assessment of the field, see Christian geologist Ralph Stearley "The Cambrian Explosion: How Much Bang for the Buck?" *Perspectives on Science and Christian Faith* 65/4 (Dec 2013), 245–67.

3. See books and articles cited in my main essay, plus the new book *Adam and the Genome* by Dennis Venema and Scot McKnight (Grand Rapids: Baker, 2017), in which Venema explains the evidence for a large population.

discussing several options that uphold the Bible while accepting the evidence in God's creation; see my essay for more. While early estimates for the size of the initial human population had large error bars, the data and methods today are more precise and clearly show a population around ten thousand individuals. It is *not* "reasonable to expect that future studies will reduce this population to only two."

God created the human population in common descent with all life on earth, yet in his image.

Ross and I clearly disagree on the origin of humans. Ross states that old-earth creationists "reject the concept of universal common descent" (p. 72), whereas evolutionary creationists see overwhelming evidence for common descent, including humans. EC points to thousands of genetic commonalities with other species[4] that go well beyond what makes sense in "common design" (the idea that God used the same genetic tools for similar functions during special creation of the species). While common design would explain why similar species share many functional genes, it does not explain why species have the same errors in non-functioning genes or why the insertion points of DNA invasions match precisely when such exact positioning is functionally unimportant. The genetic evidence points strongly to God using the natural process of evolution to create *Homo sapiens* in common descent with other species. Note that this common descent easily gives a non-miraculous explanation for the affinities of animals with humans.

EC sees God creating humans in biological continuity with all life on earth, but also as spiritual beings. God established a unique relationship with humanity by endowing us with his image and calling us to an elevated position within the created order. Our evolutionary origins do not remove our uniqueness; rather, humans are unique among animals both as God's image bearers and as the creatures that Christ died to save.

BL and RTB both present the gospel in the context of modern science, but in different ways.

Hugh Ross has a gift and calling for evangelism that I admire, and the commitment of RTB to evangelism has been inspiring for

---

4. E.g., Graeme Finlay, *Human Evolution: Genes, Genealogies and Phylogenies* (Cambridge: Cambridge University Press, 2013).

us at BioLogos as we build our own ministry. In that respect, the BL approach has more in common with RTB than with the other organizations in this book: We both present the Designer overtly as the God of the Bible, use commonalities with mainstream science to open doors in conversations with non-believers, and reject a culture-war approach. But, as mentioned above, our approaches differ in significant ways.

For some seekers, the discovery of a concordance between science and Scripture is what first piques their interest in Christianity and in some cases becomes central to their conversion. But for most seekers, science is not what points them to Christ. At BioLogos, new Christians tell us that something else has prompted their interest in Christianity—a personal crisis, a profound spiritual experience, the words of a friend or family member, or reading the Bible for the first time. Yet they had seen science as a barrier to faith and feared they would have to give up their scientific work or intellectual integrity in order to become a Christian. It wasn't until they learned about EC that the barrier was removed so that they could make a commitment to Christ, and EC then helped them grow rapidly in their faith. We also see a lot of people coming back to Christ who had left the faith because they saw Christians promoting false scientific claims. For both types of people, it becomes even more important not to tie the case for Christianity too closely to current science (which can change) and never to incorrect science.

RESPONSE FROM INTELLIGENT DESIGN

STEPHEN C. MEYER

The theory of intelligent design (ID) is an age-neutral theory that doesn't take a position on the age of the earth and the universe. Nevertheless, I am a proponent of intelligent design who happens to share Ross's view about the age issue. So, though I have little to say as a spokesman for ID in response to his old-earth arguments, I can offer a *personal* response to his perspective just as I did to Ken Ham's.

I think Ross makes a compelling case for his old-earth view. He shows how our best scientific knowledge of natural history and relevant biblical creation texts substantially agree with one another. Though I don't agree with every detail of his proposed harmonization, I do concur that this general agreement[1] provides a compelling scientific apologetic for the reliability of the biblical text.

Since I don't find much to criticize in Ross's arguments for an old earth, I would like to explain why I agree with one of his other more controversial scientific claims—one crucial to his view of natural history.

Ross notes that he and other old-earth creationists reject the theory of universal common descent (UCD), though (due to space constraints) his essay doesn't offer much scientific evidence against it. Even so, I applaud his willingness to question this part of evolutionary orthodoxy. Too many Christians in the sciences have accepted the alleged consensus in support of UCD without critically scrutinizing it.

The theory of universal common descent is a theory about the history of life. The theory affirms that all known living organisms descended from a single common ancestor. Biology textbooks today often depict this idea, as Darwin did, using a great branching tree. The bottom of the trunk represents the first primordial one-celled organism.

---

1. Stephen C. Meyer, "Qualified Agreement: Modern Science and The Return of the God Hypothesis" in *Science and Christianity: Four Views*, ed. Richard Carlson (Downer's Grove, IL: Intervarsity Press, 2000), 129–75.

The branches of the tree represent the new forms of life that developed from it. The vertical axis of the tree represents the arrow of time. The horizontal axis represents changes in biological form.

Whereas the mechanism of natural selection and random mutation describes *how* major evolutionary change allegedly happened, the theory of universal common descent asserts *that* such change *did* occur and occurred in a completely connected, rather than disconnected or discontinuous, way. Thus, UCD affirms a monophyletic view of the history of life in which all organisms are viewed as ultimately related as part of a single *connected* family tree.

Darwin argued that UCD best explains a variety of lines of biological evidence, including the succession of fossil forms, the geographical distribution of various species and the anatomical and embryological similarities among otherwise different types of organisms. Modern evolutionary biologists have added the genetic similarities (or molecular homologies) of different organisms to this list of supportive evidence.

Despite the presumed consensus in favor of UCD, there are good reasons for doubting it. Most importantly, the arguments for it depend upon an often inconclusive form of inference known as abduction.[2] In abductive reasoning, scientists (or detectives) reason from effects (or clues) in the present back to causes in the past. To see the difference between abductive and deductive inference, consider the following argument schemata:[3]

DEDUCTION:

DATA: A is given and plainly true.

LOGIC: But if A is true, then B is a matter of course.

CONCLUSION: Hence, B must be true as well.

ABDUCTION:

DATA: The surprising fact B is observed.

LOGIC: But if A were true, then B would be a matter of course.

CONCLUSION: Hence, there is reason to suspect that A is true.

---

2. Stephen C. Meyer, "Of Clues and Causes: A Methodological Interpretation of Origin of Life Studies" (PhD diss., Cambridge University, 1990). Charles S. Peirce, "Abduction and Induction," in *The Philosophy of Peirce*, ed. J. Buchler (London: Routledge, 1956), 150–54.

3. Meyer, "Of Clues and Causes," 25.

In deductive reasoning, if the premises are true, the conclusion follows with certainty. Abduction, however, does not produce certainty, but instead plausibility or possibility. Unlike deduction, in which the minor premise affirms the antecedent variable ("A"), abduction affirms the consequent variable ("B"). In deductive logic, affirming the consequent variable (with certainty) constitutes a fallacy. The error derives from failing to acknowledge that more than one cause might explain the same evidence. To see why consider the deductive fallacy:

If it rained, the streets would get wet.
The streets are wet.
Therefore, it rained.

Or symbolically:

If R, then W
W
therefore R.

Obviously, this argument has a problem. It does not follow that because the streets are wet, it necessarily rained. The streets may have gotten wet in some other way. A fire hydrant may have burst, a snow bank may have melted, or a street sweeper may have doused the streets before cleaning them. Nevertheless, that the streets are wet *might* indicate that it rained.

Oddly, abductive arguments have the same logical structure as the fallacious form of deductive arguments; they affirm the consequent. Consequently, unless these inferences are strengthened using a process of elimination showing alternative hypotheses to be implausible, they remain inconclusive.[4]

In my PhD work at Cambridge, I showed that the case for UCD is based upon several abductive inferences from various classes of biological evidence (present "clues" about the past) such as fossil succession,

---

4. In my essay on intelligent design, I showed how the case for intelligent design—which begins as an abductive inference—has been strengthened by just such a process of elimination, rendering the argument for intelligent design not just an abductive inference, but an abductive inference to the *best* explanation.

anatomical and molecular homology, embryological similarity, and bio-geographical distribution.[5] Nevertheless, as I studied the logical structure of the arguments for UCD, I discovered that the evidence in its favor was inconclusive at best. Moreover, I found that the arguments for UCD were inconclusive for exactly the reason that abductive arguments often are: For each class of evidence allegedly favoring the theory, more than one explanation—or picture of biological history—could account for it.

Consider, for example, fossil succession. According to proponents of UCD the general progression in the fossil record from less complex to more complex forms of life is exactly what proponents of the theory should expect to find. And though there are exceptions to it, the simple-to-complex rule is roughly true. Nevertheless, the fossil record also manifests large gaps or discontinuities between different groups of organisms, especially at the higher taxonomic levels of phyla, classes, and orders. With very few exceptions the major groups of organisms come into the fossil record abruptly without discernible connection to earlier alleged ancestors.

Numerous fossil radiations or explosions[6] exemplify this pattern of abrupt appearances, including the origin of life and photosynthesis with cyano-bacteria (3.85 billion years ago); putative eukaryotic cells (1.6–2.1 billion years ago); the Ediacaran fauna in the late Precambrian Avalon explosion; most new animal phyla in the Cambrian explosion, new classes and orders of animals in the great Ordovician biodiversification event, major groups of fishes in the Late Silurian/Early Devonian periods (Odontode explosion and Devonian nekton revolution), winged insects in the Carboniferous; dinosaurs, turtles, lizards (Lepidosauromorphs), crocs (Crucotarsi), and marine reptiles in the Triassic explosion, flowering plants in Late Jurassic/Early Cretaceous; the bony fishes (teleosteans) and mosasaurs in the Cretaceous; modern birds after the Cretaceous extinction (sixty-five million years ago); mammals in the Paleocene/Early Eocene; and *Homo sapiens* in the Holocene, among many others.

---

5. Meyer, "Of Clues and Causes," 77–136.

6. The scientific references documenting the various discontinuities in the fossil record described in this paragraph and the next are too extensive to be included in this essay given the format and space restrictions of this book. Nevertheless, interested readers can find complete documentation for these claims in Günter Bechly and Stephen C. Meyer, "The Fossil Record and Universal Common Ancestry" in *Theistic Evolution: A Scientific, Philosophical and Theological Critique*, eds. J. P. Moreland, Stephen C. Meyer, Chris Shaw, and Wayne Grudem (Wheaton, IL: Crossway, 2017), 323–53.

Even whales—often cited as an example of a smooth evolutionary transition—display evidence of abrupt appearance. In *The Walking Whales: From Land to Water in Eight Million Years*, leading cetacean paleontologist J. G. M. Thewissen admits that in a "dramatic transition" whales were "undergoing fast evolutionary change," with features that "change abruptly." Thewissen likens the evolution of whales from land mammals to converting a bullet train into a nuclear submarine. "Whales," he notes, "started out with a . . . perfected body adapted to life on land. They changed it, in about eight million years, to a body perfectly tuned to the ocean."[7] More recent fossil evidence shows the first fully aquatic whales, the basilosaurids, appeared even more abruptly than previously thought. Indeed, basilosaurids first appeared forty-nine million years ago perhaps within only one to two million years after the earliest Protocetidae, a family of terrestrial mammals that are supposedly ancestral to whales. The basilosaurids may even *predate* some of their supposed protocetid ancestors such as the 47.5 million-year-old "proto-whale" *Maiacetus*—a mammal that gave birth on land, had well-developed hind limbs, and lacked even rudimentary tail flukes. Indeed, the phylogenetic tree based upon cladistic analysis of fossils does not reveal a gradual origin of aquatic adaptations; instead, the defining features of true whales appear abruptly in the clade Pelagiceti.

Though common descent and its fully connected monophyletic picture of biological history can explain a progression of increasingly complex forms of fossilized life, so can a polyphyletic view. Indeed, a polyphyletic view depicts the history of life as an orchard of separate, disconnected trees in which major new groups of plants and animals are introduced into the biosphere successively, but discontinuously, just as we see in the fossil record. Moreover, a polyphyletic view would seem to better explain (or more accurately describe) the overall pattern of increasing complexity *and* abrupt appearance than would a monophyletic view.

Or consider molecular homology, the class of evidence that many evolutionary biologists think supports UCD most decisively. When biologists compare the amino acid sequences of proteins and genes in different species, they often find that they are quite similar in the

---

7. J. G. M. Thewissen, *The Walking Whales: From Land to Water in Eight Million Years* (Berkeley: University of California Press, 2014), 207.

letter-by-letter arrangement of their information-bearing subunits. Comparisons of the chimp and human genomes have indicated that the two are between 95 percent and 99 percent similar in sequence.[8] Proponents of UCD explain this similarity as the result of chimpanzees and humans having a common ancestor, one that possessed an ancestral genome that later evolved in two slightly different ways.

But that's only one possible explanation. The similarity between different genes and proteins in different organisms also might have arisen separately as the result of an intelligent designer choosing to provide similar molecular-level functional capabilities in different organisms. For example, on this view hemaglobin proteins in chimps and humans should have similar amino acid sequences or structures (as they do)[9] since they perform the same function in each animal, namely, carrying oxygen in the blood stream. Thus, as with fossil progression, the evidence of sequence similarity admits more than one explanation.

Moreover, as was the case with the fossil evidence, an alternative explanation better accounts for other aspects of the molecular evidence. Consider: If Darwin's "Tree of Life" diagram is accurate, then we should expect different types of biological evidence to point to that same phylogenetic tree. Since life had only one history, then a family history of organisms based on comparative anatomy should match one based on comparisons of DNA, RNA, and proteins. Many studies have shown, however, that trees derived from analyses of anatomy often conflict with trees based on bio-macromolecules. For example, genetic analysis of the mitochondrial cytochrome b gene produces a family tree where cats and whales wind up in the Primate order. Yet, anatomical analyses put cats in the order Carnivora and whales in Cetacea.

Worse, various molecular analyses often generate widely different evolutionary trees.[10] As biologist Michael Lynch observes, "analyses based on different genes—and even different analyses based on the same genes" can yield "a diversity of phylogenetic trees."[11] More recently, genomics experts have found thousands of genes in different organisms

---

8. See for example, Stefan Lovgren, "Chimps, Humans 96 Percent the Same, Gene Study Finds," *National Geographic News*, August 31, 2005.

9. Susan Offner, *The American Biology Teacher* 72(4) (2010): 252–56.

10. See, for example, R. Christen et al., *EMBO Journal* 10 (1991): 499–503.

11. Michael Lynch, "The Age and Relationships of the Major Animal Phyla," *Evolution* 53 (1999): 319–25.

with no known similarity to *any* other known gene.[12] The pervasiveness of these non-homologous orphan genes is completely unexpected given UCD.

Finally, there are instances where the evidence for UCD has simply crumbled. In *On the Origin of Species* Darwin claimed that embryos of different classes of vertebrates progress through similar phases of development as they grow from embryos to adults. He thought this indicated that different vertebrate classes shared a common ancestor in which that common pattern of development first originated.[13] It turns out, however, that different classes of vertebrates do not progress through similar phases of embryological development.[14] Yet, Darwin regarded alleged similarities in vertebrate development as "the strongest single class of facts in favor of" common descent.

In sum, the case for UCD rests in part upon: (1) factual claims that have evaporated, (2) circumstantial evidence that admits alternative explanation, and (3) evidence (such as fossil discontinuity and conflicting phylogenetic trees) that is better explained by a polyphyletic view of biological history.[15] Consequently, I share Ross's skepticism about universal common descent and appreciate his willingness to express it, particularly since many Christian biologists have simply acceded to a presumed consensus that doesn't pass critical scrutiny.

---

12. Richard Buggs, "The Evolutionary Mystery of Orphan Genes," Dec 28, 2016, https://natureecoevocommunity.nature.com/users/24561-richard-buggs/posts/14227-the -unsolved-evolutionary-conundrum-of-orphan-genes.

13. Charles Darwin, *On the Origin of Species*, facsimile of 1st ed., 1859 (Cambridge, MA: Harvard University Press, 1964), 442, 449.

14. Stephen Jay Gould, "Abscheulich! Atrocious!" *Natural History* (March, 2000), 42–44; Adam Sedgwick, "On the Law of Development Commonly Known as von Baer's Law; and on the Significance of Ancestral Rudiments in Embryonic Development," *Quarterly Journal of Microscopical Science* 36 (1894): 35–52.

15. For more complete documentation of these claims see Stephen C. Meyer, Scott Minnich, Jonathan Moneymaker, Paul A. Nelson, and Ralph Seelke, *Explore Evolution: The Arguments for and Against Neo-Darwinism* (Melbourne and London: Hill House, 2007); Stephen C. Meyer, *Darwin's Doubt: The Explosive Origin of Animal Life and the Case for Intelligent Design* (San Francisco: HarperOne, 2014), 114–35.

HUGH ROSS

Both Haarsma and Ham seem to have misunderstood key points in my interpretation of Genesis 1. For example, they miss my view that the animals mentioned in the day 6 passage are three subcategories of land mammals, those most critical for launching human civilization, not *all* land mammals. Thus, no conflict exists between Genesis 1 and the fact that mammals precede birds in the fossil record. I state, also, that *zera'*, *'ets*, and *peri* are references to life-forms more generic than seed, tree, and fruits. Rather, they point to three non-exhaustive examples of the much broader term *deshe'* (vegetation). In this context, the scientific literature supports my claim that continental vegetation preceded the first ocean animals.

Rather than merely "reassert that it [Genesis 1] does match [the established scientific record]" (p. 110), I show *how* it matches. My book *Navigating Genesis* explains and documents the alignment in considerable detail.

My quotations from biologists concerning the Cambrian explosion and its challenge to evolutionary models are not all, as Haarsma states, "over twenty-five years old" (p. 111). The most provocative comment dates to 2009. I agree that my quotation from Levinton is "too brief to convey [all] his views." In my book *Improbable Planet* I quote Levinton further. He writes, "The assumptions of the models of molecular evolution may influence the outcomes too strongly to allow any significant confidence in estimates of molecular dates for the divergence of the Bilateria."[1] Molecular clock evidence does not overturn the rapidity of the Cambrian explosion.

---

1. Jeffrey S. Levinton, "The Cambrian Explosion: How Do We Use the Evidence," *BioScience* 58 (October 2008): 858.

Here is additional evidence for the Cambrian explosion's suddenness:

1. Large-bodied animals could not have existed prior to the second great oxygenation event or prior to the Great Unconformity.
2. Both events occurred immediately prior to the Cambrian explosion.

At the base of the Cambrian we see not only precursors to vertebrates but also actual vertebrates.

Convergence remains a problem for evolutionary creation. Long-term evolution experiments demonstrate contingency, not convergence, and convergence does not always represent adaptation to similar ecosystems. The sandlance (fish) ecosystem, for example, differs significantly from that of the chameleon (desert reptile).

Haarsma's statement that "genetic variation in the human population today requires more genetic diversity at the beginning than two individuals could provide" (p. 112) represents a model-dependent theoretical deduction, one that is clearly contradicted by field experiments among mammals.[2] Based on recent discoveries, it seems safe to say that "errors in non-functioning genes" may not represent errors at all. These genes may well serve purposes soon to be discovered.

Genetics is a complex science. Many of the possible systematics have yet to be identified, and possible variations over time in the known systematics have yet to be determined. Even within the known systematics, accurate values for systematic errors remain unknown. To cite genetics as the basis for overturning centuries of biblical interpretation seems premature at best, if not unwarranted.

Haarsma's disagreement with me regarding scientific "predictions" in the Bible may be a matter of semantics. "Anticipation" may be a more acceptable term. Surely we can agree that the Bible makes statements about the world of nature. Thus, science, like history, can be "an appropriate tool for establishing the authority and truth of Scripture" (p. 109).

Ham's rejection of animal death before Adam's fall appears based on something other than exegesis. For some reason he cannot accept

---

2. Fazale Rana with Hugh Ross, *Who Was Adam?* 2nd ed. (Covina, CA: RTB Press, 2015): 349–53 and citations therein.

animal death as part of God's "very good" creation, despite evidence of its benefits. What's more, no biblical text explicitly rules out animal death prior to the fall. Genesis 3 says the ground was cursed "because of humanity." It's our sin that spoils creation. Much of nature's realm remains breathtakingly beautiful, and "very good," to this day.

My assertion that *yom* can literally mean a long time period is affirmed by every Old Testament Hebrew-English lexicon.[3] I agree that Job 37–39, Psalm 104, and Proverbs 8 are not creation chronologies in the way Genesis is. However, these and many other passages in the poetic books are truthful creation texts that must be considered in our interpretation of Genesis 1–2 and 6–9.

The Genesis text implies that Adam did much more on creation day 6 than name 3,600 animals. Would he not have studied them before naming them—and before realizing his lack of one special benefit they all possessed, a partner? Note that he exclaimed, "At long last!" on first seeing Eve.

While the seventh day has long been understood as God's rest, or cessation, from making new physical creatures, Ham apparently sees it differently. He says I falsely accuse him of believing "herbivores evolved rapidly into carnivores" (p. 106) after the creation days. I consider such extreme diversification over just a few centuries, even over several centuries, as unnaturally rapid.

My "ever-changing dates for Adam" (p. 106), as Ham states, simply reflect changing scientific error estimates. The dates are now recognized to be less precise. As for the claim that my statement (in footnote 2) about the constancy of physical laws is "off by 10 decimal points," let me clarify that I translated the astronomical measure to a measure consistent with physics lab measurements, which show limits on possible variability as parts/x/year. Numerous scientific articles document the measured constancy of the laws of physics. As for footnote 12, I agree it does not suggest apricot trees existed before the first ocean animals. It does affirm the early appearance of vegetation (*deshe'*).

The book (by Jonathan Sarfati) Ham cites in critique of my views is entirely dedicated to attacking my character and my competency in both

---

3. Brown, Driver, and Briggs, *Hebrew and English Lexicon*, 398–401; Gesenius, *Hebrew-Chaldee Lexicon*, 341–42; Harris, Archer, and Waltke, *Theological Wordbook of the Old Testament*, 1:370–71.

biblical and scientific study. (My name appears in the subtitle.) My book *A Matter of Days* stands on its own in addressing Sarfati's complaints.

I appreciate that Meyer, in his response, distinguished his personal position on creation and evolution from the broader stance of the Discovery Institute. I concur on nearly every point.

Despite the differences outlined in the pages of this book, I remain hopeful. The affirmations and denials set forth by the International Council on Biblical Inerrancy provide a framework for progress in closing the gaps. If we commit to thorough integration and consistency in our interpretation of God's revelation and commit to treat one another with respect as brothers and sisters in Christ, we will surely find pathways toward resolution. These pathways will equip us to bring more people from all backgrounds to faith in Jesus Christ.

EVOLUTIONARY CREATION

DEBORAH B. HAARSMA

Evolution is real. The Bible is true.

Have you ever seen those claims side by side before? If those lines feel jarring to you, you are not alone. Many people today see a conflict between evolution and the Bible. Among white evangelicals only 27 percent agree that humans and other living things have evolved over time, while among those unaffiliated with a religion, 78 percent agree.[1]

A high school student named Connor wrote to BioLogos recently telling us about his upbringing in a Christian family. At home and at his Christian school, he was taught that the earth is six thousand years old and evolution could not be true. At the same time, he was becoming more curious about science and read on his own about the strong evidence for the big bang and evolution. Faced with these competing claims, Connor wrote,

> I became convinced that the Bible was incompatible with science and therefore that the Bible was not completely true. And, if it wasn't true in one part, how can I know if anything else in it is true? This drove me to disbelief in God. He just didn't seem necessary anymore.[2]

---

1. Pew Research Center survey March 21–April 8, 2013. Other Christian groups are more likely to accept that humans evolved: 44 percent of black Protestants, 53 percent of Hispanic Catholics, 68 percent of white Catholics, and 76 percent of white mainline Protestants.

2. See Connor's full story, including how he came back to a vibrant faith in God, at http://biologos.org/blogs/archive/how-science-shook-my-faith.

Connor isn't alone. Of young people leaving the church today, 29 percent say "churches are out of step with the scientific world we live in," and 25 percent say that "Christianity is anti-science".[3]

All the authors of this book would hate to see Connor abandon his faith over science, or to see a scientist hesitate to commit her life to Christ.[4] Too often this conflict has eternal consequences, as people feel trapped in a false choice between scientific evidence and Christian faith. We all wonder, how can the church show Christian young people that the Bible is relevant? How can we show scientists that Christian faith is real?

The authors of this book propose very different responses to this challenge. At BioLogos, we present evolutionary creation as a faithful option for Christians and a reasonable option for scientists. *Evolutionary creation is the view that God created the universe, earth, and life over billions of years, and that the gradual process of evolution was crafted and governed by God to create the diversity of all life on earth.*[5] Thus, evolution is not a worldview in opposition to God but a natural mechanism by which God providentially achieves his purposes. Many people who encounter the BioLogos perspective have been brought to a *deeper* faith in Christ as they considered evolution and the Bible together, and I'm happy to say that Connor is among them.

Many leading scientists today are Christians who accept evolution, including Francis Collins, the founder of BioLogos.[6] Collins is one of the world's top biologists and leader of the Human Genome Project and the National Institutes of Health. Collins shared his testimony of becoming a Christian as an adult in the best-selling book *The Language of God.*[7] He created the term "BioLogos" from the Greek words for "life" (*bios*) and "word" (*logos*, that is Jesus Christ, John 1:1–14).

Many leading Christians since Darwin's time have been open to seeing evolution as God's hand at work even while upholding the authority

---

3. David Kinnaman and Aly Hawkins, *You Lost Me* (Grand Rapids: Baker, 2011), 137.

4. See Natasha's story and how she came to Christ at http://biologos.org/blogs/archive/stories-natasha-strande.

5. The term "theistic evolution" (TE) is also used for this view. Evolutionary creation is a subset of TE that emphasizes that the creator is the personal God revealed in the Bible and incarnated in Jesus Christ.

6. Some sentences and paragraphs in this chapter are derived from BioLogos publications.

7. Francis S. Collins, *The Language of God: A Scientist Presents Evidence for Belief* (New York: Free Press, 2006).

of Scripture. Theologian B. B. Warfield (1851–1921), an early defender of biblical inerrancy, wrote substantially on evolution as a possible (and even likely) explanation of natural development under God's governance.[8] In 1944 C. S. Lewis wrote, "We must sharply distinguish between Evolution as a biological theorem and popular Evolutionism or Developmentalism which is certainly a Myth. . . . To the biologist Evolution . . . covers more of the facts than any other hypothesis at present on the market and is therefore to be accepted."[9] In 1997 evangelist Billy Graham said "the Bible is not a book of science. . . . I believe that God created man, and whether it came by an evolutionary process and at a certain point He took this person or being and made him a living soul or not, does not change the fact that God did create man."[10] And in 2009 pastor and author Tim Keller wrote that "the supposed incompatibility of orthodox faith with evolution begins to fade away under more sustained reflection."[11]

In this chapter I present the case for evolutionary creation. I begin with the ways God reveals himself in Scripture and in nature, and the reliable means for interpreting these revelations. The middle section turns to scientific evidence and some implications. The final section addresses common questions and challenges for the evolutionary creation position.

Reading the Two Books

The metaphor of considering the natural world as a second "book" of revelation is described beautifully in The Belgic Confession, Article 2:

> We know God by two means:
> First, by the creation, preservation, and government of the
> universe,

---

8. Christian historian Mark Noll does a case study of B. B. Warfield in chapter 3 of *Jesus Christ and the Life of the Mind* (Grand Rapids: Eerdmans, 2011).

9. C. S. Lewis, Letter to Captain Bernard Acworth, September 23, 1944, quoted in Gary B. Ferngren and Ronald L. Numbers, *Perspectives on Science and Christian Faith* 48 (1996):28–43, March 1996; http://www.asa3.org/ASA/PSCF/1996/PSCF3–96Ferngren.html.

10. David Frost interviewed Billy Graham in *Billy Graham: Personal Thoughts of a Public Man* (Chariot Victor Pub., 1997), 72–74.

11. Tim Keller, "Creation, Evolution, and Christian Laypeople," BioLogos.org, 2012, http://biologos.org/blogs/archive/creation-evolution-and-christian-laypeople-part-1.

> since that universe is before our eyes like a beautiful book
> in which all creatures, great and small, are as letters
> to make us ponder the invisible things of God . . .
> Second, God makes himself known to us more clearly
> by his holy and divine Word,
> as much as we need in this life,
> for God's glory and for our salvation.

Thus, both nature and Scripture are means that God uses to reveal himself to us, showing us his character and glory. Both also reveal something of God's interaction with the natural world. God's two revelations cannot conflict, since he speaks truly in both. As my own denomination puts it, "In both creation and Scripture God addresses us with full authority."[12]

Both nature and Scripture are subject to human interpretation, in the form of the disciplines of science and biblical scholarship. It is crucial that we do not confuse our human interpretations with God's actual revelation, since we can be in error in our understanding. Conflicts appear only when our interpretation of one or both books is in error. Such conflicts rightly prompt us to reconsider our views: Are there other faithful ways to interpret the biblical text? Are there are other valid ways to understand the scientific evidence? Each discipline can provide an important corrective to the other, protecting it from overreaching and prompting it to reevaluate. But one discipline should not drive the conclusions of the other. Science should not dictate the best biblical interpretation, and biblical studies should not force the conclusions of science.

Reading the Book of Scripture

How should we interpret what Scripture has to say about creation? This was a personal challenge for me. I grew up in a Christian home and learned to love God from an early age; I read the Bible as God's word of comfort, teaching, and authority in my life. My church and my family taught the young-earth creation position and didn't know of any Christian alternatives. So when I reached my twenties and became

---

12. "Report on Biblical Authority," *Acts of Synod* (Grand Rapids: Christian Reformed Church in North America), 1972.

aware of the scientific evidence for an old universe, I was hesitant to even look at it—I feared it would jeopardize my faith. I refused to simply throw out the Genesis passages or water them down because of science. How would I uphold the authority of the Bible? How would I avoid a slippery slope to throwing out every Bible passage that was difficult to understand?

The books of the Bible were written by many human authors under the inspiration of the Holy Spirit, across a span of more than a thousand years, to tell the big, true story of God's work in the world and with his people. Those authors came from many cultures, wrote in multiple languages, and used several literary genres. That means a full and deep understanding of each passage is more complex than opening the latest English translation. If we just open the Bible and read plainly for twenty-first-century Americans, we will find puzzling language and some passages that contradict our beliefs today, like the earth being fixed on a foundation (Ps 93:1) rather than moving through space.

To understand what's going on we need to remember that this is an ancient text. As biblical scholar John Walton reminds us, all of the Bible was written *for* us, but it was not written *to* us—it was written first to peoples living in the ancient Near East.[13] While the primary messages of God's Word are clear to any reader with a good translation, we'll need to do our homework in order to understand something as complex as the Bible's relationship to modern science. Biblical scholars recommend an approach of first considering the meaning the text had for the first human author and audience, then working out the best interpretation for us today.

Note that this approach does *not* lead down a slippery slope to denying the central doctrines of Christianity. Rather, we can apply it consistently to all of Scripture. In some cases, like Psalm 93:1 ("The world is established, it cannot be moved," KJV), a consideration of the full psalm and the cultural context shows that a modern scientific meaning was *not* intended; the passage is using the fixed earth as a metaphor for the stability of God's rule. Yet the same approach in other cases, like Luke 1:1–4, reminds us that the original author and audience considered

---

13. John Walton, *The Lost World of Genesis One* (Downer's Grove, IL: InterVarsity Press, 2009) and other books.

Jesus' death and resurrection a matter of historical record, and we should do the same.

Figure 1

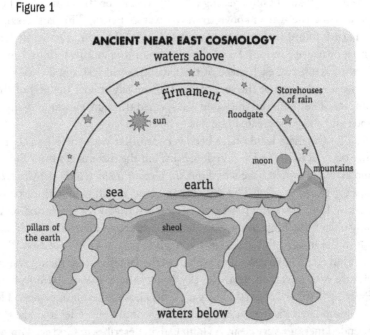

Graphic from *Origins: Christian Perspectives on Creation, Evolution, and Intelligent Design* by Deborah B. Haarsma and Loren D. Haarsma. Used with permission. Copyright © 2011 Faith Alive Christian Resources.[14]

Reading Genesis 1

Let's apply this approach to Genesis 1. It was written by and to the Israelite people, who were surrounded by other ancient Near Eastern cultures, including Egypt and Babylon. From the artwork and writings of those cultures, we know something of their understanding of the natural world (see Figure 1). They had no notion of the earth moving through space or of the earth being spherical. Rather, they believed the earth was flat, with heavens above and waters under the earth. Often

14. To order a copy of this resource please call 1–800–333–8300 or visit faithaliveresources.org.

they referred to the sky as a solid dome, with an ocean of water above it; the dome could open its floodgates, resulting in rain.

This picture helps us see Genesis 1 more clearly. On day 2 (Gen 1:6–8), we read of God creating a "vault" (NIV) or "firmament" (KJV) to separate the waters above from the waters below. This is the same structure found in Egyptian and Babylonian thought. Yet the differences between Genesis 1 and these surrounding cultures are striking. In those cultures, each piece of the natural world was a god—the god of the air, the god of the sea, the god of the sky-dome, the god of the sun, etc. They believed the world was formed through wars among these gods and the gods created humans to be slaves.

The Israelites would have been very familiar with the physical picture of a flat earth and a solid dome sky, but the differences from Egypt and Babylon would have stood out. *In Genesis, there is only one God, the sovereign Creator of all.* The sky, sea, and land are all merely things created by him. Even the powerful Egyptian sun god Ra is referred to as only one of the lights of the sky. Humans are created not as lowly slaves, but in the image of God and as a very good part of God's creation.[15]

God could have chosen to explain to the Israelites that their physical picture was mistaken, that the sky is actually a gaseous atmosphere covering a spherical earth. Instead, God chose a better approach: He accommodated his message to their understanding in order to make the intended message very clear. As John Calvin describes it, God accommodates himself to our humble capacities, even speaking in baby talk so that we can understand.[16] We can be thankful that God didn't try to explain the complexities of modern science in the Bible! God's accommodation is a gift of his grace to the original audience. Moreover, in this interpretation God's intended message does not change as science advances.

Did you notice the line of reasoning here? We started by considering Genesis 1 within its ancient context, not considering science at all. Yet we learned something relevant for our modern debates: Genesis 1

---

15. For more on ancient Near Eastern cosmology and interpretations of Genesis, see articles on the BioLogos website and books such as John H. Walton, *The Lost World of Genesis One*; Robin A. Parry, *The Biblical Cosmos* (Eugene, OR: Cascade, 2014); Kyle Greenwood, *Scripture and Cosmology* (Downer's Grove, IL: InterVarsity Press, 2015); or J. Edward Wright, *The Early History of Heaven* (Oxford: Oxford University Press, 2000).

16. John Calvin, *Institutes of the Christian Religion*, ed. John T. McNeill, trans. Ford Lewis Battles (Philadelphia: Westminster, 1960), 1.13.1.

deliberately uses concepts the first readers would understand rather than the modern scientific picture. This shows that the intent of Genesis 1 was not to address the "how" and "when" questions we ask in modern science; these were not a major concern in a pre-scientific era. Instead, the biblical text focuses on the "who" and "why" of creation. Evolutionary creationists draw similar conclusions for other Bible passages about creation. Most evolutionary creationists do not see the Bible as making scientific predictions or referring to science unknown to the ancient readers.

For me, learning about this ancient context for Genesis made all the difference. It not only resolved the concerns I had from science—it gave me a deeper understanding of God's teaching in this text and strengthened my faith. In fact, I became a bit frustrated that none of my pastors had taught me this earlier! I felt free, even called, to take a closer look at the evidence in God's creation.

Reading the Book of Nature

Like the majority of evangelical Christians today, I grew up with a generally positive view of science,[17] but I still had concerns about evolution. Can I trust the mainstream scientific picture of origins when the majority of scientists are not Christians? Are their scientific conclusions biased against God? Do we need a separate Christian version of science?

Non-Christians bring a different set of questions: Has science made religion irrelevant? Is religion anything more than superstition? Doesn't science eliminate God?

To address both sets of questions, first remember that many leaders of the scientific revolution—such as Galileo, Kepler, and Boyle—were Christians themselves. They saw their scientific work as the study of the very handiwork of God and a fitting calling for Christians. Today's militant atheists seem to forget that many first-rate scientists over the centuries were Christians, including Michael Faraday (electricity, 1791–1867), Gregor Mendel (genetics, 1822–1884), Georges Lemaître (cosmology, 1894–1966), and William Philips (Nobel prize in Physics, 1997).

---

17. Among evangelical Protestants, 48 percent believe science and religion can work in collaboration, 21 percent see them as referring to different aspects of reality, and only 31 percent see them in conflict (Elaine Howard Ecklund and Christopher Scheitle, "Religious Communities, Science, Scientists, and Perceptions: A Comprehensive Survey," http://perceptionsproject.org/multimedia-archive/religious-communities-science-and-perceptions-a-comprehensive-survey/).

Consider Robert Boyle (chemistry, 1627–1691), a devout Christian who described his scientific work as studying the "book of creatures" as a "priest of nature." He believed the natural world clearly points to God's wisdom as its creator and designer, so that "men may be brought, upon the same account, both to acknowledge God, to admire Him, and to thank Him." Yet Boyle argued strongly that Christians should *not* look to God as the "efficient" (direct) cause of the motions of particles. Instead, God creates the *mechanisms* that move particles, "those Powers, which [God] gave the Parts of Matter, to transmit their Motion thus and thus to one another." Thus, Boyle argued that the right role of the Christian studying the natural world is not to posit God as a step in the chain of cause and effect but to investigate the natural, repeatable mechanisms which God created.[18]

For similar reasons today, evolutionary creationists emphasize both (1) searching for natural mechanisms in the physical world, and (2) celebrating the God of the Bible as the creator and designer of those mechanisms. The first point is about the main task of science—looking for the natural chains of cause and effect, from gravity to chemical reactions to weather patterns. Scientists of all worldviews do this. The discoveries made by non-Christians are not automatically suspect; rather, all truth is of God, as Augustine noted long ago, "Let every good and true Christian understand that wherever truth may be found, it belongs to his Master."[19] The second point is the larger framework of our Christian faith, which makes the work of the believing scientist so distinct from scientists of other worldviews. Our view of nature as God's creation is what gives us the underlying motivation to pursue science and the ultimate praise for its discoveries. *A scientific explanation does not eliminate God.* For the Christian, a scientific explanation glorifies God by revealing his handiwork.

Is mainstream science biased against religion? It can seem like it when some vocal atheists claim that the big bang eliminates the need for a god to start things off[20] or that evolution shows "man is the result of a

---

18. Quotations from the blog series by Ted Davis, "The Faith of a Great Scientist: Robert Boyle's Religious Life, Attitudes, and Vocation," http://biologos.org/blogs/ted-davis-reading-the-book-of-nature/series/the-faith-of-a-great-scientist-robert-boyles-religious-life-attitudes-and-vocation.

19. St. Augustine, *On Christian Doctrine*, II.18.28.

20. E.g. Lawrence Krauss, *A Universe from Nothing* (New York: Atria Books, 2013).

purposeless and materialistic process that did not have him in mind."[21] Such claims go well beyond science itself, recasting the "big bang" and "evolution" as entities opposed to God. However, when scientists use these terms *scientifically*, they use them as scientific models the same way they would "gravity" or "plate tectonics." Science is limited. It simply can't prove or disprove God. Science is good at figuring out physical mechanisms, but it is not equipped to address ultimate questions of God and meaning. The same physical mechanism can be interpreted by an atheist as purposeless and replacing God while interpreted by a Christian as displaying God's creative handiwork.

What about miracles? Is evolutionary creation a slippery slope to deism, to seeing God as remote and uninvolved? No. Evolutionary creationists are passionate about seeing God's hand at work in natural processes. Natural laws are a testimony to God's faithful providential care as he upholds the existence of all matter and mechanisms moment by moment. Yet evolutionary creationists also affirm that God chose at times to act supernaturally. God acts outside his usual patterns to accomplish his kingdom purposes in human history, most powerfully in the incarnation and resurrection of Jesus Christ.

Some people ask evolutionary creationists, "Why do you believe in God if your scientific picture looks just the same as that of atheist scientists?" Well, we don't expect our science to look differently, since Christians and atheists are studying the same created world with the same divinely given minds. But for many the deeper answer is that "science isn't the reason I believe in God." Like most Christians, evolutionary creationists chose to follow Jesus Christ for other reasons, such as a deep sense of need for God, a profound spiritual experience, or the testimony of the Gospels. Having put our trust in the God of the Bible, we look through the lens of faith at the world around us—the universe, life, ourselves, human culture—and find that it all hangs together in a more powerful, compelling way than atheism. Starting from faith, we seek understanding.[22] As C. S. Lewis wrote, "I believe in Christianity

---

21. George Gaylord Simpson, *The Meaning of Evolution* (New Haven: Yale University Press, 1967), 34.

22. In *Proslogion* (the original title of which was *Faith Seeking Understanding*), eleventh-century theologian Anselm wrote: "I do not seek to understand that I may believe, but I believe in order to understand."

as I believe that the sun has risen, not only because I see it, but because by it I see everything else."[23]

The Created Order

An Ancient and Dynamic Universe

Before we look at the evidence for the age of the earth and the universe, we need to consider whether such scientific evidence is even reliable. First, how do we know that God didn't simply create everything six thousand years ago but made it appear billions of years old? The short answer is, we don't. There is no scientific way to tell the difference between an ancient universe and one that was made to look in every detail as though it were ancient. Yet there is a profound *spiritual* difference. Scripture is clear in teaching that God is a God of truth and that the heavens declare his glory. God's activity in the natural world speaks to us just as truly as his words in Scripture, and we must take it seriously.

Second, if no people were there to see it, how can we even study the universe scientifically? The short answer is, using the evidence left behind. A scientist is like a detective who gathers evidence to determine how a crime was committed. Even without an eyewitness, a detective uses evidence such as footprints, DNA, and phone records to build a strong case. Similarly, scientists can piece together what happened from the evidence we measure today. While such historical science has differences from experimental science (one can't bring a galaxy into the lab for an experiment!), it is similar in the most important respects. Just like an experimental scientist, the historical scientist builds a hypothesis, tests it against observations, then modifies the hypothesis as needed. And like the detective, when multiple lines of evidence all confirm the same hypothesis, scientists become confident that we know what happened. Historical science is reliable.

Geological Evidence

Many lines of evidence support the great age of the earth and solar system.[24] Here I will sketch just two. One is counting annual layers.

---

23. C. S. Lewis, in the concluding line of "Is Theology Poetry?" in *The Weight of Glory and Other Addresses* (New York: MacMillan, 1949).

24. See the BioLogos website for videos and articles on geological and astronomical age.

Such layers appear in glaciers, as snowfall each year is compacted into ice. Ice layers have been counted back over one hundred thousand years in Greenland and over seven hundred thousand years in Antarctica. Annual layers also appear in sedimentary rock. These rocks form at the bottom of lakes and shallow seas as sediment settles to the bottom year after year; when the layers harden into sedimentary rock, millions of years of deposits can be preserved (see Figure 2).

Figure 2

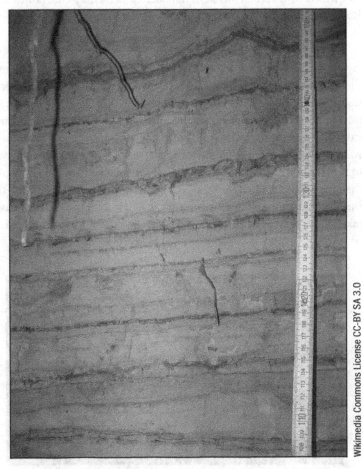

Sedimentary Rock Layers

Another is radiometric dating. Some types of atoms are radioactive and decay over time. This time period is called the "half-life," the amount of time it takes for half of the original substance to decay. For example, the half-life of potassium-40 is 1.3 billion years; during this time, half of the potassium-40 atoms decay into argon-40. Scientists can measure the ratio of potassium-40 and argon-40 in a rock and calculate the time when that rock first solidified from molten lava. A rock formation in Greenland has been dated to 3.6 billion years old, a date confirmed with several different radioactive elements in the same rocks. Rocks returned from the moon have been dated to 4.5 billion years old.

Astronomical Evidence

Again, I will sketch just two of the many lines of evidence for the age of the universe. Although light moves incredibly fast, it does take time to travel—over eight minutes just from the sun to the earth. What about travel time from a galaxy? A galaxy contains hundreds of billions of stars; our own galaxy is called the Milky Way. Figure 3 shows the spiral galaxy Andromeda, which is relatively "nearby" in space. Light takes a whopping 2.5 million years to travel from Andromeda to us. We also see galaxies with the same spiral shape that look hundreds of times smaller than Andromeda, showing that they are hundreds of times farther away. Light from those distant galaxies takes *billions* of years to reach us. The universe must be at least this old.

Figure 3

Wikimedia Commons

Andromeda Galaxy

The expansion rate of the universe can be used to determine the age of the universe as a whole. Galaxies are moving apart from one another. If we imagine rewinding the timeline of the universe, at earlier times the galaxies must have been much closer together. How long has it been since all of that material was packed together at the beginning? The expansion rate, and its change over time, has been measured carefully. We now know that the universe has been expanding for 13.80 ± 0.04 billion years.[25]

Reflections

Let's pause a moment to consider these incredible lengths of time. It's hard to imagine thousands of years of history, much less millions or billions! Yet we know that for God "a day is like a thousand years, and a thousand years are like a day. The Lord is not slow in keeping his promise, as some understand slowness" (2 Pet 3:8, 9). The vast timescales of the universe remind us that God's timing is not like ours.

Yet there is far more to this story than measuring age. For one, the universe is incredibly dynamic. It changes dramatically over time, with entire galaxies colliding, stars dying in supernova explosions, and new stars forming from the ashes. Nothing in this universe appears to be static or eternal. Rather, the universe demonstrates that God's creative work is ongoing.

Another piece of the story is God's craftsmanship. Some of the most fundamental parameters of the universe, such as the strength of gravity and the properties of atoms and particles, are precisely set ("fine-tuned") in such a way that life could develop. Scientists calculate that if these parameters were changed even slightly, stars would not be born, carbon wouldn't form, and humans wouldn't be here. From the beginning, God designed the universe so that the particles and forces would come together, assembling through natural processes to form a complex world and a home for life. Like a composer writing a symphony, God began with a rhythm and themes that start simply (the natural laws) but are designed from the beginning to repeat and grow over time to create the beautiful complex conclusion (life today).

Finally, consider the sheer extravagance of this universe. Only in the

25. Planck Collaboration, *Astronomy & Astrophysics* 594, A13 (2016): Table 4, available at https://arxiv.org/abs/1502.01589.

last century have we learned that our galaxy is one of hundreds of billions of galaxies. This vast number of galaxies were around long before humans could detect them. God appears to delight in creating extravagantly, out of his abundance. And God delights in working through systems—not creating just one galaxy, but creating the mechanisms of this universe so that billions of galaxies can form.

The Development of Life

I realize that some readers will have very negative associations with the word "evolution"—I certainly did in the church community in which I grew up. Yet this is a reaction to the false claims made by atheists in the name of evolution. Certainly, all Christians would reject the claims that science replaces God or that life is meaningless. But once the atheistic claims are rejected, the underlying science can be evaluated on its own terms. In my own journey on this issue, I was fortunate to come across the writings of Christian biologists who presented the evidence for evolution in the context of their faith rather than with an atheistic spin.

In the remainder of this section I will discuss the scientific process of evolution and the evidence that supports it. In the closing section, I return to several theological questions.

How Does Evolution Work?

In every generation, offspring of a species differ slightly from their parents. Sometimes those differences provide a reproductive advantage in their environment, meaning that individuals with particular traits are able to produce more offspring. Over successive generations those traits, or genetic differences, work their way throughout the population. For example, some of the gazelles born in one generation will run faster than others due to differences in their genetic makeup; they will be more likely to escape predators and reproduce than the slow gazelles. These fast gazelles will pass on genes to their offspring, leading to more fast gazelles in the subsequent generation. Several generations later, the traits in the entire population of gazelles will have changed. This mechanism is called "natural selection."

Sometimes one part of a population becomes isolated. Consider a flock of birds that is blown by a storm to a remote island empty of birds. The unique ecological environment on this island will favor some traits over others, and over time this will cause some genes to be selected. Over many generations, the bird population on the island will acquire traits that are distinct from the original mainland population. After enough generations pass, the characteristics of the mainland and island birds can become different enough that they are recognized as separate species. Some people call this process "microevolution." It is accepted by most Christian positions, including most young-earth creationists.

Evolutionary creationists go much further. We accept that natural selection and other evolutionary mechanisms,[26] acting over long periods of time, eventually result in major changes in body structures. Some people call this "macroevolution." Over a very long time, all species on earth arose through gradual change and are related by a "tree" of common ancestry (see Figure 4 for a portion of the tree for vertebrates, in "spindle" style). It illustrates that birds and lizards share a common reptilian ancestor, while reptiles and mice share a common vertebrate ancestor further back in time.

Figure 4

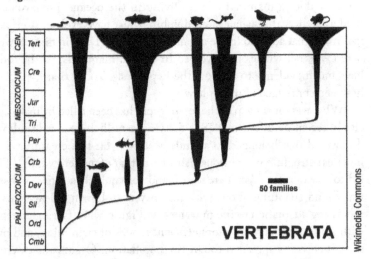

Tree of Common Ancestry for Vertebrates

---

26. See Reflections section below for more on evolutionary mechanisms.

Sometimes people wonder, "How could two individuals arise with just the right genes so that their offspring are a new species?" First, remember that evolution generally happens in *groups*, not individuals or couples. While a genetic change begins in one individual, that individual still interbreeds with the rest of the group and is not a new species. Starting a new species is a little like a pair of teenagers who try to start a fad—they may have a cool new idea, but until it spreads through their peer group, it's not a fad. Second, unlike fads, evolution takes a long time. It takes many generations for a genetic change to spread through the population. Then it takes many more generations to change enough genes that an isolated group become a separate species from their parent population.

Evidence for Evolution

The common ancestry of all species is supported by multiple independent lines of evidence.[27] For a case study, let us consider whales.

Although whales and dolphins live in the ocean, they clearly are not fish, but mammals: They are warm-blooded, they breathe air through blow holes rather gills, and they give birth to live young and nurse them. So, how does a mammal end up living in the ocean? The evolution model predicts that whales and dolphins must have evolved from land mammals that adapted to the ocean environment. Darwin himself wondered whether whales had evolved from land mammals, but he didn't have much evidence to support the hypothesis. Today that hypothesis has been confirmed in multiple ways.

What was once a gap in the fossil record has been filled by many species in recent decades. In 1978, a forty-nine-million-year-old skull was discovered that belonged to a land-dwelling wolf-like creature whose inner ear structure was curiously similar to that of modern whales. This led to a search for related creatures, and very quickly a series of fossils was found spanning about ten million years, showing clear signs of increasing adaptation to life in water (see Figure 5). Offspring emerged with spines that allowed more efficient modes of swimming, and over time such traits spread through the population. Organisms emerged

27. For more on the scientific evidence for evolution from Christian biologists, see videos and articles at BioLogos.org, particularly Dennis Venema's blog series "Evolution Basics." See also Darrel R. Falk, *Coming to Peace with Science* (Downers Grove, IL: InterVarsity Press, 2004); Denis R. Alexander, *Creation or Evolution: Do We Have to Choose?* (Oxford: Monarch Books, 2014); and Denis Lamoureux, *Evolutionary Creation* (Eugene, OR: Wipf & Stock, 2008).

with nostrils closer to the top of the skull that aided breathing during swimming, and over many generations offspring developed blow holes. In later generations, the hind legs of organisms were too small to support the animal on land. More than a thousand fossil specimens have been discovered that support this picture of whale evolution. These fossils are not all direct ancestors of whales today and small gaps remain, but they reveal a group of related species that were evolving over millions of years to adapt to ocean life. Taken together, they form an impressive picture of significant change in this lineage of mammals.

Figure 5

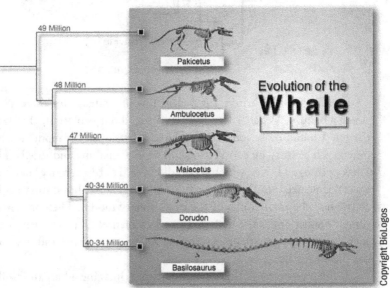

Whale Fossil Sequence

We also see the connection to land mammals in the development of whale embryos today. As the fertilized egg divides and new cells specialize, the embryo clearly shows limb buds for all four limbs, just like a land-dwelling animal. As the embryo grows, the hind limbs do not fully develop. In some species, only a pelvic bone remains in the mature whale. This evidence from embryos is independent of the fossil evidence yet points to the same story of common ancestry.

Figure 6

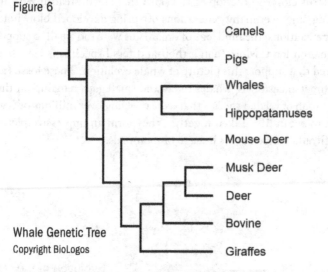

Whale Genetic Tree
Copyright BioLogos

Finally, genetics brings a powerful line of evidence for the evolutionary picture. When I was first learning about evolution, this was the one I found most convincing. Darwin developed his model in the nineteenth century by considering things like anatomy and fossils. He knew nothing of DNA, which wasn't discovered until a century later and wasn't sequenced until recently. Yet modern genetics has dramatically confirmed the predictions of the evolutionary model. The confirmation of predictions is the hallmark of good science! Genetics also gives exciting new insights that are allowing scientists to refine and develop the theory further.

To help you picture this genetic evidence, imagine a human family reunion. Say that your cousins, second-cousins, aunts, nephews, and other relatives are all gathered for a picnic. Some geneticists visit and take samples of DNA from each person present, without asking how the people are related. Considering the DNA alone, the scientists would be able to reproduce fairly closely the family tree, using only the genetic similarities and differences. In fact, they could learn about the genetic make-up of your deceased grandparents and great-grandparents based on the samples of their descendants living today. In a similar way, geneticists have studied the DNA of many modern species and used it to determine family trees of species, including how closely species are related and how long ago their common ancestor lived. Geneticists have found that whales are closely related to land animals, just as predicted in evolutionary theory and shown in the fossil record. Genetics also gives new insights, including that cows and hippos are more closely related to whales than to horses or elephants!

Reflections

As mentioned above, some Christians worry that evolutionary ideas are a result of worldview bias among scientists, perhaps a result of wishful thinking or driven by unwarranted assumptions. Or they believe that the science isn't settled—a recent survey showed that 49 percent of white evangelicals believe that scientists are divided on whether or not humans evolved.[28] But that is not the case—another survey showed that 99 percent of biologists agree that humans evolved.[29] There is a strong scientific consensus on evolution and little debate over the common ancestry of all life. The evolutionary explanation has emerged as the result of good detective skills—careful observation of evidence, formation of hypotheses, and confirmation of predictions. Christians who accept the evolutionary explanation do so because of the strength of this evidence and arguments, not out of peer pressure.

That is not to say that all aspects of evolution are completely understood. Like all fields of science, there is always more to learn. Right now there is a healthy scientific debate going on about the particular mechanisms of evolution.[30] While natural selection, the mechanism described above for the evolution of the gazelle, is a primary driver of evolution, scientists are discussing the relative importance of other mechanisms, such as embryonic development, genetic drift, the environmental impact on gene expression, and the way organisms change their environments to maximize survival. However, scientists are *not* doubting whether

---

28. Pew Research Center, "Strong Role of Religion in Views about Evolution and Perceptions of Scientific Consensus" (Oct 22, 2015). The same misconception was held by 32 percent of Hispanic Catholics, 31 percent of black Protestants, 26 percent of white Catholics, and 26 percent of white mainline Protestants; http://www.pewinternet.org/2015/10/22/strong-role-of-religion-in-views-about-evolution-and-perceptions-of-scientific-consensus/.

29. Pew Research Center "An Elaboration of AAAS Scientists' Views," July 23, 2015, http://www.pewinternet.org/2015/07/23/an-elaboration-of-aaas-scientists-views/.

30. See, for example, "Does Evolutionary Theory Need a Rethink?" in which Kevin Laland et al. and Greg Wray et al. give their positions, *Nature* 514 (Oct 2014): 161–64, http://www.nature.com/news/does-evolutionary-theory-need-a-rethink-1.16080.

evolution occurred; there is a strong consensus that all life on earth shares a tree of common ancestry.

What would it look like to praise God for his work in evolution? For me, this was a significant adjustment in my worship life.[31] But I gradually realized that in evolution we see God working through systems, systems which he crafted to bring about an extravagant abundance of variety. Biologists have identified over 350,000 species of beetles alone! A biologist is said to have quipped, "The Creator must be inordinately fond of beetles."[32] Evolutionary creationists see the interconnectedness of life as a testimony to God's creativity. He worked through simple natural processes to fashion dinosaurs and daisies, weevils and warthogs, and pine trees and people. He could have snapped his fingers to do this instantaneously, but both Scripture and the natural world reveal that God delights in working through long processes to accomplish his will.

Human Origins

Of all aspects of evolution, human origins raises the most questions for biblical interpretation and Christian theology. In my own journey through these issues, I long put off considering the topic for this very reason. Yet when I looked at it more closely, I found several options for faithful ways forward that do not deny the Bible or science. The next section will address theological questions, but let's start with the evidence in the book of nature.[33]

Evidence for Human Evolution

Archaeological studies of indigenous human cultures show that the first *Homo sapiens* left Africa around one hundred thousand years ago and had spread all over the world by ten thousand years ago. The exact

---

31. For more see Deborah B. Haarsma, "Learning to Praise God for His Work in Evolution," in *How I Changed My Mind about Evolution: Evangelicals Reflect on Faith and Science*, ed. Kathryn Applegate and J. B. Stump (Downers Grove, IL: InterVarsity Press, 2016), 40–47.

32. J. B. S. Haldane is reported to have said this often (http://quoteinvestigator.com/2010/06/23/beetles/#more-734), and wrote something similar in his 1949 book *What is Life? The Layman's View of Nature* (London: L. Drummond), 258.

33. For more on the scientific evidence regarding human origins, see infographics and articles at BioLogos.org (including blog series by Dennis Venema on human genetics) and books cited above.

timeline of human migration is still being investigated, but it is clearly inconsistent with the first modern humans living only in the Middle East six thousand years ago.

Human anatomy clearly has many similarities to chimpanzees, gorillas, and other primates, including color vision, hands with opposable thumbs, and flat faces. Humans are not "just apes"—we certainly have abilities beyond other primates—but we are also closely related to this family of creatures. The evolutionary model predicts that humans share a common ancestor with other great apes.

Fossils have been found for over six thousand individual creatures in several species in the time between that common ancestor and modern *Homo sapiens*. Over the last several million years, these creatures show a gradual transition toward bipedal walking, greater height, and greater brain size. The exact line of descent to *Homo sapiens* is not yet known, but many new fossils and entire new species continue to be discovered from this period, filling in the evolutionary picture.

Genetic Evidence for Human Origins

Genetics strongly confirms the prediction that humans share common ancestry with great apes and with all life on earth. Here's one striking example. Chimpanzees have twenty-four pairs of chromosomes, while humans have just twenty-three. If humans share a common ancestor with other great apes, evolution predicts that two chromosomes fused in the line descending to humans, but did not fuse in the line descending to chimps.

Before testing this prediction, here's some background on the structure of chromosomes. While each chromosome contains various genes, all chromosomes have two common features. The first is telomeres. Telomeres are repetitive sequences at each end of the chromosome, which act kind of like the plastic bits on the end of your shoelace that prevent it from fraying. The second feature in common is the centromere, a region closer to the middle of the chromosome that is important during cell division. If two chromosomes fused together in humans at some point in our ancestral past, then we would have only twenty-three chromosomes instead of twenty-four, and the fused chromosome would be nearly identical to that of two chimp chromosomes laid end to end. Furthermore, the human chromosome would have an extra telomere sequence in the middle, as well as an extra centromeric sequence. This is like finding a shoelace laid down end to end with two plastic bits right in the middle; the telomere pieces no longer serve their original purpose. It turns out that this is exactly what we find in one of our chromosomes, confirming the prediction that chimps and humans share a common ancestor. It is very hard to explain these and many other genetic features apart from common ancestry.

Figure 7

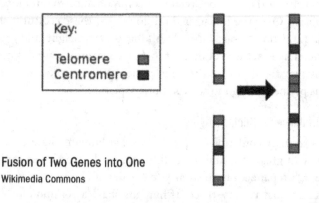

Fusion of Two Genes into One
Wikimedia Commons

In addition to common ancestry, the human genetic evidence also reveals two other key results that inform our theology. Both arise from considering the genetic variation across the whole human population. One is that humans are remarkably similar to one another; we clearly are all descended from the same progenitors, debunking the idea that different human groups or races arose independently. *Genetics shows that we are one human family*, as taught throughout the Bible.

The other result is that humans, like other animal species, emerged as a population rather than as two individuals. While modern humans have a lot of similarities across our population, we have much more variation than could arise from only two people. The early *Homo sapiens* population was several thousand individuals, living about two hundred thousand years ago. This is one of the most startling results for Christians because of the impact on doctrines tied to Adam and Eve.

Adam and Eve

How are we to understand the biblical accounts of Adam and Eve? At least three types of views are available for those who desire to remain faithful to Scripture and take science seriously.

First, the scientific evidence does not rule out the historicity of Adam and Eve; it only rules them out as sole progenitors. Adam and Eve could have been historical, real people living in a real place; it's just that other humans would have been living at the same time. (This may resolve some longstanding challenges in the Gen 4 text, which refers to other people who do not seem to be descended from Adam and Eve including those in cities and Cain's wife.) Some Christian leaders (including evangelist Billy Graham[34] and pastor Tim Keller[35]) see evolution as compatible with a historical Adam and Eve. In one version, minister John Stott[36] suggests that God entered into a special relationship with a pair *of ancient representatives of humanity* about two hundred thousand years ago in Africa. In this view, Genesis retells this historical event using cultural terms that the Hebrews in the ancient Near East could understand.

In another version (accepted by biologist Denis Alexander[37]) Adam and Eve are *recent representatives*, living perhaps six thousand years ago in the ancient Near East rather than Africa. By this time, humans had dispersed throughout Earth. God then revealed himself specially to a pair of farmers we know as Adam and Eve—real people whom God chose as spiritual representatives for all humanity.

Other Christians, including Alister McGrath,[38] have suggested a *non-historical* model. In this view, Adam and Eve were not historical figures and the early chapters of Genesis are symbolic stories in the genre of other ancient Near Eastern literature. They convey important, inspired theological truths about God and humanity, but the texts are

34. Grant Wacker, *America's Pastor: Billy Graham and the Shaping of a Nation* (Cambridge, MA: Belknap, 2014), summarizes, "Graham nowhere claimed that the Bible answered questions of history and science, but it did answer everything that truly counted" (see 38–40).

35. Tim Keller, "Creation, Evolution, and Christian Laypeople: Part 4," BioLogos.org, 2012.

36. John R. W. Stott, *Understanding the Bible: Expanded Edition* (Grand Rapids: Zondervan, 1999).

37. Denis Alexander, *Creation or Evolution: Do We Have to Choose* (Oxford: Monarch, 2008).

38. Alister McGrath, video interview for *Test of Faith*, http://www.testoffaith.com/resources/resource.aspx?id=276.

not historical in the sense people today use the word or in the way that the Gospel of Luke was written based on eyewitness reports of Jesus' life, death, and resurrection.

If these options for Adam and Eve are new to you, then likely you are full of questions and concerns at this point. Each of the views raises various hermeneutical and theological challenges, and I'll comment on some of those below. You may also be thinking of ways to mix and match these views or other variations; if so, you are in good company, as the study of Adam and Eve has become an active area for many evangelical scholars in recent years.[39]

Questions and Challenges

What happens to Christian theology if evolution is true? The stakes seem high. Evolution touches on central doctrines such as the image of God, original sin, and God's work in creation.[40]

Yet the stakes may not be as high as they look at first. Each of these doctrines has been debated and discussed for centuries, long before modern science. While all Christians uphold these key doctrines, Christians often disagree about the precise meaning of the doctrines (let's call these various meanings *doctrinal theories*[41]). For example, all Christians believe that humans are created in the image of God, but for centuries theologians have proposed different doctrinal theories for what this means (see more below). New scientific discoveries are prompting us to take another look at these doctrinal theories, but that doesn't mean the doctrines themselves are at risk. In my own struggles with questions raised by evolution, I've found hope in the treasure trove of theological resources developed over the history of the church. For example, the church has *not* always held to a literal interpretation of Genesis 1; Augustine himself argued against it.[42] Modern scientific discoveries are providing new insights into age-old debates but need not lead to a rejection of core doctrines.

---

39. For a good overview, see *Four Views on the Historical Adam* (Grand Rapids: Zondervan, 2014); see also BioLogos.org for other recommended books and articles from multiple viewpoints.

40. For further reading on all of these topics, visit BioLogos.org.

41. Benno van den Toren, "Not All Doctrines Are Equal: Configuring Adam and Eve," BioLogos.org, February 17, 2014.

42. Augustine, *The Literal Meaning of Genesis*, Ancient Christian Writers 41 (New York: Newman Press, 1982).

Image of God. The doctrine derives from Genesis 1:26, in which God creates humanity in his image. In the common Latin phrase, we are endowed with the *imago dei.* The idea is not discussed often in Scripture, leaving much room for theological speculation. Traditionally this doctrine has been tied closely to the miraculous creation of humans, so that many find it hard to reconcile the *imago dei* with the idea of humans sharing a common ancestor with chimpanzees. But let's consider for a moment some of the doctrinal theories. Some theologians see the *imago dei* as primarily about human abilities, such as intelligence, language, and rationality, particularly those abilities that make us distinct from animals. Science is giving new information about aspects of these abilities in animals, showing that these precursors are consistent with evolutionary models while also showing how the abilities in humans are at distinctly higher levels. Other theologians see the *imago dei* as primarily about our spiritual capacities and our relationship with God. And still other theologians see the *imago dei* as primarily about our commission to represent God's kingdom on earth, referring to the ancient Near Eastern practice where kings set up statues (images) of themselves around their country to represent their rule. So, do any of these doctrinal theories require the miraculous creation of humans? Evolutionary creationists would say no. Whether God chose to create humankind through a miracle or through evolution, God governed the process and gave us our abilities. God established a unique relationship with humanity, giving us spiritual capacities and calling us to an elevated position within the created order.

Original Sin. For some theological traditions, original sin is the most challenging question raised by evolution. Romans 3:23 and many other passages teach the core doctrine: All people are sinners and no one is righteous apart from Christ's redeeming work. This is central to the gospel. But precisely *what* happened historically when sin entered the world, and *when* it happened, and *why* God permitted it, are doctrinal theories that have been debated by theologians for centuries. Lutheran theologian George Murphy writes,

> The Christian claim is that a savior is needed because all people are sinners. That is simple. *Why* all people are sinners is an important question, but an answer to it is not required in order to recognize the need for salvation. None of the gospels uses the

story in Genesis 3 to speak of Christ's significance. In Romans, Paul develops an indictment of the human race as sinful and then presents Christ as God's solution to this problem in chapters 1–3 before mentioning Adam's sin in chapter 5.[43]

Questions about original sin become intertwined with questions about the historicity of Adam and Eve. Romans 5:12 teaches that "Just as sin entered the world through one man, and death through sin, and in this way death came to all people, because all sinned." However, two humans are present in Genesis 3, so some theologians read Romans 5:12 as allowing other humans to be alive at the time of Adam. Others read Paul as referring to Adam as an archetypal figure; the story of the fall in Genesis 3 involves some symbolic elements—a talking snake, miraculous trees—that suggest to some biblical scholars that it may not be literal history in the modern sense. Different theological and hermeneutical traditions tend to emphasize different issues; for some the key element is the historicity of the two individuals in the cultural context described in Genesis 4–5, while for others it is the original goodness and righteousness of humanity prior to the fall. These are important and challenging questions! Yet proponents of these differing views can still agree on the essentials: Sin is rebellion against God's revealed will, all humans have sinned, and none are righteous apart from Christ's atoning work.

Death before the Fall. The record of fossils in God's creation clearly shows that many animals died before humans appeared. (Note that this is a challenge for any position that accepts the ancient dates of fossils, even if evolution is rejected.) How does this long history of death square with passages such as Genesis 2–3 and Romans 5:12, which describe death as the punishment for human sinfulness? First, note that neither passage mentions animal death but refers directly to human death. Second, these passages could be speaking primarily of spiritual death rather than physical death; in Genesis 2:17, God says, "in the day that you eat from it you will surely die" (NASB), yet the immediate consequence for Adam and Eve was not physical death but a curse and ejection from God's presence.

Natural Evil. Evolution involves the suffering, death, and extinction

---

43. George Murphy, "Roads to Paradise and Perdition: Christ, Evolution, and Original Sin," *Perspectives in Science and Christian Faith* 58 (June 2006): 109–18.

of creatures. Of course, the existence of suffering is one of the biggest challenges in Christian theology—how could an all-powerful and all-loving God allow it? Again, Christians have debated this long before the discovery of evolution (the answers that have been proposed are called theodicies). Thus, the challenge for the evolutionary creation view is not "How could a loving God allow suffering?" but "Does evolution change the debate over theodicy?" Of the theodicies that have been proposed in the past, some now seem less plausible in light of evolution, such as the idea that all death and suffering are a consequence of human sin. Other theodicies are still viable, such as the idea that some suffering may be part of God's pre-fall creation (e.g., Gen 1–2 speaks of a good world, not a perfect one; in Job 38–39 God delights in predators). Many evolutionary creationists accept some form of the argument that God designed a system that works best for his purposes and our overall good, even if that system involves suffering. And we must remember that God's ultimate answer to our suffering is personal—in Christ, God himself took on suffering and death in his own body, for our sakes.

It is important to note that the scientific picture of suffering is not as extreme as is often portrayed. While some have painted evolution as "nature, red in tooth and claw,"[44] the evolutionary process actually reduces suffering in some ways, as it allows species to adapt and survive in new environments. Yet evolution is about far more than survival and competition; *cooperation* is at least as big a factor. Evolutionary biologists Michod and Roze write, "Cooperation is now seen as a primary creative force behind greater levels of complexity and organization in biology,"[45] arguing that cooperation is the common theme for several major transitions in the history of evolution. Cooperation increases in the transition from single-celled to multi-cellular organisms, from asexual to sexual reproduction, from individual behavior to social behavior, and from animal cooperation to the impressive levels of human social cooperation. In fact, some biologists say that cooperation is so important that we should not call evolution "the struggle for existence" but the "snuggle for existence."[46]

---

44. A line from Alfred Tennyson's poem, *In Memoriam*, which was published ten years before Darwin published *On the Origin of the Species*.

45. R. E. Michod and D. Roze, "Cooperation and Conflict in the Evolution of Multicellularity," *Heredity* 86/1 (Jan 2001): 1–7, http://www.ncbi.nlm.nih.gov/pubmed/11298810.

46. Martin Nowak and Roger Highfield, *Supercooperators: Altruism, Evolution, and Why We Need Each Other to Succeed* (New York: Free Press, 2011), xix.

Randomness. While some atheists put a nihilistic worldview spin on evolution, calling it random and thus meaningless, they are going far beyond what is warranted by the science itself. The evolutionary process does rely on random genetic variation, but also the non-random process of selection. Even for the random side of the process, the word "random" is used in the scientific sense of "unpredictable," not in the everyday sense of "meaningless." In fact, random (unpredictable) processes can actually have purposeful functions. Consider the videogame designer who chooses to incorporate random elements into a game. She does this deliberately because an unpredictable game is more interesting and enjoyable, and the random element will better accomplish her goals. Similarly, many Christians see God using intentional randomness, deliberately choosing to include some random elements in creation to bring more variety. The evolutionary process produces not just one kind of flower but an extravagant variety of flowers of every shape and color and scent.

Purpose and Directionality. Biologist Stephen Jay Gould is among some biologists who think that "we are a momentary cosmic accident that would never arise again if the tree of life could be replanted . . ."[47] The first half of this statement is pure worldview spin, but the second is a biological claim that evolution might have led to very different outcomes if the process were repeated. Other biologists, such as Simon Conway Morris, present a different scientific picture.[48] They point out that evolution converges on the same features again and again. The eye evolved independently several times, as did wings (e.g., bats are descended from land mammals, not birds). In this view, if the process were replayed, many of the same body features would arise. Many evolutionary creationists see God as designing the evolutionary process with the intention of producing life with these features.

Conclusion

Christians hold multiple views on questions of creation and evolution, as Christians do on many theological issues. While not everyone will agree with evolutionary creation, I've made the case that this view is a faithful option for serious Christians. It upholds the authority of the

---

47. Stephen Jay Gould, *Full House* (Cambridge, MA: Harvard University Press, 1996), 18.
48. E.g., Simon Conway Morris, *The Runes of Evolution* (West Conshohocken, PA: Templeton Press, 2015) and http://www.mapoflife.org/.

Bible and core theological doctrines, even while reinvigorating ancient discussions of how to interpret the Bible and various doctrinal theories. For Christians who are encountering the scientific evidence for the first time, evolution need not push them away from their faith.

I've also shown that evolutionary creation is a reasonable option for serious scientists. This view accepts the scientific case for evolution while showing that it need not lead to rejection of God or a nihilistic worldview. For science lovers who are considering Christ for the first time, evolution need not be a barrier to coming to faith.

The way we talk about this issue matters for both the church and the world. Christ calls the church to unity (John 17). Unity does not mean uniformity, but it does mean a deep love for fellow believers who hold different views than our own and certainly from refraining from accusations of stupidity or weak faith. Unity means taking the time to listen and understand those with whom we disagree, celebrating our areas of agreement even while seriously debating our areas of disagreement. I pray that this book becomes a useful tool to further gracious dialogue in the church. Through such dialogue, may the world see the fragrance of Christ among us; they will know we are Christians by our love.

While issues of creation and evolution are important, they are not the only science issue facing the church today. The church also needs to be engaged in issues like medical care for the needy, responsible use of new technologies, and caring for the environment. I pray that Christian young people today will hear God's call to bring their scientific talents and a biblical witness in these areas as well as origins.

Finally, in the midst of these discussions, we must never forget the biblical call to praise God for his glory and power displayed in creation. As an astronomer, I have a front-row seat to the wonders of the universe. I continually marvel that the One who created all of this is also my own Savior and Lord. As John writes in the opening of his Gospel, "In the beginning was the Word . . . through him all things were made." The living Word, Jesus Christ, is fully God and the creator of this entire cosmos, from billions of galaxies to thousands of species of beetles. Yet the Word also became flesh and dwelt among us, moving into our neighborhood (John 1:14, NIV, The Message) to walk the dust of this earth and bear our sins on the cross. Jesus Christ is our cosmic creator *and* our incarnate savior. To him be the glory!

KEN HAM

Sadly, there is not much in Dr. Haarsma's chapter that I can agree with. I do agree with her that God has revealed Himself in Scripture and in nature. Obviously, that is true of Scripture, and the Bible also clearly says so regarding nature (e.g., Rom 1:18–20; Acts 14:15–17; Pss 19:1; 97:6; and Job 12:7–10). But notice carefully what Haarsma, the Bible, and the Belgic Confession (which she quotes) say that nature reveals: it reveals *God* (His existence and at least some of His attributes). Those verses also teach that nature reveals God *infallibly* so that every nonbeliever is inexcusably guilty for not worshiping God. But neither the Bible nor the historic confessions teach that nature reveals how and when it came into existence.[1]

Related to this, I agree that both creation and Scripture are subject to human interpretation. However, we must remember that Scripture is *verbal* revelation and nature speaks *nonverbally*, which is less clear. Furthermore, Scripture is perfect and inerrant (Ps 19:7–8), and Jesus promised His Holy Spirit to lead believers into the truth (John 16:13; 1 John 2:27) as they study His Word diligently (2 Tim 2:15), interpreting it in its historical and grammatical context and by comparing Scripture with Scripture. On the other hand, nonverbal nature is cursed and in slavery to corruption (Gen 3:17; 5:29; 8:21; Rom 8:19–22), thereby making it difficult to interpret. Therefore, Scripture must be used to interpret nature, not vice versa, especially when it comes to the question of origins.

I agree with Haarsma that genetics shows there is only one human family (i.e., one race) and that man is made in the image of God. I also agree that the evolution story impacts central doctrines of the Christian faith, as I explained in my chapter. I agree that Romans 3:23 teaches that

---

1. For a thorough discussion of these two sources of revelation (also called general revelation and special revelation), see Richard L. Mayhue, "Is Nature the 67th Book of the Bible?" in *Coming to Grips with Genesis*, eds. Terry Mortenson and Thane H. Ury (Green Forest, AR: Master Books, 2008), 105–30.

"all people are sinners and that no one is righteous apart from Christ's redeeming work." Finally, I agree with her that Christ calls Christians to unity (John 17:21–23). But Christian unity can only be achieved and maintained as we are committed to the supreme truth of His Word in our lives (John 17:17; John 8:31–32; Acts 20:28–32; 1 Tim 3:15; 2 Tim 2:15–18). Where that shared commitment is lacking, there will be division, and the greater the differences in our understanding of and submission to Scripture, the greater our disunity. We cannot sacrifice biblical truth for the sake of a superficial unity.

This fundamental point is where I see great weakness in Haarsma's chapter. She discusses very little Scripture. She touches on one word in Genesis 1:6–8 to talk about the ancient Jewish picture of the world. She refers to Genesis 1:26 in saying that there has been considerable debate in the church about man being in the image of God.[2] She says the various theories about that don't rule out the idea that God created man by evolution from lower life forms, but she discusses no verses to support that claim, and in fact the idea cannot be defended from the Bible.[3] In dealing with the origin of sin and death and the issue of death before the fall she only vaguely refers to Genesis 1–3, Romans 5:12, and Job 38–39, ignoring all the specific verses that I discussed in my chapter.

Under the influence of John Walton, Haarsma assumes and asserts that the ancient Israelites had a view of the world just like Israel's pagan neighbors, implying that the Israelites believed in a flat earth (which is unlikely[4]) with a solid dome[5] (also unlikely[6]) and states that God "accommodated

---

2. For a thorough discussion of the historical and biblical teaching about the image of God in man, see David Casas, "Adam and the Image of God" in *Searching for Adam: Genesis and the Truth about Man's Origin*, ed. Terry Mortenson (Green Forest, AR: Master Books, 2016), 195–228.

3. Ibid. See in-depth analysis of all relevant verses in the Bible in chapters 1, 2, 4, and 5.

4. Job 26:7, 10; Proverbs 8:27; and Psalm 19:6 indicate that the biblical authors and their believing ancient readers believed in a spherical earth resting on nothing. For a discussion of the firmament (Gen 1:6–8) see Danny Faulkner (PhD, astronomy), *The Created Cosmos: What the Bible Reveals about Astronomy* (Green Forest, AR: Master Books, 2016), 39–43.

5. Haarsma picks up on "vault" in the NIV 2011 translation of Genesis 1:6–7 (though the NIV 1984 translates the Hebrew as "expanse"). Walton no longer believes "vault" is a correct translation. See his "Response from the Archetypal View," in *Four Views on the Historical Adam*, eds. Matthew Barrett and Ardel B. Caneday (Grand Rapids: Zondervan, 2013), 67–68.

6. It is very questionable if many of the ancients believed in a flat earth and a hard dome. More likely, modern scholars who don't believe Genesis have interpreted literally the words of the ancients that were intended as metaphors. Regarding this and the diagram Haarsma used, see William Barrick (Hebrew scholar), "Old Testament Evidence for a Literal, Historical Adam and Eve" in *Searching for Adam*, ed. Terry Mortenson, 45–49. Jeffrey Burton Russell

his message to their [erroneous] understanding." This accuses God of using error to teach truth, something the God of the Bible would never do. But Walton's and other scholars' insistence that we must use ancient Near East literature to interpret Genesis 1–11 is mistaken in many ways.[7]

On the question of death and natural evil before the fall, she rejects the young-earth view by saying that Romans 5:12 doesn't speak of animal death. But in my chapter I did not say that Romans 5:12 does. She also says that this verse and Genesis 2:17 "could be speaking primarily of spiritual death rather than physical death" (p. 151). But it is speaking of both. In Genesis 3:8 we see spiritual death (separation from God) while in 3:19 God pronounces their eventual physical death. The contexts of Romans 5:12 and 1 Corinthians 15:21–22 show that Paul is referring to the physical death of both Jesus and Adam. In any case, Haarsma's quite brief comments on this very important topic provide no basis for believing in millions of years of animal death, disease, and extinction before the fall of Adam.

With respect to all the scientific "evidence" that Haarsma presents for evolution and millions of years, I will only respond to a few points and encourage readers to consider resources cited in the footnotes.

One problem is that she never defines what she means by "evolution." Nor does she define what she means by "new species" forming. All young-earth creationists accept natural selection and mutations, which can even form new species within the original created kinds. But those changes do not produce microbe-to-microbiologist change that adds brand new genetic information causing one kind to change into a very different kind.

Haarsma uses vague diagrams and generalities to claim that the fossil record proves evolution. But two of America's greatest evolutionists at Harvard University informed us otherwise. In 1977 Stephen J. Gould said,

> The extreme rarity of transitional forms in the fossil record persists as the trade secret of paleontology. The evolutionary trees that adorn our textbooks have data only at the tips and nodes of their branches; the rest is inference, however reasonable, not the evidence of fossils.[8]

(professor of history), *Inventing the Flat Earth* (New York: Praeger, 1991), shows that the ancients did *not* believe in a flat earth.

7. See the critique by Steve Ham, "What's Lost in John Walton's *The Lost World of Adam and Eve?*" in *Searching for Adam*, ed. Terry Mortenson, 165–94.

8. Stephen J. Gould, "Evolution's Erratic Pace," *Natural History* 86/5 (May 1977): 14.

Ernst Mayr said essentially the same in 2001:

> Given the fact of evolution, one would expect the fossils to document a gradual steady change from ancestral forms to the descendants. But this is not what the paleontologist finds. Instead, he or she finds gaps in just about every phyletic series. . . . The discovery of unbroken series of species changing gradually into descending species is very rare.[9]

Sinonyx jiashanensis
Lived 56 million years ago
6 feet long

Ambulocetus natans
Lived 49 million years go
11 feet long

Rodhocetus kasrani
Lived 47 million years ago
15 feet long

Dorudon atrox
Lived 39 million years ago
20 feet long

Basilosaurus isis
Lived 39 million years ago
60 feet long

From Dr. Carl Werner's *Evolution: The Grand Experiment* (2014, 3rd ed.), 131. Used with permission.

But what about her specific example of whale evolution? The solid lines in Haarsma's "Whale Genetic Tree" should be dotted lines (as in older evolutionist diagrams), indicating to the reader that they represent evolutionist imagination, not the fossil evidence. But furthermore, compare her "Whale Fossil Sequence" diagram with this one (right) from the University of Michigan, where Dr. Phil Gingerich is the expert

9. Ernst Mayr, *What Evolution Is* (New York: Basic Books, 2001), 14.

whale paleontologist.[10] The University of Michigan diagram seems more convincing as it shows a land animal gradually changing into a sea creature, compared to Haarsma's diagram, which makes a very abrupt change from land to sea between the third and fourth creature.

But the first and third creatures don't agree in these two diagrams. So, which evolutionist is telling us the truth? Also, in 1983 Gingerich (who found the fossils of *Pakicetus*) confidently said that it "is the oldest and most primitive whale yet discovered . . . it is an important transitional form linking Paleocene carnivorous land mammals and later, more advanced marine whales."[11] He even showed *Pakicetus* in its ocean habitat (below left) based solely on some skull bones and teeth. But by 2001 almost the whole skeleton had been found, and a technical article in *Nature* described it as "no more amphibious than a tapir" (pig-like creature),[12] like this on the right.[13]

10. Diagram photographed by Carl Werner when he interviewed Phil Gingerich at the University of Michigan in 2001. Carl Werner, *Evolution: The Grand Experiment*, 3rd ed. (Green Forest, AR: New Leaf, 2014), 129–46. See also the associated DVD by the same title.

11. Phil Gingerich, "Evidence for Evolution from the Vertebrate Fossil Record," *Journal of Geological Education* 31 (1983): 140–44.

12. J. G. M. Thewissen, E. M. Williams, L. J. Roe, and S. T. Hussain, "Skeletons of Terrestrial Cetaceans and the Relationship of Whales to Artiodactyls," *Nature* 413 (Sept 2001): 277–81.

13. Art by Carl Buell at http://www.amnh.org/exhibitions/whales-giants-of-the-deep/whale-evolution/. See further, Terry Mortenson, "Fossil Evidence for Whale Evolution?" https://answersingenesis.org/aquatic-animals/fossil-evidence-of-whale-evolution/.

Gingerich also admitted that the flippers and fluke on *Rodhocetus* were speculations, not the evidence of fossils.[14] Whale evolution from land animals is a myth, just like the rest of the macroevolutionary story, including the story about *Tiktaalik*.[15] None of it stands up to scrutiny.

Genetics doesn't support evolution either. It confirms the literal truth of Genesis about Adam, including how long ago he was created.[16] Lightner and DeWitt refute the evolutionist claim about the fusion of two chimp genes into one human gene.[17] Sanford demonstrates that mutations are fatal to the hypothesis of macroevolution.[18] Lenski's amazing research on *E. coli* bacteria doesn't prove evolution either.[19]

Regarding geology, Haarsma documents none of her claims. Evolutionists *assume* layers of ice and sediments were formed annually. But careful inspection shows that interpretation is erroneous.[20] The assumptions and interpretations involved in radiometric dating are equally flawed.[21] Regarding astronomy, scientists have not *observed* an expanding universe; they have observed the redshift of starlight and *interpreted* it (based on naturalistic *assumptions*, again) as an expanding universe. But that may not be the correct interpretation. Even if it is correct, that doesn't prove the universe started from an almost infinitely small bit of matter, energy, and space. Many top-notch secular scientists reject the big bang theory,[22] and creationist researchers are working on

---

14. Gingerich's admission is reported in Werner, *Evolution: The Grand Experiment*, 141 and 143. See also in a DVD by the same title. A video clip of that admission in the DVD is at https://www.youtube.com/watch?v=R7e6C6yUqck.

15. David Menton, "Is Tiktaalik Evolution's Greatest Missing Link?" https://answersin-genesis.org/missing-links/is-tiktaalik-evolutions-greatest-missing-link/.

16. Nathaniel Jeanson and Jeff Tomkins, "Genetics Confirms the Recent, Supernatural Creation of Adam and Eve" in *Searching for Adam*, ed. Terry Mortenson, 287–330.

17.Jean Lightner, "Chromosome Tales and the Importance of a Biblical Worldview," https://answersingenesis.org/genetics/dna-similarities/chromosome-tales-and-importance-biblical-worldview/; and David DeWitt, "What about the Similarity between Human and Chimp DNA?" https://answersingenesis.org/genetics/dna-similarities/what-about-the-similarity-between-human-and-chimp-dna/.

18. John Sanford, *Genetic Entropy* (FMS Publications, 2014).

19. Georgia Purdom, "Bacteria Evolve Key Innovation or Not?" https://answersingenesis.org/blogs/georgia-purdom/2012/11/08/bacteria-evolve-key-innovation-or-not/.

20. Jake Hebert, "ICR and AIG Refute BioLogos Old-Earth Argument," http://www.icr.org/article/9761. The technical article backing up this summary article is in its footnote 15.

21. Andrew Snelling, "Radiometric Dating: Problems with the Assumptions," https://answersingenesis.org/geology/radiometric-dating/radiometric-dating-problems-with-the-assumptions/.

22. Eric J. Lerner, "Bucking the Big Bang," *New Scientist* 2448 (May 22, 2004): 20. Originally signed by thirty-four scientists in ten countries, it was eventually signed by more than

several models to deal with the distant starlight problem (which is similar to the evolutionists "horizon problem").[23]

The Bible clearly teaches the supernatural origin of all kinds of plants and animals along with man, to reproduce only variation within each kind, and the supernatural creation of earth and the heavenly bodies. Evolutionist scientific claims are *interpretations* of some of the physical evidence based on naturalistic (atheistic) religious *assumptions*, which is why the "evidence" for evolution and millions of years does not stand up to scrutiny. Adding God to the story doesn't make it true either.

four hundred scientists in over fifty countries; https://web.archive.org/web/20140401081546/ http://cosmologystatement.org/. See also Hilton Ratcliffe, "The First Crisis in Cosmology Conference," *Progress in Physics* 3 (Dec 2005): 19–24; and Paul J. Steinhardt, "The Inflation Debate: Is the Theory at the Heart of Modern Cosmology Deeply Flawed?" *Scientific American* 304:4 (April 2011): 36–43.

23. Jason Lisle, "Does Distant Starlight Prove the Universe is Old?" https://answersin genesis.org/astronomy/starlight/does-distant-starlight-prove-the-universe-is-old/.

HUGH ROSS

D r. Haarsma and I share the core belief that "both nature and Scripture are means that God uses to reveal himself" (Belgic Confession, Article 2). While my position aligns with the International Council on Biblical Inerrancy's statements on how we are to interpret God's revelations in science and Scripture, I have yet to learn where Haarsma stands on these statements.

Haarsma's passion for science, like mine, is motivated by our shared "view of nature as God's creation" (p. 133). Christianity, after all, gave birth to both the scientific method and scientific revolution. I especially endorse Haarsma's admonition that we express "deep love for fellow believers who hold different views than our own, . . . taking the time to listen and understand those with whom we disagree" (p. 154). My heart joins with hers in praying that this book will become "a useful tool to further gracious dialogue" (p. 154).

Reading Haarsma's testimony gave me a deeper appreciation for her reluctance to use science as an evangelism resource. Steeped in young-earth creationism until her twenties and hesitant until then to examine scientific evidence for the universe's age, she understandably concludes that science "is not equipped to address ultimate questions of God and meaning" (p. 134). She found answers apart from science. My story is different in that God used science to point me toward answers to ultimate questions, to show me the reliability of Scripture, where I met and surrendered to Christ, Creator and Savior of mankind.

I freely acknowledge many come to Christ through "a deep sense of need for God, a profound spiritual experience, or the testimony of the Gospels" (p. 134). However, for a considerable portion of our population, connecting science with Scripture provides the motivation to pick up a Bible, listen to a Christian testimony, or open up to spiritual experience.

As Hebrews 11:6 declares, "Anyone who comes to him must believe that he exists and that he rewards those who earnestly seek him." In my experience, people with negative, little, or no contact with Christians need a nudge from the book of nature to become convinced God exists, that he is the biblical God, and that the Bible is worth taking seriously and personally.

Haarsma asserts that biological evolution was a gradual process. Yet gradualism faces multiple challenges. The fossil record, repeated mass extinction and speciation events, and long-term field observations show discontinuities separated by long periods of stasis or minor oscillations back and forth about a mean. Naturalists lack a plausible scenario, let alone an established model, to explain many of these discontinuities. Meanwhile, the fact that each leap serves a specific purpose in making possible the existence and redemption of billions of humans strongly suggests God's supernatural involvement in those leaps.

While Haarsma says, "We don't expect our science to look differently [from nontheistic science]" (p. 134), Romans 1 and other biblical texts lead me to conclude that differences will be apparent. From an evolutionary creationist perspective, science carries no apologetics significance. The Bible, however, explicitly states that nature provides a clear and compelling testimony of God's existence and divine attributes, the bedrock of our accountability to respond to him in faith.

For her biblical hermeneutics, Haarsma cites John Walton, saying the Bible was written *for* us, not *to* us, and was not intended to address the "how" and "when" of creation. She endorses Walton's accommodation view, belief that God's inspiration of Scripture includes accommodating mistaken understandings of the physical realm held by the biblical authors' contemporaries. Her example: supposed biblical references to a solid dome above a flat earth. Lexicons list "expanse," not "vault," as the primary definition of the Hebrew word *raqia*.[1] In Genesis 1:8 God calls the *expanse* "sky." In Genesis 1:20, birds fly across the *expanse*. Job 36–38 and Isaiah 5:6 indicate that the ancient Hebrews knew rain came from clouds, not from holes in a brass dome. While it's true some ancient Mesopotamians believed a brass dome sat above a flat earth, I see no compelling evidence suggesting Bible writers shared or expressed such beliefs.

Most evolutionary creationists see no scientific predictions in

---

1. R. Laird Harris, Gleason L. Archer, and Bruce K. Waltke, *Theological Wordbook of the Old Testament* (Chicago: Moody, 1980), 2:862.

Scripture, yet they do acknowledge its accuracy in making historical predictions. Why the difference? Similarly, they believe God miraculously intervened in human history and intervenes today in believers' lives. Again, it seems inconsistent to assume God would not also miraculously intervene in natural history.

Like other evolutionary creationists, Haarsma affirms macroevolution and the relationship of all life through "a 'tree' of common ancestry." However, we note that the fossil record frequently is more accurately described as a "lawn" rather than as a tree (see figure). If the evolutionary model is correct, fossil record dates should match molecular clock dates. They rarely do, with discordances sometimes larger than two hundred million years. In our view, the same data set better fits a picture of common design—God's repeated use of optimal designs in different kinds of life he creates—rather than common descent.

Timing of Phyla

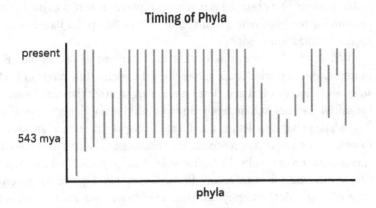

Instead of new phyla branching off in a tree-like manner from previously existing phyla, they appear as a lawn, like blades of grass originating without apparent connection to one another.

Convergence and results from long-term evolution experiments fit well with a common design perspective. According to our day-age model, God ceased from making new life-forms once he created humans. What we see throughout the human era (the seventh day) is microevolution, the adaptability of life and emerging diversity within kinds, not the generation of new and more advanced kinds.

Real-time (seventh-day), long-term experiments show that natural evolutionary outcomes are contingent.[2] Natural processes don't converge on the same features again and again. However, hundreds of examples of virtually identical features appear in species widely separated in any evolutionary tree. These repeated outcomes speak of God's efficiency, his use of common, optimal designs throughout the six creation eras.

It seems ironic that Haarsma cites whales as evidence for macroevolution and common ancestry. Conservation biology and evolutionary principles reveal that whales possess a high probability of rapid extinction and low probability of evolutionary advance. In part, their huge body sizes, low population levels, long generation times, few progeny per adult, and sensitivity to environmental stresses explain these probabilities. Thus, whales have the lowest imaginable probability of generating transitional forms.

Why, then, do we see so many whale species over the past forty million years? The observed progression is precisely timed to help compensate for the brightening sun and to help build up the bio-resources human civilization needs.[3]

Whale speciation events cannot be described as sequential. For example, modern whales appear explosively, with a full range of body sizes and dietary diversity. They appear right after the extinction of "primitive" whales and undergo limited evolutionary change thereafter. The whale pelvis is no longer considered vestigial. It serves as an attachment for muscles used in reproduction. Haarsma's claimed evolutionary transformation of a wolf-like land dweller into "primitive" whales in just five to nine million years seems unrealistically rapid, given the magnitude of anatomical and physiological alterations. Special creation acts offer a more plausible explanation of the whale fossil record.

The familiar objection to this intervention explanation is to label it a "God-of-the-gaps fallacy." However, gaps in our knowledge and understanding of nature's book are opportunities for testing our creation model alongside other models.

All models have gaps. The question is what happens to the gaps as

2. Hugh Ross, *More Than a Theory: Revealing a Testable Model for Creation* (Grand Rapids: Baker, 2009), 169–70; Fazale Rana, "Inability to Repeat the Past Dooms Evolution," *Today's New Reason to Believe*, Reasons to Believe, August 7, 2008, http://www.reasons.org/articles/inability-to-repeat-the-past-dooms-evolution.

3. Hugh Ross, "Thank God for Whales," *Today's New Reason to Believe*, Reasons to Believe, August 23, 2010, http://www.reasons.org/articles/thank-god-for-whales.

scientists learn more. Do they shrink or widen, become more numerous and problematic or less? The past forty years of whale research has progressively made evolutionary explanations more intractable, not less. Meanwhile, whale research offers increasing evidence of rapid, comprehensive, and nearly simultaneous changes optimally timed to serve humanity's needs. Such changes, their timing, and outcomes increasingly reflect what one would expect from a God intent on supporting and redeeming billions of humans.

A more dramatic example of the efficacy of this "gaps test" comes from origin-of-life research. Over the past seven decades, scientists have made astounding progress in understanding the chemical pathways critical to life's origin and Earth's chemical environment at the time of life's origin. This research has shown an increasingly (not decreasingly) delicate degree to which laboratory conditions must be controlled to simulate the essential chemical pathways for life's origin. Such degree of control implies the necessity for a Controller with greater capacities and resources than even brilliant biochemists at the best laboratories.

Meanwhile, outside of living organisms and the decay products of living organisms, no ribose, arginine, lysine, or tryptophan—building blocks critical for assembling proteins, RNA, and DNA—have been found either on Earth or anywhere else in the universe. While they may exist below a few parts per billion, such scarcity would seem to rule out naturalistic origin-of-life models. In this case, the absence of evidence implies evidence of absence. If evolutionary creationists would acknowledge that life's origin reasonably can be considered a supernatural event, we would be a major step closer to resolving our differences.

Haarsma found genetics evidence "most convincing" for biological evolution, including evidence indicating humanity came from a population, not a pair. Population geneticists, however, have yet to identify the full range of systematic effects, let alone measure the systematic errors. This systematics problem likely explains why field experiments yield results discordant with predictions from genetics models. For example, field studies of orangutans, horses, and sheep show genetic diversity of generation is consistently much greater than what current genetics models predict. These results indicate we should hesitate to draw conclusions about the human ancestral population from present genetics models.

DNA comparisons of modern species do, as Haarsma states, show relatedness among species. This relatedness, however, aligns just as reasonably, if not more so, with common design as with common descent.

It comes as no surprise that 99 percent of surveyed biologists from the American Association for the Advancement of Science agree that "humans evolved over time." Given the broad definitions of these terms, the most ardent creationist would likely agree. Furthermore, since most humans will choose autonomy over submission to God, no matter how strong the scientific case against naturalistic evolution, we can expect a majority of researchers will refuse to credit God.

While human anatomy resembles ape anatomy, no such similarity exists in brain structure and brain chemistry. In these features, humans more closely resemble corvids and rodents, respectively. Ravens, not chimpanzees, most closely match human intellectual capacities. Darwin's prediction on this matter has been falsified.

We have good reason to celebrate the recent explosion of hominid fossil finds. These new fossils help overturn the hypothesis of "a gradual transition toward bipedal walking, greater height, and greater brain size." Rather than affirming this evolutionary scenario, they throw it into chaos. Again, the evolutionary tree transforms into a lawn.

Human chromosome 2 may appear as two chimpanzee chromosomes fused together. However, the extra telomeres and centromere in this chromosome only roughly resemble telomeres and a centromere. If chromosome 2 does, indeed, prove a fusion of two chromosomes, it speaks of a super-intelligent, supernatural Creator. Chromosomal fusion and fission events in nature almost always prove catastrophic, and biochemists have yet to achieve a successful chromosomal fusion.

Personally, I see defense of a literal Adam and Eve, the progenitors of all humanity, as crucial to the defense of biblical inspiration and inerrancy. Genesis 3:20, Acts 17:26, Romans 5:12–19, and 1 Corinthians 15:20–22 affirm the descent of all humans from a single pair and the inheritance of our sin nature from Adam. Genesis 1–2 uses the verbs *bara'* (create), *'asah* (make), and *yatsar* (fashion) in describing the origin of Adam and Eve. These verbs imply direct special creation by God.

I am hopeful that differences between evolutionary creationists and day-age creationists can be resolved through ongoing research and study. If we respectfully commit to thorough integration and consistency in our interpretation of God's two inerrant books, we will find pathways to resolution. Those pathways will equip us to bring more people to faith in Jesus Christ.

STEPHEN C. MEYER

Deborah B. Haarsma defends a position she calls "evolutionary creation" or what others have called "theistic evolution." She explains that evolutionary creationists equate the evolutionary process or mechanism(s) with the creative activity of God. She asserts that "evolution is . . . *a natural mechanism* by which God providentially achieves his purpose" (p. 126, emphasis added). As she argues, natural selection acting on random mutations generates not just small-scale variations in the expression of pre-existing traits but also large-scale changes in living forms. As she explains, evolutionary creationists "accept that natural selection and other evolutionary mechanisms, acting over long periods of time, eventually result in major changes in body structures. Some people call this 'macroevolution'" (p. 140).

Since the term "evolution" can have many different meanings, Haarsma's care in defining the kind of evolution she has in mind is admirable. Yale biologist Keith Stewart Thomson noted that evolution can refer to: (1) change over time, (2) universal common ancestry, and/or (3) the natural mechanisms that produce change in organisms—whether (a) small-scale "microevolutionary" change in the frequency of expression of existing traits or (b) large-scale "macroevolutionary" changes that result in genetic and morphological novelty.[1] Evolutionary creationists don't just affirm the generic idea of change over time, or even the common ancestry of all organisms. Instead, as Haarsma makes clear, they also affirm that the mechanism of natural selection and random mutation (and perhaps other unspecified mechanisms) generate "major changes in body structures."

Oddly, however, Haarsma offers no evidence for the creative power of natural selection and random mutation (or other alleged mechanisms

---

1. Keith S. Thomson, "The Meanings of Evolution," *American Scientist* 70 (1982): 521–39.

of macroevolutionary innovation). Nor does she address the well-documented scientific reasons for doubting its creative power.

In my essay making the case for intelligent design (p. 178ff.), I explained one of those reasons. Since natural selection can only "select" what random mutations first generate, random mutations alone must produce the genetic information necessary for building novel protein structures (i.e., folds). Yet, given the extreme rarity of functional genes and proteins within the set of all possible combinations of DNA or amino acid sequences, random mutational searches for new information-rich genes capable of building new protein folds are *overwhelmingly* more likely to fail than succeed, even granting billions of years to perform the searches.

More Discoveries, More Trouble

There are many other scientific reasons for doubting the creative power of the mutation/selection mechanism. First, though evolutionary biologists have long touted mutations as a kind of silver bullet capable of generating unlimited innovation, developmental biologists have discovered that only mutations that occur early in embryological development can alter an entire animal body plan—that is, produce *major* evolutionary change. Mutations that occur late or mid-way through animal development only affect individual somatic cells, or isolated cell clusters, not whole body architectures. This discovery poses difficulty for all theories of macroevolution that rely on mutations to generate major changes in form. Why? Because developmental biologists have also discovered that mutations early in an animal's development are *inevitably lethal*. This problem of "embryonic lethals" has created a dilemma for evolutionary theorists: The kind of mutations needed to generate new body plans—i.e., early-acting *beneficial* body-plan altering mutations—never occur. The kinds of mutations that do occur—early, lethal mutations or late-acting mutations that affect only small clusters of somatic cells—don't generate new body plans. How then could the evolutionary process overcome this difficulty to produce major changes in animal form? Mainstream evolutionary biologists have not answered this question—and neither have evolutionary creationists such as Haarsma.

Consider a related difficulty: Developmental biologists have also discovered that building a new animal form requires more than new genes and proteins. It also requires integrated networks of genes and proteins called developmental gene regulatory networks (dGRNs). These networks regulate the timing of gene expression as animals develop. The products of the genes in these integrated networks transmit signals (known as transcriptional regulators or transcription factors) that influence how individual cells develop and differentiate during this process.

Cal-Tech biologist Eric Davidson explored the regulatory logic of animal development more deeply than perhaps anyone.[2] In the course of his investigations, he discovered not only what these networks do but also what they never do: namely, change significantly. Davidson explained why. The integrated complexity of the dGRNs (which he likened to integrated circuits) makes them stubbornly resistant to fundamental restructuring without breaking. As he explained, mutations affecting the dGRNs that regulate body-plan development inevitably lead to "catastrophic loss of the body part or loss of viability altogether. . . . There is always an observable consequence if a dGRN subcircuit is interrupted. Since these consequences are always catastrophically bad, flexibility is minimal."[3]

So, building new animal body plans requires not just new genes and proteins but new dGRNs. But to build a new dGRN from a preexisting dGRN requires altering the preexisting dGRN—the very thing Davidson showed does not occur without catastrophic consequences.[4] Given this, how could a new animal body plan—and the new dGRN necessary to produce it—ever evolve from a preexisting body plan and dGRN? Neither mainstream evolutionary biologists, nor evolutionary creationists have answered this question.

Consider another difficulty: Recent studies in embryology show that DNA alone does not carry all the instructions for building a whole organism or animal. Instead, DNA helps to direct and regulate the timing of the synthesis of proteins within cells. Yet, by itself DNA does not determine how individual proteins assemble themselves into larger systems of proteins that service different cell types. Nor does it solely

2. Isabelle S. Peter and Eric H. Davidson, *Genomic Control Processes: Development and Evolution* (New York: Academic Press, 2015).

3. Eric Davidson, "Evolutionary Bioscience as Regulatory Systems Biology," *Developmental Biology* 357 (2011): 35–40.

4. Eric Davidson and Douglas Erwin, "An Integrated View of Precambrian Eumetazoan Evolution," *Cold Spring Harbor Symposia on Quantitative Biology* 74 (2009): 1–16.

determine how different cell types arrange themselves into different types of tissues or how different of types of tissues and organs arrange themselves into body plans. Instead, other factors—such as the three-dimensional organization of the cytoskeleton and the distribution of protein binding "targets" on cell membranes as well as yet unknown sources of epigenetic (beyond the gene) information—play important roles in determining body plan formation.

An analogy may help to clarify the point. Electronic circuits are composed of many components, such as resistors, capacitors, and transistors. Manufacturing such components can be automated using machine assembly instructions, but the instructions for building these lower-level components will not determine their arrangement on an integrated circuit board. Additional instructions are needed. Similarly, the information in DNA is necessary but not sufficient to build whole organisms.

This poses another problem. Neo-Darwinism holds that natural selection acting on random genetic variations in DNA generates new biological form and structure. Yet if the genetic information in DNA is not wholly responsible for the construction of animal body plans, then DNA sequences can mutate indefinitely, regardless of available time, and still not produce a new body plan. Consequently, the mechanism of natural selection acting on random mutations in DNA cannot *in principle* generate the epigenetic information necessary to produce a new body plan.

These various difficulties have led many evolutionary biologists to doubt the creative power of the mutation/selection mechanism and to reject textbook neo-Darwinism. At a recent conference of the Royal Society of London called in part to address this problem, Austrian evolutionary biologist Gerd Müller began the conference by outlining "the explanatory deficits" of neo-Darwinism, including its inability to explain the "origin of biological complexity" and the origin of major "novelties." He and co-author Stuart Newman have elsewhere argued that neo-Darwinism has "no theory of the generative."[5] Other biologists have explained that mutation and selection can account for "the survival, but not the arrival of the fittest"—that is, minor but not major changes.

Accordingly, many biologists are pursuing new theories of evolution

5. Gerd Müller and Stuart Newman, *On the Origin of Organismal Form* (Boston: MIT Press, 2003).

based upon various proposed evolutionary mechanisms as part of an "extended evolutionary synthesis." Yet, as I show in *Darwin's Doubt*, none of these newly proposed mechanisms explains the origin of the genetic and epigenetic information necessary to generate biological novelty.[6]

Consequently, there is no consensus within evolutionary biology in support of the creative power of *any* of these proposed new mechanisms. This raises a question for Haarsma: Why attempt to reconcile claims about the creative power of evolutionary mechanisms with a biblical understanding of divine creation if the scientific evidence increasingly casts doubt on the creative power of those mechanisms?

Logically or Theologically Problematic

Haarsma also ignores the theological difficulties attendant in her attempted synthesis of evolutionary theory and Christian doctrine—especially those that arise in response to considering the *cause* of biological change and whether evolution should be viewed as a directed or undirected process.

Where theistic evolution or evolutionary creation affirms the third meaning of evolution—the idea that the selection/mutation mechanism can generate major biological change—the concept becomes deeply problematic. Depending on how theistic evolutionists (or evolutionary creationists) conceive of God's role in this evolutionary mechanism, the version of theistic evolution that affirms this third meaning of evolution results in either (1) logical contradictions, (2) theological problems, or (3) a scientifically vacuous affirmation.

First, if theistic evolutionists affirm the standard neo-Darwinian view of the mutation/selection mechanism as an *un*directed process while simultaneously affirming that God is causally responsible for the origin of new forms of life, then they imply that God somehow *guided* an *unguided* process. Yet, logically, no intelligent being—not even God—can *direct* an *un*directed process. As soon as He directs it, the undirected process is no longer undirected.

Alternatively, many theistic evolutionists, like mainstream evolutionary biologists, *deny* that God directs the evolutionary process. For example, Kenneth Miller, a leading theistic evolutionist, has repeatedly

---

6. Stephen C. Meyer, *Darwin's Doubt: The Explosive Origin of Animal Life and the Case for Intelligent Design* (San Francisco: HarperOne), 291–335.

stated in editions of his popular textbook that "evolution works without either plan or purpose . . . Evolution is random and undirected."[7]

This version of theistic evolution holds that God created the universe and its laws at the beginning and constantly upholds those laws on a moment-by-moment basis. Nevertheless, it denies that God actively directs the mutation/selection mechanism. Instead, it conceives of God's role in the *creation* of life (as opposed to His maintenance of physical law) as mainly passive rather than actively directive. Undirected evolutionary mechanisms are seen as the causally active "agents of creation."

This version of theistic evolution is theologically problematic, at least for those who derive their understanding of divine action from the biblical text. The Bible describes God as not only creating the universe in the beginning and upholding it in its ongoing orderly concourse, it also describes God acting discretely as an agent within the natural order that He otherwise upholds. (See Gen 1:27: "God created [*bara'*] human beings" [NLT]; and Exod 10:13: "and the LORD *caused* an east wind to blow" [NLT].) Moreover, if God is not at least directing the evolutionary process, then the origin of biological systems must be attributed, in some part, to nature acting independently of God's direction. This entails a diminished view of God's sovereignty and involvement in creation, one at odds with traditional readings of Scripture. Moreover, many theistic evolutionists have reasoned that if God does not (or did not) direct or control the evolutionary process, then He could not have known what that process would have produced, including whether it would have produced human beings—a conclusion at odds with divine providence and omniscience.

Indeed, many theistic evolutionists who embrace this view insist that the evolutionary process might just as well have produced "a big-brained dinosaur" as big-brained bipedal hominids—i.e., human beings.[8] Moreover, since on this view God does not direct the evolutionary

---

7. Kenneth Miller and Joseph S. Levine, *Biology* (Upper Saddle River, NJ: Prentice Hall: 1998), 658.

8. Kenneth Miller, *Finding Darwin's God: A Scientist's Search for Common Ground Between God and Evolution* (New York: HarperCollins, 1999); idem, "Evolution and Intelligent Design: An Exchange" (paper presented at the Shifting Ground: Religion and Civic Life in America conference, Bedford, NH, sponsored by the New Hampshire Humanities Council, March 24, 2007); John G. West, "Nothing New Under the Sun," in *God and Evolution: Protestants, Catholics, and Jews Explore Darwin's Challenge to Faith*, ed. Jay Wesley Richards (Seattle, WA: Discovery Institute Press, 2010), 40–45.

process, what that process produces cannot be said to express His specific intentions in creation—contrary to the biblical claim that God made man expressly in His own image and that He "foreknew" him (Rom 8:29).

A Vague and Ambiguous Formulation

Given this dilemma, many evolutionary creationists, including Francis Collins, perhaps the best-known proponent of this position, have been reluctant to clarify what they think about this issue. In *The Language of God*, Collins seems to assume the adequacy of standard evolutionary mechanisms but does not clearly say whether he thinks those mechanisms are directed or undirected—only that they could be. Perhaps, Haarsma would like to clarify her position here. When she affirms evolutionary creation what does she mean by evolution—a directed or an undirected process? I'd be interested to know.

DEBORAH B. HAARSMA

I appreciate the thoughtful responses of the other authors. Several of their concerns were addressed in my responses to their chapters, including geological evidence, first life, convergent evolution, common design, protein folding, and approaches to the book of nature and apologetics. I will address most other concerns here.

Biblical and Theological Differences

Ham feels my chapter is fundamentally weak because I discuss very little Scripture. Since I discuss several passages from throughout the Bible, I expect his concern is more about interpretation than quantity.

Ross asks why EC would accept historical predictions of Scripture but not scientific predictions. Certainly many biblical predictions are fulfilled later in the Bible for events in human history and the coming kingdom of God. It does not necessarily follow that the Bible makes predictions for science and natural history, peripheral to kingdom purposes and opaque until the twentieth century.

Meyer asks why EC would attempt to reconcile the Bible with scientific claims that he sees as weak and failing. However, my arguments regarding biblical interpretation (pp. 130–32 of my chapter) are explicitly *not* driven by scientific claims; they are driven by the authority of Scripture, hermeneutical best practices, and the ancient context of the text.

Meyer asks about BioLogos' views on divine action. BioLogos explicitly affirms that God works with purpose and intent (Ken Miller, while a theistic evolutionist, does not represent most evolutionary creationists on this point). Many of us see signs of purpose and intent in convergent evolution, the role of cooperation,[1] or other aspects of evolution. All of us believe that God planned, created, governs, and continually sustains the process of evolution; this is an active role for God, not a passive or distant one. God in his sovereignty has chosen to use random processes as part of his design, but that does not require God to explicitly determine the outcome of every random event. These questions are not unique to evolution but have been discussed by theologians for millennia.[2] Jesus taught that God feeds the birds (Matt 6:26), but does God select each worm for each bird? The psalmist taught that God knits together a fetus in the womb (Pss 139:13–16), but does that require God to act in some special way? Even in ancient times, bird behavior and fetal development were seen as the regular working of the natural world and part of God's providential care, without any diminishment in his activity or sovereignty.

Scientific Differences

Ross lists several areas of scientific disagreement, as I did in my response to him. Ham and Meyer discuss fewer areas but with longer arguments, which I address below. For any of these scientific disagreements, the lay reader is put in the challenging place of judging between two expert authors who each assert that the other is wrong. It may come down to which voices a reader trusts; I encourage lay people to read more to help them decide.[3]

Ham describes a paleontologist's 1983 publication regarding a transitional whale fossil and a 2001 publication that showed a change in the researcher's conclusions after more fossil evidence was discovered. Ham then makes a great leap to conclude, "Whale evolution from land animals is a myth" (pp. 159–60). Far from the case! His example actually shows the proper workings of science, as researchers modify and develop their understanding in response to new data. What Ham doesn't say is that in those eighteen years many other fossils were found for several species between land mammals and whales, showing

---

1. E.g., R. E. Michod and D. Roze, "Cooperation and Conflict in the Evolution of Multicellularity," *Heredity* 86 (Jan 2001): 1–7.

2. For more from several Christian theologians and philosophers, see "The Divine Action Series," BioLogos.org, May–June 2016, http://biologos.org/blogs/jim-stump-faith-and-science-seeking-understanding/series/divine-action.

3. Ross and I expand our conversation in Kenneth Keathley, J. B. Stump, and Joe Aguirre, eds., *Old Earth or Evolutionary Creation? Discussing Origins with Reasons to Believe and BioLogos* (Downers Grove, IL: InterVarsity Press, 2017).

a group of creatures that led to the whales we know today.[4]

Meyer introduces arguments regarding evolutionary mechanisms beyond natural selection, including epigenetics and the genetic regulation of embryonic development. As I argued in my response to his chapter, many mechanisms are under discussion today as evolutionary biologists investigate the details of how evolution works. Those discussions in no way question common ancestry or the strength of the overall evolutionary picture. Consider Meyer's example of developmental gene regulatory networks (dGRNs). Meyer correctly notes Eric H. Davidson as a world leader in this area. Yet a simple Google search shows that Davidson does not call evolution into question; in fact, Davidson clearly rejects anti-evolution arguments. Rather, the Davidson paper that Meyer quotes weighs in on the debate over mechanism, showing the importance of dGRNs and arguing that dGRNs in the time of the Cambrian had the polyfunctionality needed to produce many body plans at the level of Phylum and Class. He argues that since then dGRNs have become more hierarchical, giving stability over geological timescales for body plan basics while allowing the development of variations at the levels of class, order, family, genus, and species. Davidson's paper develops our understanding of how evolution works.

These examples are part of an unfortunate pattern in anti-evolution arguments: A Christian will cite a mainstream research paper that debates *how* evolution works as if the research shows evolution does *not* work at all. Such arguments give Christians a false picture of what we know about God's creation and give scientists the false impression that they are not welcome in Christianity.

Fundamental Unity

All four authors affirm Christian faith. Christ calls us to unity despite our clear differences. As Ham notes, that unity is founded on the essential beliefs of Christianity. Yet the call to unity also includes living with our differences on secondary issues (e.g., Rom 14). I pray this book will help Christians discuss their differences on creation and evolution in a spirit of truth and grace.

---

4. For more on whale evolution, see Dennis Venema "Understanding Evolution: Theory, Prediction and Converging Lines of Evidence," BioLogos.org, March–April 2012, http://biologos.org/blogs/dennis-venema-letters-to-the-duchess/series/understanding-evolution-theory-prediction-and-converging-lines-of-evidence. For a detailed whale genetic tree (using solid lines, the current standard), see Andrew D. Foote et al., *Nature Genetics* 47 (2015): 272–275.

INTELLIGENT DESIGN

STEPHEN C. MEYER

A Brief History of—and Scientific Argument for—Intelligent Design

In December 2004 the renowned British philosopher Antony Flew made worldwide news when he repudiated a lifelong commitment to atheism, citing, among other factors, evidence for intelligent design in the DNA molecule. In that same month, the American Civil Liberties Union filed suit to prevent a Dover, Pennsylvania school district from informing its students that they could learn more about the theory of intelligent design from a supplementary science textbook in their school library. The following February, *The Wall Street Journal*[1] reported that an evolutionary biologist at the Smithsonian Institution with two doctorates had been punished for publishing a peer-reviewed scientific article making a case for intelligent design.

Since then the theory of intelligent design has been the focus of a frenzy of international media coverage, with prominent stories appearing in *The New York Times*, *Nature*, *The Washington Post*, *The London Times*, *Sekai Nippo* (Tokyo), *The Times* of India, *Der Spiegel*, *The Jerusalem Post*, and *Time* magazine to name just a few. Pope Benedict, the Dalai Lama, and former President George W. Bush have all made statements supporting the theory of intelligent design. Meanwhile, mainstream science organizations have denounced the theory as "pseudo-science," "religion," or "creationism in a cheap tuxedo." Similarly, the federal judge who heard the *Kitzmiller* case in Dover eventually ruled that

---

1. David Klinghoffer, "The Branding of a Heretic," *The Wall Street Journal*, January 28, 2005, W11.

teaching students about the theory, at least in the central Pennsylvania district over which he had jurisdiction, represented an unconstitutional incursion of religion into public science instruction.

In the wake of his ruling, many critics of intelligent design claimed interest in the theory was "over after Dover." Yet, the controversy generated by the theory has hardly abated. In 2008, over one million people saw the film *Expelled* in movie theatres in North America. The film, featuring actor Ben Stein, told the stories of Richard Sternberg (the aforementioned Smithsonian scientist punished for his publishing decision) and other scientific proponents of intelligent design whose academic freedom had been similarly abridged. In 2009, a major book advocating intelligent design published by a prominent mainstream trade publisher was named book of the year by the London *Times Literary Supplement*.[2] In 2013, another prominent book advancing the theory debuted at number seven on the *New York Times* bestseller list.[3] And since 2004, when the first peer-reviewed scientific article advocating intelligent design caused the uproar at the Smithsonian, one hundred new peer-reviewed articles supporting the theory have been published in other scientific journals.[4]

But what is this theory of intelligent design, where did it come from, and why does it inspire such determined efforts to suppress it?

According to a spate of recent media reports, intelligent design is a new faith-based alternative to evolution based on religion rather than scientific evidence. As the story goes, intelligent design is just biblical creationism repackaged by religious fundamentalists in order to circumvent a 1987 United States Supreme Court prohibition against teaching creationism in the public schools. Over the past several years, major newspapers, magazines, and broadcast outlets, as well the federal judge in the Dover case have repeated this trope. But is it accurate?

Intelligent Design: What It Is and Where It Came From

As one of the architects of the theory of intelligent design and the director of a research center that supports scientists developing the theory,

---

2. Stephen Meyer, *Signature in the Cell: DNA and the Evidence for Intelligent Design* (San Francisco: HarperOne, 2009).

3. Stephen Meyer, *Darwin's Doubt: The Explosive Origin of Animal Life and the Case for Intelligent Design* (San Francisco: HarperOne, 2013).

4. "Peer Reviewed Papers Supporting Intelligent Design," See: http://www.discovery.org/id/peer-review.

I know that this media stereotype isn't accurate. The modern theory of intelligent design predates the legal setback for creationists in 1987, having first been proposed in the early 1980s by a group of scientists— Charles Thaxton, Walter Bradley, and Roger Olson—who were trying to account for an enduring mystery in modern biology: the origin of the digital information encoded along the spine of the DNA molecule. Thaxton and colleagues came to the conclusion that the information-bearing properties of DNA provided strong evidence of a designing intelligence. They wrote a book proposing this idea in 1984, three years before the US Supreme Court decision (in *Edwards v. Aguillard*) outlawing the teaching of creationism.

Contemporary scientific interest in the design hypothesis not only predates the US Supreme Court rulings against creationism, but the formal theory of intelligent design is clearly distinct from creationism in both method and content. The theory of intelligent design, unlike creationism, is not based upon the Bible. Instead, the theory is based on recent scientific discoveries and what we know about the cause-and-effect structure of the world—specifically, what we know about patterns of evidence that indicate *intelligent* causes. Thus, intelligent design is not a deduction from, or an interpretation of, a religious text but an inference from scientific evidence.

The propositional content of the theory of intelligent design also differs from that of creationism. The theory of intelligent design attempts to explain the observed complexity and information-rich structures found in living systems and other features of life and the universe. Creationism or creation science, as defined by the US Supreme Court, defends a particular reading of the biblical book of Genesis, typically one that asserts that God created the earth in six twenty-four hour periods a few thousand years ago. In contrast, the theory of intelligent design does not offer an interpretation of the book of Genesis, nor does it posit a theory about the length of the biblical days of creation or the age of the earth. Consequently, intelligent design proponents may have a variety of positions on such issues (or none at all).

But if the theory of intelligent design is not creationism, what is it? As it applies to biology (the focus of this essay), intelligent design is an evidence-based scientific theory about life's origin and development that challenges strictly materialistic views of evolution. According to

Darwinian biologists such as Oxford's Richard Dawkins, living systems "give the appearance of having been designed for a purpose."[5] But for modern Darwinists, that appearance of design is entirely illusory. Why? According to them, wholly undirected processes such as natural selection and random mutations are fully capable of producing the intricate designed-like structures in living systems. In their view, evolutionary processes can mimic the powers of a designing intelligence without themselves being directed by an intelligent agent in any way.

Conversely, the theory of intelligent design holds that there are telltale features of living systems and the universe—for example, the digital code in DNA, the miniature circuits and machines in cells,[6] and the fine tuning of the laws and constants of physics[7]—that are best explained by an intelligent cause rather than an undirected material process. The theory does not challenge the idea of evolution defined as either change over time or common ancestry, but it does dispute the Darwinian idea that the cause of biological change is wholly blind and undirected. Either life arose as the result of purely undirected material processes or a guiding intelligence played a role. Design theorists affirm the latter option and argue that living organisms look designed because they really were designed.

A Brief History of the Classical Design Argument

By making a case for design based on evidence in nature, contemporary advocates of intelligent design have resuscitated the classical design argument. For centuries before Darwin's *On the Origin of Species* appeared in 1859, most Western thinkers held that life arose from the activity of a purposeful designer. Design arguments based on observations of the natural world were made by Greek and Roman philosophers such as Plato[8] and Cicero,[9] by Jewish philosophers such as Maimonides, and by Christian thinkers such as Thomas Aquinas.[10]

The idea of design also figured centrally in the scientific revolution

---

5. Richard Dawkins, *The Blind Watchmaker* (London: Norton, 1986), 1.

6. Michael Behe, *Darwin's Black Box* (New York: Free Press, 1996).

7. Fred Hoyle, *The Intelligent Universe* (London: Michael Joseph Limited, 1983).

8. Plato, *The Laws*, trans. A. E. Taylor (London: Everyman, 1960), 279.

9. Cicero, *De Natura Deorum*, trans. H. Rackham (Cambridge, MA: Harvard University Press, 1933), 217.

10. John Hick, *Arguments for the Existence of God* (London: Macmillan, 1970), 1.

(1300–1700). As historians of science have often noted,[11] many of the founders of early modern science assumed that the natural world was intelligible and amenable to rational scientific investigation precisely because they also assumed that it had been designed by a rational mind. In addition, many individual scientists—Johannes Kepler in astronomy,[12] John Ray in biology,[13] and Robert Boyle in chemistry[14]—made specific design arguments based upon empirical discoveries in their respective fields.

This tradition attained an almost majestic rhetorical quality in the writings of Sir Isaac Newton, who made sophisticated design arguments based upon biological, physical, and astronomical discoveries. Writing in the General Scholium to the *Principia*, Newton suggested that the stability of the planetary system depended not only upon the regular action of universal gravitation but also upon the precise initial positioning of the planets and comets in relation to the sun. As he explained, "though these bodies may, indeed, continue in their orbits by the mere laws of gravity, yet they could by no means have at first derived the regular position of the orbits themselves from those laws." Thus, he concluded, "this most beautiful system of the sun, planets, and comets, could only proceed from the counsel and dominion of an intelligent and powerful Being."[15]

Or as he wrote in the *Opticks*:

How came the Bodies of Animals to be contrived with so much Art, and for what ends were their several parts? Was the Eye contrived without Skill in Opticks, and the Ear without Knowledge of Sounds? . . . And these things being rightly dispatch'd, does it not appear from Phænomena that there is a Being incorporeal, living, intelligent, omnipresent . . .[16]

11. Neal C. Gillespie, "Natural History, Natural Theology, and Social Order: John Ray and the 'Newtonian Ideology,'" *Journal of the History of Biology* 20 (1987): 1–49.

12. Johannes Kepler, *Mysterium Cosmographicum [The Secret of the Universe]*, trans. A. M. Duncan (New York: Arabis Books, 1981), 93–103. Johannes Kepler, *Harmonies of the World*, trans. Charles Glen Wallis (New York: Prometheus, 1995), 170, 240.

13. John Ray, *The Wisdom of God Manifested in the Works of the Creation* (London, 1701).

14. Robert Boyle, *Selected Philosophical Papers of Robert Boyle*, ed. M. A. Stewart (Manchester: Manchester University Press, 1979), 172.

15. Isaac Newton, *Newton's Principia: Motte's Translation Revised (1686)*, trans. Andrew Motte, rev. Florian Cajori (Berkeley: University of California Press, 1934), 543–44.

16. Isaac Newton, *Opticks* (New York: Dover, 1952), 369–70.

Scientists continued to make design arguments well into the early nineteenth century, especially in biology. By the later part of the eighteenth century, however, some enlightenment philosophers began to express skepticism about these arguments. David Hume, in his *Dialogues Concerning Natural Religion* (1779), argued that the design argument depended upon a flawed analogy with human artifacts.[17] He admitted that artifacts derive from intelligent artificers and that biological organisms have certain similarities to complex human artifacts. Eyes and pocket watches, for example, both depend upon the functional integration of many separate and specifically configured parts. Nevertheless, he argued, biological organisms also differ from human artifacts—they reproduce themselves, for example—and the advocates of the design argument fail to take these dissimilarities into account. Since experience teaches that organisms always come from other organisms, Hume argued that analogical argument ought to suggest that organisms ultimately come from some primeval organism (perhaps a giant spider or vegetable), not a transcendent mind or spirit.

Despite his objections, Hume's categorical rejection of the design argument did not prove decisive. Thinkers as diverse as the Scottish Presbyterian Thomas Reid,[18] the Enlightenment deist Thomas Paine,[19] and the rationalist philosopher Immanuel Kant[20] continued to affirm[21] various versions of the design argument after the publication of Hume's *Dialogues*. Moreover, with the publication of William Paley's *Natural Theology*, science-based design arguments would achieve new popularity, both in Britain and on the European continent. Paley catalogued a host of biological systems that suggested the work of a superintending intelligence.[22] Paley argued that the astonishing complexity and superb

---

17. David Hume, *Dialogues Concerning Natural Religion*, ed. Richard H. Popkin (Indianapolis: Hackett, 1980), 61–66.

18. Thomas Reid, *Lectures on Natural Theology (1780)*, ed. Elmer Duncan and William R. Eakin (Washington, DC: University Press of America, 1981), 59.

19. Thomas Paine, *The Life and Works of Thomas Paine, Vol. 8: The Age of Reason* (New Rochelle, New York: Thomas Paine National Historical Association, 1925), 6.

20. Immanuel Kant, *Critique of Pure Reason*, trans. Norman Kemp Smith (London: Macmillan, 1963), 523.

21. Kant sought to limit the scope of the design argument but did not reject it wholesale. Though he rejected the argument as a proof of the transcendent and omnipotent God of Judeo-Christian theology, he still accepted that it could establish the reality of a powerful and intelligent author of the world (*Critique of Pure Reason*, 523).

22. William Paley, *Natural Theology* (Boston: Gould and Lincoln, 1852), 8–9.

adaptation of means to ends in such systems could not originate through the blind forces of nature any more than could a complex machine such as a watch. Paley also responded directly to Hume's claim that design inferences rested upon a faulty analogy. A watch that could reproduce itself, he argued, would constitute an even more marvelous system than one that could not. Thus, for Paley, the differences between artifacts and organisms only strengthened the conclusion of design. Thus, despite Hume's objections, many scientists continued to find Paley's watch-to-watchmaker reasoning compelling well into the nineteenth century.

Darwin, Neo-Darwinism, and the Eclipse of Design

Acceptance of the design argument began to abate during the late nineteenth century with the emergence of increasingly powerful materialistic explanations of "apparent" design in life, particularly Charles Darwin's theory of evolution by natural selection. Darwin argued in 1859 that living organisms only *appeared* to be designed. To show this, he proposed a concrete mechanism, natural selection acting on random variations, to explain the adaptation of organisms to their environment (and other evidences of apparent design) without invoking an intelligent agency. Darwin thought that natural selection could accomplish the work of a human breeder, and thus that blind nature could come to mimic, over time, the action of a selecting intelligence—a designer. If the origin of biological organisms could be explained naturalistically, as Darwin argued,[23] then explanations invoking an intelligent designer were unnecessary (and even vacuous).

Thus, it was not ultimately the arguments of the philosophers that destroyed the popularity of the design argument, but a scientific theory of biological origins. This trend was reinforced by the emergence of other fully naturalistic origin theories in astronomy, biology, and geology throughout the nineteenth century.

Though the design argument in biology went into retreat after *On the Origin of Species* was published, it never quite disappeared. Darwin was challenged by several leading scientists of his day, most forcefully by the great Harvard naturalist Louis Agassiz, who argued that the sudden appearance of the first complex animal forms in the Cambrian

---

23. Charles Darwin, *On the Origin of Species* (Cambridge, MA: Harvard University Press, 1964), 481–82.

fossil record pointed to an "intellectual power" and attested to "acts of mind." Similarly, the co-founder of the theory of evolution by natural selection, Alfred Russel Wallace, argued that some features of human beings, such as their consciousness and capacity to use language, were better explained by reference to the work of a "Higher intelligence" than to Darwinian evolution.[24] There seemed to him "to be evidence of a Power" guiding the laws of organic development "in definite directions and for special ends." Wallace further insisted that "so far from this view being out of harmony with the teachings of science, it has a striking analogy with what is now taking place in the world." And in 1897 Oxford scholar F. C. S. Schiller argued that "it will not be possible to rule out the supposition that the process of Evolution may be guided by an intelligent design."[25]

Continued interest in the design hypothesis was made possible in part because the mechanism of natural selection had a mixed reception in the immediate post-Darwinian period. As the historian of biology Peter Bowler has noted,[26] classical Darwinism entered a period of eclipse during the late nineteenth and early twentieth centuries mainly because Darwin lacked an adequate theory for the origin and transmission of new heritable variation. Natural selection, as Darwin well understood, could accomplish nothing without a steady supply of variation, the ultimate source of new biological structure. Nevertheless, both the blending theory of inheritance that Darwin had assumed and the classical Mendelian genetics that soon replaced it, implied limitations on the amount of genetic variability available to natural selection. This in turn implied limits on the amount of novel structure that natural selection could produce.

By the late 1930s and 1940s, however, natural selection was revived as the main engine of evolutionary change as developments in several fields clarified the nature of genetic variation. The resuscitation of the variation/natural selection mechanism by modern genetics and

---

24. Alfred Russel Wallace, "Sir Charles Lyell on Geological Climates and the Origin of Species," in *An Anthology of His Shorter Writings*, ed. Charles H Smith (Oxford: Oxford University Press, 1991), 33–34.

25. F. C. S. Schiller, "Darwinism and Design Argument," in *Humanism: Philosophical Essays* (New York: Macmillan, 1903), 141.

26. Peter J. Bowler, *Theories of Human Evolution: A Century of Debate, 1844–1944* (Baltimore: Johns Hopkins University Press, 1986), 44–50.

population genetics became known as the neo-Darwinian synthesis. According to it, natural selection, acting upon a special kind of random variations known as genetic mutations, could account for the origin of novel biological forms and structures. These random mutations (conceived of as copying errors or alterations in hereditary material) supplied the variations upon which natural selection could act and from which new biological form and structure would arise. Small-scale microevolutionary changes could, then, be extrapolated indefinitely to account for large-scale macroevolutionary development.

With the revival of the natural selection mechanism, the neo-Darwinists would assert, like Darwinists before them, that they had found an entirely undirected natural process or mechanism that explained the appearance of design in biology. As Harvard evolutionary biologist Ernst Mayr explained, "[T]he real core of Darwinism . . . is the theory of natural selection. This theory is so important for the Darwinian because it permits the explanation of adaptation, the 'design' of the natural theologian, by natural means."[27] By the centennial celebration of Darwin's *On the Origin of Species* in 1959, many scientists assumed that natural selection could fully explain the appearance of design and that, consequently, the design argument in biology was dead. As Julian Huxley proclaimed at the Centennial celebration, "Future historians will perhaps take this Centennial Week as epitomizing an important critical period in the history of this Earth . . . when the process of evolution, in the person of inquiring man, began to be truly conscious of itself."[28]

The Evidence and the Argument for Intelligent Design

Despite such pronouncements, and the perceived triumph of neo-Darwinism, new discoveries would resuscitate the question of design. Indeed, discoveries in the burgeoning field of molecular biology during the 1950s, some made just before the 1959 Centennial celebration, would suggest that at least one key appearance of design in biology had not been explained by natural selection and random mutation or by any other purely materialistic mechanism of evolution.

---

27. Ernst Mayer, "Foreword" to *Darwinism Defended* by Michael Ruse (Reading, MA: Addison Wesley, 1982), xi–xii.

28. Julian Huxley, *Evolution After Darwin*, ed. Sol Tax (Chicago: University of Chicago Press, 1960), 3:249–61.

The DNA Enigma and the Appearance of Design

When Watson and Crick discovered the structure of DNA, they also discovered that DNA stores information in the form of a four-character alphabetic code. Strings of precisely sequenced chemicals called *nucleotide bases* store and transmit assembly instructions—the information—for building the crucial protein molecules and protein machines that cells need to survive.

Crick further developed this idea with his now famous "sequence hypothesis," according to which the chemical subunits of DNA (the nucleotide bases) function like letters in a written text or digital characters or symbols in computer software. Just as letters in an English sentence or digital characters in a computer program may convey information depending on their arrangement, so too do certain sequences of chemical bases along the spine of the DNA molecule convey precise instructions for arranging the amino acids from which the proteins are made. (Proteins perform most of the life-maintaining functions in cells. For example, they function as enzymes catalyzing chemical reactions at rates much faster than would otherwise occur; they process genetic information; and they form the structural parts of molecular machines.)

Moreover, the sequences of nucleotide bases in DNA do not just possess information in the strictly mathematical sense of the theory of information developed by the famed MIT scientist Claude Shannon in the late 1940s. Shannon developed a mathematical theory of information[29] that equated the amount of information transmitted with the amount of uncertainty reduced or eliminated by a series of symbols or characters.[30] In Shannon's theory, the more improbable an event or sequence the more uncertainty it eliminates and the more information it conveys. Shannon generalized this relationship by stating that the amount of information conveyed by an event or sequence of characters is inversely proportional to the probability of its occurrence. The greater the number of possibilities, the greater the improbability of any one being actualized, and thus the more information transmitted when a particular possibility occurs.

---

29. Claude Shannon, "A Mathematical Theory of Communication," *Bell System Technical Journal* 27 (1948): 379–423, 623–56.

30. Fred Dretske, *Knowledge and the Flow of Information* (Cambridge, MA: MIT Press, 1981): 6–10.

Nevertheless, Shannon's mathematical formalism could not measure or detect whether a sequence of characters is meaningful—or whether it performs a communication function. To see the distinction between a merely improbable sequence of characters (that is, one possessing Shannon information alone) and a sequence possessing *both* Shannon information and *functional* information, consider these two sequences:

inwehnsdysk]ifhsnmcpew,m.sa
Time and tide waits for no man.

Although it would be very improbable for, say, a blind man typing at a standard keyboard to generate either of these exact strings of characters, only the bottom string performs a communication function, while the top string does not. Thus, while the top string contains Shannon information, the bottom also contains what has been called "functional" or "specified information."

Why does this distinction matter? It turns out that the specific arrangements of bases on the DNA molecule, like the arrangement of characters in an English sentence or section of computer software, do not just exhibit a high degree of mathematical improbability. Instead, the *specific* way in which the nucleotide bases in DNA are arranged is crucial to the function of the DNA molecule in the cell. That is, the arrangement of nucleotide bases in the coding regions of DNA also exhibits "specificity." As Francis Crick explained in 1958, "Information means here the *precise* determination of sequence, either of bases in the nucleic acid [DNA] or on amino acid residues in the protein."[31]

Thus, DNA not only has Shannon information, it also contains information in the ordinary sense of alternative sequences or arrangements of characters *that produce a specific effect*. DNA base sequences convey instructions that produce proteins that perform functions and produce specific effects. Thus, they not only possess Shannon information but also specified or functional information.

Further, the presence of functionally specific, information-bearing sequences in DNA represents a striking appearance of design. As Richard Dawkins notes, "the machine code of the genes is uncannily

31. Francis Crick, "On Protein Synthesis," *Symposium for the Society of Experimental Biology* 12 (1958): 138–63, esp. 144, 153.

computer-like,"[32] and software developer Bill Gates has observed, "DNA is like a computer program."[33] And after the early 1960s, further discoveries made clear that the digital information in DNA and RNA is only part of a complex information processing system—an advanced form of nanotechnology that both mirrors and exceeds our own in its complexity, design logic, and information storage density.

But if this is true, how did the functional information in DNA arise? Biologists know that all forms of life, and all living cells in every organism, require genetic information to construct the crucial protein molecules that cells and organisms need to live. This implies that building new forms of life during the history of life required new functional genetic information. How did that new information arise?

When I was a college professor I used to ask my students a question: "If you want your computer to acquire a new function or capability, what do you need to give it?" Typically, student answers would cluster around terms such as "new code," "instructions," "software," or "information." All these answers are correct, of course—and we now know that the same is true of living organisms. To build new forms of life from simpler preexisting forms, or to build the first cell from simpler non-living chemicals, would have required new functional information.

But if that is so, is it plausible to think natural selection acting on random mutations, or other undirected evolutionary mechanisms, could have produced the information in DNA necessary to generate new forms of life? There are several compelling reasons to think not. Indeed, explaining the origin of the digital information stored in DNA—again, a striking appearance of design—has turned out to be a formidable problem for both branches of evolutionary theory—for biological evolutionary theory, which attempts to explain the origin of new forms of life from simpler preexisting forms of life, and for chemical evolutionary theory, which attempts to explain the origin of the first life from simpler non-living chemicals.

Biological Evolution and the Origin of Genetic Information

According to neo-Darwinism, new genetic information arises when random mutations occur in the DNA of existing organisms. "Random" here

---

32. Richard Dawkins, *River Out of Eden* (New York: Basic Books, 1995), 17.
33. Bill Gates, *The Road Ahead* (New York: Viking, Penguin Group, 1995), 188.

means "without respect to functional outcome," implying that there can be no directionality or *telos* to mutational events. When mutations arise that, strictly by chance, confer a functional advantage on the organisms possessing them (thereby increasing their reproductive output), the resulting genetic changes will be passed on by natural selection to the next generation. As such changes accumulate, the features of a population will change over time.

Yet natural selection can only "select" what random mutations first generate. Thus, for natural selection to preserve any significant functional innovation, random mutations must first produce new genetic information for building new proteins (from a new arrangement of amino acids). Without new functional mutations, natural selection will have nothing advantageous to preserve and pass on to the next generation—in which case no significant evolutionary change will occur. Natural selection necessarily awaits the deliverances of the mutational process because it is there that a new selectable function (and morphological novelty) first arises.

If mutation is occurring without direction, however, the evolutionary mechanism faces what amounts to a needle-in-the-haystack problem, or what mathematicians call a "combinatorial search problem." In mathematics, the term "combinatorial" refers to the number of possible ways a set of objects can be arranged or combined.

For example, as the length of a required gene or protein grows, the number of possible nucleotide base (in the case of DNA) or amino-acid sequences (in the case of proteins) of that length grows exponentially. For example, using the twenty protein-forming amino acids, there are 20^2 or 400 ways to make a two-amino-acid combination, since each position could feature any one of twenty different amino acids. Similarly, there are 20^3 or 8,000 ways to make a three-amino-acid sequence, and 20^4 or 160,000 ways to make a sequence four amino acids long, and so on. Yet, most functional proteins are made of *hundreds* of amino acids. Thus, even a relatively short protein of, say, 150 amino acids, represents one sequence among an astronomically large number of other possible amino acid combinations (approximately 10^{195}). Intuitively, this suggests that the probability of finding even a single functional sequence—i.e., a working gene or protein—as the result of random mutational search may be prohibitively small because of the sheer number of possible sequences that must be searched by mutations in the available time.

To see why consider a simple bicycle locks with four *dials* with ten *settings* on each dial. A thief encountering one of these locks (and lacking bolt cutters) faces a combinatorial search problem because there are 10 × 10 × 10 × 10, or 10,000 possible ways of combining the possible settings on each of the four dials. Yet, there is only one combination that will open the lock. Randomly trying possible combinations is unlikely to yield the correct setting, unless the thief has a lot of time on his hands to search exhaustively.

Imagine, however, that we now encounter a really committed bicycle thief who patiently searches the "sequence space" of possible lock combinations at a rate of one combination every ten seconds. If our hypothetical thief had fifteen hours and took no breaks he could generate more than half (5,400 out of 10,000) of the total possible combinations on a four-dial bike lock. Given this, the probability that he will happen upon the right combination exceeds the probability that he will fail. In that case, he would be more likely (than not) to *succeed* in opening the lock by random search. And the chance hypothesis—i.e., the hypothesis that he will succeed in opening the lock via a random search—is, therefore, also more likely to be *true* than false.

But now imagine a much more complicated lock. Instead of four dials, this lock has ten dials. Instead of 10,000 possible combinations, this lock has 10^{10} or 10 billion possible combinations. With only one combination that will open the lock out of 10 billion—a prohibitively small ratio—it is much more likely that the thief will fail *even if he devotes his entire life to the task.*

A little math shows this to be true. If the thief did nothing but sample combinations at random, one every ten seconds for an entire one-hundred-year lifetime, he would still sample only about 3 percent of the total number of combinations on a lock that big. In this admittedly contrived case, he would most likely *fail* to open the lock by random search. And in such a case, the chance hypothesis—the hypothesis that the thief will succeed in finding the combination by a random search—is also much more likely to be *false* than true.

So what about relying on random mutations to "search" for a new DNA base sequence capable of directing the construction of a new functional protein? Would such a random search for new genetic information be more likely to succeed—or to fail—in the time available to the evolutionary process? In other words, is a random mutational search for a new gene capable of producing a new protein more like the search for the combination on the four-dial lock or on the ten-dial lock?

As our examples show, the ultimate probability of the success of a random search—and the plausibility of any hypothesis that affirms the success of such a search—depends upon both the *size of the space* that needs to be searched and *the number of opportunities* available to search it.

But it happens that scientists need to know something else to determine the probability of success in the case of genes and proteins. They need to know how rare or common functional arrangements of DNA bases capable of generating new proteins are among all the possible arrangements for a protein of a given length. That's because in genes and proteins, unlike in our bike lock example, there are *many functional* combinations of bases and amino acids (as opposed to just one) among all the combinations. Thus, in order to assess the plausibility of a random search, we need to know the overall ratio of functional to non-functional sequences in the DNA.

Until recently molecular biologists didn't know how many of the possible combinations in a given stretch of genetic information were functional. They didn't know—in effect—how many of the possible combinations would "open the lock." But recent experiments in molecular biology and protein science have settled the issue.

While working at Cambridge University from 1990–2003, molecular biologist Douglas Axe set out to answer this question using a sampling technique called "site directed mutagenesis." His experiments revealed that for every one DNA sequence that generates a short *functional* protein of just 150 amino acids in length, there are 10^{77} *non*-functional combinations—that is, 10^{77} amino acid arrangements that will *not* fold into a stable three-dimensional protein structure capable of performing a biological function.[34]

In other words, there are unimaginably more ways of arranging nucleotide bases that result in non-functional sequences of DNA than there are sequences resulting in functional genes. (Consequently, there

---

34. Douglas Axe, "Estimating the Prevalence of Protein Sequences Adopting Functional Enzyme Folds," *Journal of Molecular Biology* 341 (2004): 1295–1315. For an earlier estimate also derived from mutagenesis experiments see John Reidhaard-Olson and Robert Sauer, "Functionally Acceptable Solutions in Two Alpha-Helical Regions of Lambda Repressor," *Proteins: Structure, Function, and Genetics* 7 (1990): 306–16.

are also vastly more ways of arranging amino acids that result in non-functional amino-acid chains than there are ways of arranging amino acids to make functional proteins). Indeed, Axe's experimentally derived estimate placed that ratio—the size of the haystack in relation to the needle—at 10^{77} non-functional sequences for every functional gene or protein. That ratio implies that the difficulty of a mutational search for a new gene or protein *is equivalent to the difficulty of searching for just one combination on a lock with 10 digits on each of 77 dials.*

Could random genetic mutations effectively search a space of possibilities that large in the time available to the major evolutionary transitions documented in the fossil record, or even in the entire history of life on Earth? Clearly 10^{77} power represents a huge number. (To put that number in context, consider that there are only 10^{65} atoms in our galaxy.) Yet, to assess whether the mutation/selection mechanism could effectively search such a large number of possible combinations in the time available, we also need to know how many opportunities the evolutionary process would have had to search this huge number of possibilities.

Consider that every time an organism reproduces and generates a new organism an opportunity occurs to generate and pass on a new DNA sequence as well. But during the entire 3.85 billion year history of life on Earth, only 10^{40} individual organisms have ever lived—meaning that at most only 10^{40} such opportunities have occurred. Yet 10^{40} represents only a small fraction of 10^{77}—only one ten trillion, trillion, trillionth to be exact.

Thus, for even a single relatively simple functioning protein to arise, the mutation selection mechanism would have time to search just a tiny fraction of the total number of relevant sequences—one ten trillion trillion trillionth of the total possibilities. That is, the number of trials available to the entire evolutionary process turns out to be incredibly small in relation to the mind-bendingly large number of possible sequences that need to be searched. The size of the relevant spaces that need to be searched by the evolutionary process dwarfs the time available for searching—even taking into account evolutionary deep time.

It follows that it is overwhelmingly more likely (than not) that a random mutational search would have failed to produce even one new functional (information-rich) DNA sequence and protein in the entire history of life on earth. Consequently, it also follows that the hypothesis that such a random search succeeded is more likely to be false than true. And, of course, the building of new plants and animals required many new proteins, not just one.

When our bicycle thief faced many more combinations than he had time to explore, it was much more likely that he would fail than it was that he would succeed in opening the lock. Likewise, the mutation and selection mechanism is much more likely to fail than to succeed in generating even a single new protein—and the genetic information necessary to produce it—in the known history of life on Earth. It follows that the neo-Darwinian mechanism does not provide an adequate explanation for the origin of the genetic information necessary to produce the major innovations in biological form that have arisen during the history of life on Earth. In my book *Darwin's Doubt*, I note that many leading evolutionary biologists now acknowledge the inadequacy of the neo-Darwinian mechanism of natural selection and random mutation for this and other reasons. I also show that attempts to replace or supplement this mechanism as part of new, but still strictly materialistic, theories of evolution (such as self-organization, neo-Lamarckian inheritance, neutral theory, natural genetic engineering) also fail to solve the problem of the origin of biological information.

Chemical Evolutionary Theory and the Origin of Information

Explaining the origin of genetic information poses an even more acute difficulty for scientists attempting to explain the origin of life in the first place. Recall that Darwin's theory sought to explain the origin of new forms of life from simpler forms. It did not purport to explain how the first life—presumably a simple one-celled organism—might have arisen to begin with. During the 1930s a Russian biochemist named Alexander I. Oparin attempted to remedy this lacuna in the evolutionary story by suggesting that life could have first evolved through a long series of undirected chemical reactions over hundreds of millions of years. Yet, neither he nor anyone else in the 1930s fully appreciated the complexity of even the simplest cells.

Though Oparin's theory appeared to receive experimental support in 1953 when Stanley Miller simulated the production of the amino acid "building blocks" of proteins under ostensibly pre-biotic atmospheric conditions, his textbook version of chemical evolutionary theory is riddled with difficulties. Miller's simulation experiment is now understood by origin-of-life researchers to have little, if any, relevance to explaining how amino acids—let alone their precise sequencing, which is necessary to produce proteins—could have arisen in the actual atmosphere of the early earth.

Moreover, like other biologists, origin-of-life researchers (also known as chemical evolutionary theorists) now recognize the centrality of information to even the simplest living systems. They recognize that building a living cell in the first place requires assembly instructions stored in DNA or some equivalent molecule. But how did such functional digital information and the cell's complex information processing system arise? Today these questions lie at the heart of origin-of-life research. As researcher Bernd-Olaf Küppers has explained, "The problem of the origin-of-life is clearly basically equivalent to the problem of the origin of biological information."[35]

Clearly, the informational features of the cell at least *appear* designed. They also would seem to require some kind of explanation. Yet, since Oparin proposed his theory of chemical evolution before the elucidation of the structure of DNA and the formulation of the sequence hypothesis, he did not initially propose any explanation for the origin of the information present in the DNA and RNA of even the simplest living cells. Since the 1960s, however, scientists have proposed three broad types of materialistic explanations for the origin of the information necessary to produce the first cell—explanations based upon (1) chance, (2) self-organizational laws (or physical-chemical "necessity") or (3) some combination of the two. In *Signature in the Cell*, I show that all three of these types of explanations have failed to explain the ultimate origin of genetic information.

In brief, theories of chance fail because the probability of generating a functional (i.e., information-rich) gene or protein from simpler nonliving chemicals turns out to be even smaller than the probability of building a new functional gene or protein from a preexisting gene or protein in an already existing organism (i.e., the probability calculated above)—even taking into account all the opportunities for such an event to have occurred since the beginning of the universe. For this and other

---

35. Bernd-Olaf Küppers, *Information and the Origin of Life* (Cambridge, MA: MIT Press, 1990), 172.

reasons, serious origin-of-life researchers now consider "chance" an inadequate causal explanation for the origin of biological information.[36]

Moreover, the information in DNA has also been shown to defy explanation by reference to "self-organizational" laws or forces of chemical attraction, though some earlier origin-of-life scientists did propose that both DNA and proteins might have originated this way. These scientists thought that just as electrostatic forces draw sodium (Na+) and chloride ions (Cl-) together into highly ordered patterns within a crystal of salt (NaCl), so too might amino acids with special affinities for each other, or nucleotide bases with special affinities for each other, arrange themselves into information-bearing protein and DNA molecules. Nevertheless, proteins and DNA are not like crystals. While crystals are characterized by highly *ordered* or *repeating* sequences of their chemical constituents, information-rich sequences, whether in software, a passage of English text, or in DNA, defy reduction to such rigidly repeating patterns. Instead, the bases sequences in DNA vary in unpredictable ways and, consequently, can convey (uncertainty-reducing) information. In the case of DNA, the underlying forces of attraction that hold the molecule together do not determine the exact sequences of the information-carrying nucleotide bases. As a result, the sequences can vary in innumerable ways, unlike a crystal. Just as magnetic letters can be combined and recombined to form various sequences on a metal surface, so too can each of the four bases (represented with the letters A, T, G, and C) attach to any site on the DNA backbone with equal facility, making all sequences equally probable (or improbable). Thus, instead of its chemical subunits making a rigidly repeating or highly ordered sequence (such as Na-Cl Na-Cl Na-Cl . . .) the information-bearing subunits in DNA are aperiodic and highly complex. Yet, for just this reason the bases in DNA can carry information (as opposed to repetitive order) and function as an instructional molecule. If every DNA sequence was characterized by the same rigidly repeating pattern, DNA would not be able to provide instructions for building the many thousands of different proteins in cells—but, at best, only one. DNA contains functional information for building numerous different proteins precisely because it does not exhibit rigidly repeating patterns

---

36. Christian de Duve, "The Constraints of Chance," *Scientific American* 271 (1996): 112; Francis Crick, *Life Itself* (New York: Simon & Schuster, 1981), 89–93.

of the kind that can self-organize by the laws of chemical attraction. As I show in *Signature in the Cell* in more detail, molecular biology has revealed that self-organizational forces of attraction between the information-bearing constituents in DNA (and RNA and proteins) do not explain the sequence specificity (the information) in these large information-bearing molecules. Saying otherwise would be like saying that a newspaper headline might arise as the result of the chemical attraction between ink and paper.

Finally, other chemical evolutionary theories have attempted to combine the two types of explanations—those based on chance and those that invoke law-like processes. The most popular theory of this type, "the RNA world," invokes chance variations and a law-like process of "pre-biotic natural selection."

This theory is based upon the discovery that RNA molecules are capable of both storing information like DNA and catalyzing some enzymatic reactions like proteins. For this reason, some origin-of-life scientists proposed that life might have first arisen out of a group of self-copying RNA molecules competing with each other on the early earth. RNA world proponents imagined sections of RNA with different sequences of bases arising by chance on the pre-biotic earth, with some eventually acquiring an ability to make copies of themselves. In such a scenario, the capacity to self-replicate would favor the survival of those RNA molecules that could do so and would, thus, also favor the specific sequences that the first self-replicating molecules happened to have.

Numerous difficulties with the RNA-world scenario have emerged, however. First, synthesizing (and maintaining) many essential building blocks of RNA molecules under realistic conditions has proven either difficult or impossible.[37] Second, naturally occurring RNA catalysts (so-called "ribozymes") possesses very few of the specific enzymatic properties of proteins necessary to extant cells. Third, RNA-world advocates offer no plausible explanation for how primitive RNA replicators might have evolved into modern cells that allow proteins to process and translate genetic information and regulate metabolism.[38]

---

37. Robert Shapiro, "Prebiotic Cytosine Synthesis: A Critical Analysis and Implications for the Origin of Life," *Proceedings of the National Academy of Sciences, USA* 96 (1999): 4396–4401.

38. Yuri I. Wolf and Eugene V. Koonin, "On the Origin of the Translation System and the Genetic Code in the RNA World by Means of Natural Selection, Exaptation, and Subfunctionalization," *Biology Direct* 2 (2007): 14.

Most importantly, the RNA-world hypothesis presupposes, but does not explain, the origin of sequence specificity or information in the original functional RNA molecules. To date scientists have been able to design RNA catalysts that will copy only about 10 percent of themselves.[39] Yet, for strands of RNA to perform even this much, they must have very *specific* arrangements of constituent building blocks (nucleotides on the RNA strand). Further, the strands must be long enough to fold into complex three-dimensional shapes. Thus, any RNA molecule capable of even limited self-copying must have possessed considerable (specified) information. Yet explaining how the building blocks of RNA arranged themselves into functionally specified sequences has proven no easier than explaining how the parts of DNA might have done so, especially given the high probability of destructive cross-reactions between desirable and undesirable molecules in any realistic pre-biotic soup. As Nobel laureate biochemist Christian de Duve noted in a critique of the RNA-world hypothesis, "Hitching the components together in the right [information-rich] manner raises additional problems . . . that no one has yet attempted to [solve] in a prebiotic context."[40] He explained further that all theories of pre-biotic natural selection "need information which implies they have to presuppose what is to be explained in the first place."[41]

In any case, attempts to enhance the limited catalytic and self-replicating properties of RNA molecules in "ribozyme engineering" experiments inevitably require extensive investigator manipulation, thus simulating, if anything, the need for intelligent design, not the efficacy of an undirected chemical evolutionary process.

The Mystery of Life's Origin and the "Intelligent Cause" Hypothesis

It was the crisis in origin-of-life research (already, but not fully, apparent by 1984) led chemist Charles Thaxton, polymer scientist Walter Bradley, and geochemist Roger Olsen to write *The Mystery of Life's Origin*—the

---

39. Wendy Johnston et al., "RNA-Catalyzed RNA Polymerization: Accurate and General RNA Templated Primer Extension," *Science* 292 (2001): 1319–25.

40. Christian De Duve, *Vital Dust: Life as a Cosmic Imperative* (New York: Basic Books, 1995b), 23.

41. Theodosius Dobzhansky, "Discussion of G. Schramm's Paper," in *The Origins of Prebiological Systems and of their Molecular Matrices*, ed. Sidney W. Fox (New York: Academic, 1965), 310.

first contemporary book to advance the idea of intelligent design. In *Mystery*, Thaxton and his colleagues critiqued all then current chemical evolutionary theories. They showed that the Miller-Urey experiment did not simulate early earth conditions; that the existence of an early earth pre-biotic soup was a myth; that chemical evolutionary transitions were subject to destructive interfering cross-reactions; and that neither chance nor self-organizational laws could account for the information in proteins and DNA.

But it was in the book's epilogue that the three scientists proposed a radical alternative. There they suggested that the information-bearing properties of DNA might point to an "intelligent cause." Drawing on the work of the famed chemist Michael Polanyi, they argued that chemistry and physics alone couldn't produce information any more than ink and paper could produce the information in a book. Instead, they argued that our uniform experience suggests that information (or what they called specified complexity) is the product of an "intelligent cause."[42] *Mystery* also argued that intelligent causes could be considered legitimate scientific hypotheses within the historical sciences, a mode of inquiry they called *origins science*.

Intelligent Design: A Better Explanation?

Mystery marked the beginning of interest in the contemporary theory of intelligent design. It also inspired a generation of younger scholars and scientists to investigate whether there is evidence of actual design, or just the appearance of design, in living organisms. When the book was first published, I was working as a geophysicist in Dallas where Charles Thaxton happened to live. In 1985 I met him at a scientific conference and learned about the hypothesis he was developing about DNA. I began meeting him after work to discuss the arguments he had made in his book.

Intrigued with his thesis but not yet fully convinced, the next year I left my job as a geophysicist to pursue a PhD at the University of Cambridge in the history and philosophy of science. During my PhD research, I investigated questions that had emerged in my discussions with Thaxton. What methods do scientists use to study biological

---

42. Charles Thaxton et al., *The Mystery of Life's Origin: Reassessing Current Theories* (New York: The Philosophical Library, 1984), 211.

origins? Do they use a distinctive method of historical scientific inquiry? After completing my PhD, I would take up another question: Was it possible to formulate a rigorous scientific case for intelligent design based upon the presence of the digital information in DNA?

As I began to study the method of reasoning that historical scientists use to identify causes responsible for events in the remote past, I discovered that these scientists often make inferences with a distinctive logical form, known technically as *abductive inferences*.[43] Geologists, paleontologists, evolutionary biologists, and other historical scientists reason like detectives, inferring *past* conditions or causes from *present* clues. As Stephen Jay Gould notes, historical scientists typically "infer history from its results."[44]

Nevertheless, as many philosophers have noted, this kind of historical reasoning can be problematic because more than one cause can often explain the same effect or clue. This makes reasoning from present clues tricky because the evidence may point to more than one causal explanation or hypothesis. To address this problem in geology, the nineteenth-century geologist Thomas Chamberlain delineated a method of reasoning he called "the method of multiple working hypotheses."[45]

Contemporary philosophers of science such as Peter Lipton have called this the method of "inference to the best explanation."[46] That is, when trying to explain the origin of an event or structure from the past, scientists often compare various hypotheses to see which would, if true, best explain it. They then provisionally affirm the hypothesis that best explains the data as the one most likely to be true.

But that raised an important question: Exactly what makes an explanation *best*? As it happens, historical scientists had already developed criteria for deciding which cause, among a group of competing possible causes, provides the best explanation for some event in the remote past. The most important of these criteria is called "causal adequacy." This

43. C. S. Peirce, *Collected Papers, Volumes 1–6*, eds. C. Hartshorne and P. Weiss (Cambridge, MA: Harvard University Press, 1932), 2:375.

44. Stephen J. Gould, "Evolution and the Triumph of Homology: Or, Why History Matters," *American Scientist* 74 (1986): 61.

45. Thomas C. Chamberlain, "The Method of Multiple Competing Hypotheses," *Science* 148 (1965): 754–59.

46. Peter Lipton, *Inference to the Best Explanation* (London and New York: Routledge, 1991), 1.

criterion requires that historical scientists, as a condition of a successful explanation, identify causes known to have the power to produce the kind of effect, feature, or event in question. In making these determinations, historical scientists evaluate hypotheses against their present knowledge of cause and effect. Causes known to produce the effect in question are judged better candidates than those that are not. For instance, a volcanic eruption provides a better explanation for an ash layer in the earth than an earthquake because volcanic eruptions have been observed to produce ash layers, whereas earthquakes have not.

One of the first scientists to develop this principle was the geologist Charles Lyell, who also influenced Charles Darwin. Darwin read Lyell's magnum opus, *The Principles of Geology*, on the voyage of the *Beagle* and employed its principles of reasoning in *On the Origin of Species*. The subtitle of Lyell's *Principles* summarized the geologist's central methodological principle: *Being an Attempt to Explain the Former Changes of the Earth's Surface, by Reference to Causes Now in Operation*. Lyell argued that when scientists seek to explain events in the past, they should not invoke unknown causes, the effects of which we do not know. Instead they should cite causes known from our uniform experience to have the power to produce the effect in question.[47] Historical scientists should cite "causes now in operation"—that is, presently acting causes. This was the idea behind his uniformitarian dictum: "The present is the key to the past."

Darwin himself adopted this methodological principle as he sought to demonstrate that natural selection qualified as a *vera causa*, that is, a true, known, or actual cause of significant biological change.[48] He sought to show that natural selection was *causally adequate* to produce the effects he was trying to explain.

Both philosophers of science and leading historical scientists have emphasized causal adequacy as the key criterion for assessing competing hypotheses. Philosophers of science have also noted that assessments of explanatory power lead to conclusive inferences only when it can be shown that there is *only one known cause* for the effect or evidence in

---

47. Charles Lyell, *Principles of Geology: Being an Attempt to Explain the Former Changes of the Earth's Surface, by Reference to Causes Now in Operation*, 3 vols. (London: Murray, 1830–33), 75–91.

48. V. Kavalovski, "The Vera Causa Principle: A Historico-Philosophical Study of a Meta-theoretical Concept from Newton Through Darwin" (PhD diss., University of Chicago, 1974), 78–103.

question.[49] When scientists can infer a *uniquely* plausible cause, they can avoid the fallacy of affirming the consequent—the error of deciding on one causal explanation while ignoring other causes that also may have the power to produce the same effect.[50]

What did all this have to do with the origin of biological information, what I have called "the DNA enigma?" As a PhD student I wondered if a case for an intelligent cause could be formulated and justified in the same way that historical scientists would justify any other causal claim about an event in the past. My study of historical scientific reasoning and origin-of-life research suggested to me that it was possible to formulate a rigorous scientific case for intelligent design as an inference to the best explanation, specifically, as the best explanation for the origin of biological information. The creative action of a conscious and intelligent agent clearly represents a known (presently acting) and adequate cause for the origin of information. Uniform and repeated experience affirms that intelligent agents can produce large amounts of functional or specified information, whether in software programs, ancient inscriptions, or Shakespearean sonnets. Minds are clearly capable of generating specified information.

Further, the specified information in the cell also points to intelligent design as the *best* explanation for the origin of biological information. Why? Experience shows that large amounts of functional information (especially when expressed in a digital or alphabetic form) invariably originate from an intelligent source—from a mind or personal agent. In other words, intelligent activity is *the only known cause of* the origin of functionally specified information (at least, in amounts sufficient to produce a new protein fold—the minimal unit of biological innovation. See footnote for an explanation of this caveat).[51] Since intelligence is the

49. Michael Scriven, "Explanation and Prediction in Evolutionary Theory," *Science* 130 (1959): 480.

50. Stephen Meyer, "Of Clues and Causes: A Methodological Interpretation of Origin of Life Studies" (PhD diss., Cambridge University, 1990), 96–108.

51. Building a new form of animal life requires innovation in form and structure. New protein folds—the subunits of large-scale structure out of which whole proteins are made—constitute the smallest unit of *structural* innovation in the history of life. Thus, a novel protein fold represents the smallest unit of innovation that natural selection can detect. Since building fundamentally new forms of life requires structural innovation, mutations must generate new protein folds for natural selection to have an opportunity to preserve and accumulate structural or morphological innovations. Thus, the ability to produce new protein folds represents a *sine qua non* of macroevolutionary innovation. For this reason, Douglas Axe's experiments tested

only known cause of specified information, the presence of functional or specified information in even the simplest living systems points decisively to the past existence and activity of a designing intelligence.[52]

Ironically, this generalization—that intelligence is the only known cause of specified information—has received support from origin-of-life research itself. During the last fifty years, every materialistic model proposed has failed to explain the origin of the functionally specified genetic information required to build a living cell.[53] It also has received confirmation from new developments in evolutionary biology, where not only neo-Darwinism but—as I demonstrate in *Darwin's Doubt*—more recently proposed mechanisms of evolutionary change also have failed to explain the origin of novel information—again, at least in amounts sufficient to produce new protein folds. Thus, intelligence, or what philosophers call "agent causation," now stands as the only known cause to be capable of generating large amounts of specified information.[54] As a result, the presence of specified information-rich sequences in even the simplest living systems, and in the large increases of biological

---

the difficulty of generating new protein folds, not just new protein functions within an existing folded structure. Though random mutations may produce slight changes in protein functions within a common proteins fold (i.e., without producing a new fold), Axe's work showing that the extreme rarity (and isolation) of novel folds within amino acid sequence space suggested that generating a novel fold requires more new information than could be reasonably expected to arise given the probabilistic resources available to earth's evolutionary history. Thus, Axe's experiments also suggested an *informational* limit to the creative power of the mutation and selection. See Meyer, *Darwin's Doubt* (pp. 221–27) and David Klinghoffer, ed., *Debating Darwin's Doubt: A Scientific Controversy That Can No Longer Be Denied* (Seattle: Discovery Institute Press, 2016) for examples of failed attempts to demonstrate that mutation and natural selection can generate novel protein folds.

52. My conclusions were reinforced by the work of mathematician William Dembski in his book, *The Design Inference* (Cambridge: Cambridge University Press, 1998). Chapter 16 of *Signature in the Cell* explains how Dembski's criteria and method of design detection relate to the idea of specified information.

53. Thaxton et al., *The Mystery of Life's Origin*, 42–172; Robert Shapiro, *Origins: A Skeptic's Guide to the Creation of Life on Earth* (New York: Summit, 1986); Klaus Dose, "The Origin of Life: More Questions Than Answers," *Interdisciplinary Science Review* 13 (1988): 348–56; Hubert P. Yockey, *Information Theory and Molecular Biology* (Cambridge: Cambridge University Press, 1992), 259–93; Charles B. Thaxton and Walter L. Bradley, "Information and the Origin of Life" in *The Creation Hypothesis: Scientific Evidence for an Intelligent Designer*, ed. J. P. Moreland (Downers Grove, IL: InterVarsity Press, 1994), 193–97. Meyer, *Signature in the Cell*.

54. Of course, the phrase "large amounts of specified information" begs a quantitative question, namely, "How much specified information would the minimally complex cell have to have before it implied design?" In *Signature in the Cell*, I justify a precise quantitative answer to this question. I show that the de novo emergence of five hundred or more bits of specified information reliably indicates design. See also endnote 53.

information that arise throughout the history of life, points to the activity of a designing intelligence.

Scientists in many fields recognize the connection between intelligence and information and make inferences accordingly. Archaeologists assume that a scribe produced the inscriptions on the Rosetta stone. The search for extraterrestrial intelligence (SETI) presupposes that any specified information imbedded in electromagnetic signals coming from space would indicate an intelligent source.[55] As yet, radio astronomers have not found any such information-bearing signals, but closer to home, molecular biologists have identified specified information-rich sequences and systems in the cell, suggesting, by the same logic, the past existence of an intelligent cause for those effects.

Indeed, our uniform experience affirms that specified information—whether inscribed in hieroglyphics, written in a book, encoded in a radio signal, or produced in an RNA world "ribozyme engineering" experiment—*always* arises from an intelligent source, from a mind, not a strictly material process. So the discovery of the functional digital information in the DNA molecule, and the evidence that large infusions of such new information have entered the biosphere during the history of life, provides strong grounds for inferring that intelligence played a role in the origin of that information. Indeed, whenever we find specified information and we know the causal story of how that information arose, we invariably find that it arose from an intelligent source. It follows that the best, most causally adequate explanation for the origin of the specified, digitally encoded information in DNA is an intelligent source. Intelligent design best explains the origin of biological information—the DNA enigma.

Philosophical Objections to Intelligent Design

In response to arguments for intelligent design summarized here, opponents have often responded with philosophical rather than evidential objections. The two of the most common are: (1) that the theory of intelligent design is an argument from ignorance, and (2) that intelligent design is "not science." Let's examine each of these arguments in turn.

---

55. Thomas R. McDonough, *The Search for Extraterrestrial Intelligence: Listening for Life in the Cosmos* (New York: Wiley, 1988).

An Argument from Ignorance?

Opponents of intelligent design frequently characterize the theory as an argument from ignorance. According to this criticism, anyone who makes a design inference from the presence of specified information in the biological world uses our present ignorance of an adequate materialistic cause of such information as the basis for inferring an intelligent cause. Since, the objection goes, design advocates can't imagine a natural process that can produce biological information, they resort to invoking the mysterious notion of intelligent design. In this view, intelligent design functions not as an explanation but as a placeholder for ignorance.

But arguments from ignorance occur when evidence against a proposition is offered as the sole grounds for accepting an alternative proposition. The arguments for intelligent design made by contemporary design theorists don't commit this fallacy. True, the design arguments employed by contemporary advocates of intelligent design do depend in part upon negative assessments of the causal adequacy of competing materialistic hypotheses. And clearly, the lack of an adequate materialistic cause does provide part of the grounds for inferring design from information-rich structures in the cell. Nevertheless, this lack is only part of the basis for inferring design. Proponents of intelligent design also infer design because we *know* that intelligent agents can and do produce specified information-rich systems. As the information theorist Henry Quastler observed, "Information habitually arises from conscious activity."[56] Indeed, we have positive, experience-based *knowledge* of an alternative cause sufficient to have produced the effect in question—and that cause is intelligence or mind. Thus, design theorists infer intelligent design not just because natural processes do not explain the origin of specified information in biological systems, but also because we *know*, based upon our uniform experience, that intelligent agents, and only intelligent agents, produce this effect. That is to say, we have positive, experience-based knowledge of an alternative cause (intelligence) that is sufficient to produce specified information.

That contemporary arguments for design necessarily include critical evaluations of the causal adequacy of competing hypotheses is, therefore,

---

56. Henry Quastler, *The Emergence of Biological Organization* (New Haven: Yale University Press, 1964), 16.

entirely appropriate. All historical scientists must compare the causal adequacy of competing hypotheses in order to make a judgment as to which hypothesis is best. We would not say, for example, that an archeologist had committed a "scribe of the gaps" fallacy simply because—after rejecting the hypothesis that an ancient hieroglyphic inscription was caused by a sand storm—he went on to conclude that the inscription had been produced by a human scribe. Instead, we recognize that the archeologist has made an inference based upon his experience-based *knowledge* that information-rich inscriptions invariably arise from intelligent causes, not solely upon his judgment that there are no suitably efficacious natural causes that could explain the inscription.

By reasoning in this manner, contemporary design advocates employ the standard uniformitarian method of reasoning used in all historical sciences. In all cases where we know how specified information arose, experience has shown that intelligent design played a causal role. Thus, when we encounter such information in the bio-macromolecules necessary to life, we may infer—based upon our *knowledge* of established cause-effect relationships (i.e., "causes now in operation")—that an intelligent cause operated in the past to produce the information necessary to the origin of new forms of life or life in the first place.

But Is It Science?

Of course, many simply refuse to consider the design hypothesis on grounds that it does not qualify as scientific. Such critics[57] affirm the extra-evidential principle known as methodological naturalism. Methodological naturalism asserts that, as a matter of definition, for an explanation to qualify as scientific, it must invoke only materialistic entities. Thus, critics say, the theory of intelligent design does not qualify. Yet, even if one grants this definition, it does not follow that some nonscientific (as defined by methodological naturalism) or metaphysical hypothesis couldn't constitute a better, more causally adequate explanation of some phenomena than competing materialistic hypotheses. Design theorists argue that, whatever its classification, the intelligent design hypothesis does constitute a better explanation than its materialistic rivals for the origin of biological information as well as

57. Michael Ruse, "McLean v. Arkansas: Witness Testimony Sheet" in *But Is It Science?*, ed. M. Ruse (Amherst, New York: Prometheus Books, 1988), 103.

other indicators of design such as the irreducible complexity of cellular molecular machines and the fine-tuning of the laws and constants of physics. Surely, simply classifying an argument as "not scientific" does not refute it.

In any case, methodological materialism now lacks justification as a normative definition of science. First, attempts to justify methodological materialism by reference to metaphysically neutral (that is, non-question begging) demarcation criteria have failed.[58] Second, to assert methodological naturalism as a normative principle for all of science has a negative effect on the practice of certain scientific disciplines, especially those in the historical sciences. In origin-of-life research, for example, methodological materialism artificially restricts inquiry and prevents scientists from considering some hypotheses that might provide the best, most causally adequate explanations. To be a truth-seeking endeavor, the question origin-of-life researchers must address is not "Which materialistic scenario seems most adequate?" but rather "What actually caused life to arise on Earth?" Clearly, it's at least logically possible that the answer to the latter question is this: "Life was designed by an intelligent agent that existed before the advent of humans." If one accepts methodological naturalism as normative, however, scientists may never consider that design hypothesis as possibly true. Such an exclusionary logic diminishes the significance of any claim of theoretical superiority for any remaining hypothesis and raises the possibility that the best scientific explanation (as defined by methodological naturalism) may not be the best in fact.

As many philosophers of science now recognize, scientific theory-evaluation is an inherently comparative enterprise. Theories that gain acceptance in artificially constrained competitions can claim to be neither most probably true nor most empirically adequate. At best, such theories can be considered the most probably true or adequate among an artificially limited set of options. Thus, openness to the

58. Stephen C. Meyer, "The Scientific Status of Intelligent Design: The Methodological Equivalence of Naturalistic and Non-Naturalistic Origins Theories" in *Science and Evidence for Design in the Universe* (San Francisco: Ignatius Press, 2000b). L. Laudan, "The Demise of the Demarcation Problem" in *But Is It Science?*, ed. M. Ruse (Amherst, New York: Prometheus Books, 2000a), 337–50. L. Laudan, "Science at the Bar—Causes for Concern" in *But Is It Science?*, ed. M. Ruse (Amherst, New York: Prometheus Books, 2000b), 351–55; A. Plantinga, "Methodological Naturalism?" *Origins and Design* 18.1 (1986a): 18–26; A. Plantinga, "Methodological Naturalism?" *Origins and Design* 18.2 (1986b): 22–34.

design hypothesis would seem necessary to any fully rational historical science—that is, to one that seeks the truth "no holds barred."[59] A historical science committed to following the evidence wherever it leads will not exclude hypotheses a priori on metaphysical grounds. Instead, it will employ only metaphysically neutral criteria—such as explanatory power and causal adequacy—to evaluate competing hypotheses. This more open, and seemingly rational, approach to scientific theory evaluation suggests the theory of intelligent design as the best, most causally adequate explanation for the origin of certain features of the natural world, including the origin of the specified information necessary to build new forms of life.

Conclusion

Of course, many continue to dismiss intelligent design as nothing but "religion masquerading as science." They point to the theory's obviously friendly implications for theistic belief as a justification for dismissing the theory as religion. But such critics confuse the implications of a theory with its evidential basis. The theory of intelligent design may well have theistic implications. Indeed, I think it does precisely because it suggests the design we observe in nature is real, not just apparent—just as a traditional theistic, and indeed a biblical, worldview would lead us to expect. Though intelligent design is not *based upon* religious belief, it does affirm a key tenet of a biblical worldview—namely, that life and the universe are the products of a designing intelligence—an intelligence that I, and other Christians, would attribute to the God of the Bible.

Nevertheless, the theistic implications of intelligent design are not grounds for dismissing it. Scientific theories must be judged by their ability to explain evidence, not by whether they have undesirable implications. Those who say otherwise overlook the testimony of the history of science. For example, many scientists initially rejected the big bang theory because it seemed to challenge the idea of an eternally self-existent universe and pointed to the need for a transcendent cause of matter, space, and time. But scientists eventually accepted the theory despite such potential implications because the evidence strongly supported it. Today a similar metaphysical prejudice confronts the theory

---

59. Percy Williams Bridgman, *Reflections of a Physicist*, 2nd ed. (New York: Philosophical Library, 1955), 535.

of intelligent design. Nevertheless, it too must be evaluated on the basis of the evidence, not our philosophical preferences or concerns about its possible religious implications. As Professor Antony Flew, the long-time atheistic philosopher who came to accept the case for intelligent design, advised: We must "follow the evidence wherever it leads."

KEN HAM

Young-earth creationists find much that we can agree with in the theory of intelligent design (hereafter ToID) presented by Dr. Meyer. But at the outset I think it is important to point out the difference between intelligent design *arguments* on the one hand and on the other hand the *strategy* of the ID movement (hereafter IDM) developed by Phillip Johnson, William Dembski, and others associated with the Discovery Institute, of which Meyer is a key leader.

Probably all young-earth creationist speakers and writers have used intelligent design arguments as part of their defense of the truth of Genesis, and they did so long before the modern IDM was born. For decades after joining Henry Morris at the Institute for Creation Research in 1970, Duane Gish spoke and wrote frequently on the incredible design of the bombardier beetle, the monarch butterfly, and dinosaurs, which defy evolutionary explanations for their origin. Every issue of AiG's *Answers Magazine* (which teaches a biblical worldview) has at least one article on the amazing design of one of God's creatures, and AiG sells many books and DVDs (including some produced by people connected to the IDM) that argue for the existence of God from the design we see in nature. Intelligent design arguments are perfectly consistent with the Bible's teaching in Romans 1:20, Acts 14:15–17, Psalm 19:1, Job 12:7–10, and other passages. Since God designed and created this universe, we expect to see all kinds of evidence of intelligent design. Young-earth creationists are grateful for the way that IDM leaders have ratcheted up the sophistication and philosophical depth of ID arguments.

But the IDM and its strategy for dealing with evolution and its influence in science and the culture is a different matter. We certainly agree with Dr. Meyer that, contrary to what many secularists think, ToID is not simply repackaged biblical creation. It is indeed distinct from young-earth creation in both method and content. It is important to note Meyer's statement that "the theory does not challenge the idea of evolution defined as either change over time or common ancestry, but it does dispute the Darwinian idea that the cause of biological change is wholly blind and undirected" (p.181). So, in the IDM, neither theistic evolution nor billions of years of history for the universe and earth are ruled out: only *atheistic* evolution is rejected. That explains why the IDM and Discovery Institute bring together people of diverse religious (even agnostic) viewpoints. As a result, the Bible (especially Genesis) is almost completely left out of their ID arguments, as it has been in Meyer's chapter.

I and most young-earth creationists think this is a mistaken strategy. The fact is that the Intelligent Designer of heaven and earth and everything in them is the God of the Bible, and He is not silent. He has spoken, and the Bible is His inspired, inerrant Word. Anyone who claims to be a Christian and to believe that about the Bible cannot justifiably ignore what it says or treat its text in a superficial way. And we must remember: "So faith comes from hearing, and hearing through the word of Christ" (Rom 10:17 ESV).

This strategy of arguing for design but ignoring Genesis was tried in the early nineteenth century but it failed to derail the deism and atheism that were increasingly taking over in science, resulting in first the idea of millions of years and then evolution. And it won't stop these ideas now. It won't "split the foundations of naturalism"[1] and break naturalism's control of science or the culture. While scientific evidence and arguments are extremely important in Christian apologetics, ultimately the creation vs. evolution battle is a spiritual one. It can only be successfully waged and won in the heart of an individual by the Spirit of God using the Word of God. That's why young-earth creationists use God's Word *and* evidences and arguments, not just the latter. And that is why ID arguments moved Anthony Flew to accept an intelligent designer of some kind, but he did not "follow the evidence wherever it leads." Having rejected or never considered the overwhelming evidence that the Bible is God's Word, he died, apparently, as a Christ-rejecting sinner who sadly will spend eternity in hell. It is not sufficient for cul-

---

1. Phillip E. Johnson's subtitle to his book is *The Wedge of Truth*.

ture change or a person's eternal destiny simply to get people to believe in the existence of an intelligent designer. Only Christ and His Word can change a life and impact the culture. I and others in the biblical creation movement freely admit that our aim is to not convert people to be creationists but to help them trust in Jesus Christ for salvation.

All young-earth creationists would agree with Meyer's discussion of the evidence for intelligent design in the complex, information-loaded DNA molecule in every living creature. He helpfully demonstrates that no natural process, including natural selection and mutations, can cause information to arise in non-living matter to form the first living cell. Nor can those processes create new genetic information to transform that first single-celled creature into all the diverse plants, animals, and people, no matter how much time is allowed. In fact, as Sanford argues,[2] time is the enemy of evolution, because over time harmful mutations are increasing in the DNA of all creatures. All scientific and non-scientific investigations of the world show that information does not come from matter but from an intelligent mind, and life comes from life. Meyer is right: We *know* this. But Paul tells us (Rom 1:18–20) that people suppress this truth in their sinful rebellion against God. The God of the Bible is the living, eternal, and infinitely intelligent Creator not only of the genetic information but also of the various kinds of organisms that function and reproduce "after their kind" (Gen 1). God is not guiding natural selection and mutations to create living creatures because natural selection and mutations do not produce the new information needed for molecules-to-man evolution.

Meyer and other ID proponents are correct to see and expose naturalism's (i.e., atheism's) control of the sciences concerned with biological origins (chemistry, biology, genetics, and anthropology). He also correctly sees that Darwin based his idea of biological evolution squarely on Charles Lyell's naturalistic, uniformitarian theory of geological evolution over millions of years, as I also documented in my chapter. But IDM leaders are failing to deal with naturalism's control of geology (and cosmology), and most of them apparently accept the evolutionist claim about millions of years.

Meyer mentions Thomas Chamberlain (1843–1928), an American

---

2. John Sanford, *Genetic Entropy* (Livonia, NY: FMS Foundation, 2014).

geologist who developed the method of multiple working hypotheses. He studied geology in 1868–1869 at the University of Michigan, which like all universities was already locked into millions of years and probably Darwinian evolution. Chamberlain's method was never followed, however, because from the late eighteenth century to the present geologists generally have denied the eyewitness testimony of the Creator. Except for young-earth creationists, they have never entertained the idea that a supernatural creation about six thousand years ago and Noah's flood could be the key to deciphering the history of the geological record. Their multiple working hypotheses have all been naturalistic and were never provisional regarding the age of the earth. In fact, most geologists rejected the flood and biblical chronology before even the world's first geological society was formed in London in 1807.[3]

Young-earth creationists also agree with Meyer about the significant difference between experimental science (e.g., chemistry and physics) and historical or origin science (e.g., geology, paleontology, and cosmology). He is right that in historical science investigators are like detectives trying to determine the past cause(s) that produced the evidence we see in the present. But here I find some deficiencies in Meyer's analysis. He apparently fails to consider the role of eyewitness testimony in reconstructing the unrepeatable and unobserved past. No good detective would ignore truthful eyewitness testimony; in fact, he would regard it as most important and the key to correctly interpreting the physical evidence of a crime. But all old-earth origin scientists ignore (or worse, twist) God's eyewitness testimony in Genesis in their efforts to interpret the physical evidence from events of the past.

If we had no reliable eyewitness testimony about the origin and history of the creation, then we would be left with just the physical evidence in the present and could only reason from the present processes to reconstruct the past. But we do have that testimony, and IDM leader Phillip Johnson was exactly right when he said, "If God has spoken, then we need to build on that foundation rather than try to fit what God has done into some framework that comes from human philosophy."[4] Unfortunately, Johnson and most other IDM leaders have never given

---

3. See Terry Mortenson, *The Great Turning Point*, 27–33.
4. Phillip E. Johnson, *The Wedge of Truth* (Downers Grove, IL: InterVarsity Press, 2000), 158.

serious consideration (at least in any of their writings or lectures, as far as I know) to what God said in Genesis 1–11 about creation, the flood, and the age of the earth. So, they have been open to the acceptance of millions of years (and other evolutionary beliefs) and have not exposed and opposed naturalism's control of geology and cosmology. Young-earth creationists are the only fully consistent origin scientists because they alone take full account of the eyewitness testimony of the God who knows everything, always tells the truth, and saw every event in history from the first moment of creation.

One other weakness of the IDM and ToID is the failure to deal with a major point that I discussed in my chapter, namely the problem of death, disease, and suffering before the fall. The theory of intelligent design is simply not an adequate explanation for the world we live in. The creation not only bears witness to God's intelligent creative work but also to His judgments in the world at the fall and the flood. But the witness of nature to those judgments can only be recognized and properly understood in the light of God's written witness in Scripture. To avoid the question of the age of the earth or to embrace the millions of years is in effect to reject the Bible's teaching about the original "very good" creation and the fall, i.e., to reject what God has said.

So, the IDM intelligent design arguments are much appreciated, but the IDM strategy of leaving the Bible, or at least Genesis, out of the discussion leads to compromise with millions of years and the big bang and other ideas that undermine the truth and authority of Scripture. This in turn undermines biblical morality and the gospel in the culture, thereby keeping people from embracing the saving work of Jesus Christ. The IDM is not a Christian movement, whereas biblical creationists are overtly and unashamedly Christian.

Meyer's focus on the teleological argument for an intelligent designer seems wise. For millennia the teleological argument has consistently remained among the most popular lines of evidence for God's existence.

As a Christian astronomer, I appreciate Meyer's appeal to cosmic fine-tuning as evidence for intelligent design (ID). Cosmic fine-tuning and big bang cosmology have clear theistic implications, specifically Christian implications. The long history of negative reaction to the big bang by non-theistic astronomers and physicists traces back to these implications. Thanks to accumulating evidence in support of a big bang origin event and counter to competing models, big bang cosmology has gained increasing acceptance. However, since cosmic fine-tuning and the big bang align with Christian theology, scientific resistance lingers, and I suspect it always will.

I applaud Meyer's emphasis on life's origin. Life's origin is the scientifically best opportunity for testing the evolutionary paradigm, yielding the most unambiguous and rigorous evidence for ID. Consequently, Reasons to Believe has published four books on life's origin.[1]

Meyer correctly identifies that biomolecules possess not just order but extreme levels of specified complexity. Meyer's reference to ribozyme engineering experiments' requiring sophisticated laboratories and "extensive investigator manipulation" (p. 199) strengthens his argument for direct intervention in life's origin by an intelligent Designer. At a minimum these experiments establish that Someone with vastly greater

---

1. Fazale Rana and Hugh Ross, *Origins of Life*, 2nd ed. (Covina, CA: RTB Press, 2014); Fazale Rana, *The Cell's Design* (Grand Rapids: Baker, 2008); Fazale Rana, *Creating Life in the Lab* (Grand Rapids: Baker, 2011); Hugh Ross, *Improbable Planet* (Grand Rapids: Baker, 2016).

resources than the scientists conducting these experiments must have been responsible for assembling life some 3.825 billion years ago.

Meyer's philosophical approach to ID research is one I share. His appeal to abductive reasoning, or "inference to the best explanation," enables us to distinguish sharply between a merely deistic interpretation of life's history and a theistic interpretation, also between a theistic interpretation and an explicitly Christian interpretation. I would add that in astronomy we can do more than infer best explanations of past events. Thanks to light's finite and constant velocity, we can directly observe the past.

Design research has been part of my ministry since before the founding of Reasons to Believe and the founding of the ID movement. What differentiates my team's approach from other ID proponents is our acknowledgement of a biblical foundation. Our aim is to construct and communicate a testable, falsifiable, and predictive creation model that integrates all scientific disciplines and all books of Scripture. Such a model can be presented in virtually any setting because it identifies the design Source and the specific ways and times God intervened in the natural order.

From an evangelistic perspective, Meyer pays a steep price for refraining from taking a stand on the designer's identity, Earth's age, the Genesis creation days, and dates for life's and humanity's origins. He makes a number of sacrifices:

1. He cannot use some of the best scientific evidences for the Christian faith.
2. He arouses suspicion among scientists, suspicion of a hidden agenda.
3. He may seem to endorse the scientific credibility of young-earth creationism.
4. He relinquishes opportunities to address Bible questions that inevitably arise from discussion of design evidence.
5. He inadvertently reinforces a widely held misinterpretation of the US Supreme Court ruling on creation teaching.

Yes, the US Supreme Court did outlaw "the teaching of creationism." However, what the court, in fact, outlawed was the teaching of young-earth creationism in public school science classrooms. Why? Because the advocates failed to establish for the court any scientific merit for their creation model. The court was clear that if such merit could be established, the content would be permissible.[2]

According to famed physicist Paul Davies, anyone presenting a model identifying the designer, citing specific dates, locations, and means of design, showing how their model could be falsified, and making short-range predictions of what scientists should discover (distinct from other models' predictions), has earned a seat at the science research and education tables.[3] Commitment to such a model opens doors to discussion in public universities. It also elicits valuable critique from non-Christian research scientists and provides opportunities to draw them toward faith in Jesus Christ.

Meyer and fellow ID proponents appear noncommittal on young-earth creationism, evolutionary creationism, and other religious and non-religious creationism models. Meyer "does not challenge" such beliefs as "common ancestry," though he does dispute that "the cause of biological change is wholly blind and undirected" (p. 181). What he writes here is exactly what Haarsma would say. This similarity leads me to ask whether Meyer sees specific instances where the Designer's intervention in the "common descent" process is unambiguously revealed?

One of Meyer's main arguments for design in life's origin exemplifies the importance of field testing apologetics arguments, trying them out on research scientists active in relevant disciplines. Meyer's argument that biochemical information cannot arise through chance processes seems convincing to lay audiences, but we note it has little to no impact on origin-of-life researchers and biochemists. Attempts to use this argument in a university setting can lead to embarrassment.

Evolutionary biochemists think Meyer's argument misrepresents the processes they believe generated information-rich molecules. For example, they cite recent research that shows protein space is far more densely populated by functional proteins than what Meyer acknowledges.[4]

---

2. I document this in chapter 15 of my book, *More Than a Theory* (Grand Rapids: Baker, 2009).

3. Davies made this comment during a dialogue with me on *Unbelievable?*, a program hosted by Justin Brierley on Premier Christian Radio in the UK.

4. Jeffrey Skolnick and Mu Gao, "Interplay of Physics and Evolution in the Likely Origin of Protein Biochemical Function," *Proceedings of the National Academy of Sciences USA* 110 (June 2013): 9344–49, doi:10.1073/pnas.1300011110.

This critique that Meyer's probability numbers are exaggerated does not imply all biochemical information arguments for a Designer should be avoided. It simply means we must use ones that origin-of-life researchers openly acknowledge as major, if not intractable, problems for naturalistic models. Here are a few examples, some of which Meyer references in his other writings:

1. No known natural mechanism can account for the algorithmic nature of biochemical information. Information harbored in biomolecules works like computer software. It exerts highly specified and sequentially timed control over the operation of biochemical machines and biochemical systems.

2. Biochemical systems employ three different codes: the genetic code, the histone code, and the even parity code of DNA. Only beings at least as intelligent as humans can design such complex codes.

3. Rules making up the genetic code are better designed for minimizing errors than any other conceivable code.

4. Information-based biochemical systems display language structure as complex as human language.

5. Even with high-tech lab facilities, biochemists cannot make RNA or DNA with genuine self-replication capability. Furthermore, laboratory biochemical evolution studies have failed to yield any evidence that evolutionary processes can generate information under conditions that existed on Earth at the time of life's origin. Lab experiments designed to provide an evolutionary explanation for life's origin provide evidence that Someone more capable and intelligent than the brightest humans created life.

Robust biochemical information arguments for the Designer are complex and challenging to present. Much simpler arguments can be made for the necessity of a Designer and, when integrated with other evidences, of the biblical Designer. Here's a partial list:

1. *Scarcity of building blocks.* Outside of living organisms and their decay products, scientists find no ribose, arginine, lysine, or tryptophan—molecules critical for assembling proteins, RNA,

and DNA—either on Earth or anywhere else in the universe. While these building blocks may exist somewhere below the detection limits of a few parts per billion, such scarcity would seem to rule out a naturalistic origin of life.

2. *Lack of a source for homochiral molecules.* Protein assembly requires that all the amino acids involved possess a left-handed config-uration. DNA and RNA assembly requires that all the ribose sugars involved be "right-handed." Outside of organisms, organic decay products, and controlled laboratories, no source has been found, either on Earth or elsewhere in the universe, for this homochirality. Nature provides a mixture of right- and left-handed molecules. No conceivable naturalistic scenario is able to generate large, stable ensembles of homochiral ribose and homochrial amino acids.

3. *Short lifespans of building blocks.* Many of the critical building block molecules cannot last outside of organisms and their decay product for more than just days, hours, or minutes.

4. *Assembly challenges.* The more (building block) isomers link together on a mineral substrate, the harder for additional isomers to join the linkage, and the more difficult for the isomer chain to separate from the substrate. In the most recent laboratory exper-iments, chains of fewer than fifty amino acids or nucleobases represent the upper limit, a number far short of what's needed for life.

5. *Presence of primordial oxygen.* Even the tiniest amount of oxygen shuts down the chemical pathways to a naturalistic origin of life. Early earth's abundance of uranium and thorium would have (by their radiometric decay) split enough of Earth's surface water into hydrogen and oxygen to shut down those pathways.

6. *Rapidity of life's origin.* The measured time window between Earth's deadly hostile environment for life—even for complex biochemical reactions—and an abundance of life is narrower than some millions of years.

7. *Early date of life's origin.* Life originated on Earth under the most hostile conditions life has ever faced and yet early enough to set in motion the plate tectonics needed for later advanced life to exist.

8. *Diversity of Earth's first life.* According to isotope analysis, Earth's earliest life included not just one microbial species with a few hundred gene products but rather dozens or more different forms manifesting multiple independent metabolic chemistries, including photosynthesis. Some possessed at least fifteen thousand gene products.

9. *Relevance to human existence.* If not for the remarkable abundance and diversity of microbes on Earth as early as the laws of physics and the universe's gross features would allow, Earth's geologic and chemical transformation (propelled by that early life) would have had insufficient time to attain survivable conditions for humans and human civilization before the ever-brightening sun becomes too bright.

10. *Relevance to redemptive purpose.* Nothing less than the appearance of life at the earliest moment physics would permit and the maximum diversification and abundance of life from that time forward, for as long as physics would allow, could possibly account for the availability of resources for the existence of humans in the billions, much less for development of the technologies that permit dissemination of the gospel message to all peoples of the earth.

Let me reiterate that Meyer is right to make the origin of life the linchpin of his ID argument. I encourage him, though, to listen more carefully to critiques from origin-of-life researchers. This topic, the origin of life, could be the key to resolving the differences this book presents. For example, if the four authors were given the assignment to research the science and theology of life's origin and to develop our findings into a compelling approach for bringing nonbelieving adults to faith in Jesus Christ, that exercise, by itself, might resolve most of our theological and scientific differences. We would also see many more scientists and students of science becoming Christ's followers.

I also want to emphasize that Meyer's response to methodological naturalism is on target: "Simply classifying an argument as 'not scientific' does not refute it" (p. 207). Although I would like to see ID proponents reframe their agenda and become open to identifying the Designer, such a change would mean a seismic shift of major proportions. I can't help but imagine what such a shift would accomplish for the advance of Christ's kingdom.

Meyer's closing comment about "scientific theory-evaluation" as "an inherently comparative enterprise" (p. 208) holds great promise for progress toward greater unity. My prayer is that the comparative enterprise and open competition of ideas this book facilitates will become a model for both the Christian community and the scientific research community.

DEBORAH B. HAARSMA

I'm grateful for this opportunity to interact with Stephen C. Meyer and the views of the Discovery Institute on Intelligent Design, continuing several exchanges between our scholars over the years.

Evolutionary Creation (EC) and Intelligent Design (ID) agree on important areas of design and science.

EC joins ID in believing that an intelligent designer crafted the universe and life with purpose and intent. Who is this intelligent agent? The Discovery Institute (and the ID argument itself) avoid any reference to organized religion or God and count agnostics, Muslims, and Jews among their adherents. However, Stephen C. Meyer and many advocates of ID share with EC a belief that this Intelligent Designer is the God of the Bible.

Scientifically, ID has important areas of agreement with EC. Meyer clearly states that he accepts the evidence for an ancient universe and the long time scale of development of life on earth.[1] Moreover, I was pleased (and surprised) to read his statement that ID does not challenge the common ancestry of all life, since most ID advocates reject common ancestry.

*Evolutionary Creation sees design in what science **can explain**.*

The Intelligent Design argument is framed on the contrast between "undirected material process" vs. "intelligent cause" and sets a full natural explanation in opposition to the design argument. Meyer quotes skeptics who think a natural explanation reduces design to merely "apparent" design and renders the design argument "vacuous."

---

1. Note, however, that some ID proponents argue for a young earth and some young-earth creationists adopt the language of the Intelligent Design movement.

EC argues instead that we can perceive design in nature even when scientists have a complete natural explanation. While ID points to supposed flaws in evolutionary explanations, EC sees design in the whole fabric of the universe that makes life (and evolution) possible.[2] Following Robert Boyle and other Christian leaders in the scientific revolution, evolutionary creationists are motivated by a Christian world-view to discover the *natural* mechanisms that God is using. Although some atheist scientists are slow to consider other models because of their atheistic worldview (e.g., the big bang), in many cases Christians like Galileo, Boyle, Mendel, and Lemaître were scientific pioneers who saw their work as following God's call to investigate the natural processes in creation. Sometimes the term "methodological naturalism" (MN) is used for this project of searching only for material causes, but MN is not inherently atheistic (the term was coined in contrast with *metaphysical* naturalism). Evolutionary creationists delight in natural mechanisms as descriptions of the ongoing, regular activity of God in the natural world. Without God's sustained action, all natural laws and matter itself would cease to exist. God also works in non-regular (i.e., miraculous) ways at times, most notably in the incarnation and resurrection of Christ. Yet a completely natural explanation never negates God as the designer.

Some Christians are concerned that the EC approach is not a convincing apologetic. It's true that an atheist can look at a complete natural explanation and conclude that there is no need for God. Yet many scientists, even atheist scientists, do not see a scientific explanation as ruling out spirituality. And for many laypeople, greater scientific understanding leads to a greater appreciation of design and the Designer; recent studies of people watching nature documentaries (with sweeping scenery and beautiful animals) found that the viewers were more likely to perceive something beyond a materialist explanation.[3] From a Christian perspective, scientific explanations elicit even deeper praise, as they reveal new examples of God's beauty, power, intricacy, and craftsmanship.

---

2. Curiously, ID sees design this way in the fine-tuning of cosmology and physics, but not in the history of life.

3. Jeff Hardin "Is Science 'Awe'some for Christians?" BioLogos.org Sept 25, 2016, http://biologos.org/blogs/deborah-haarsma-the-presidents-notebook/is-science-awesome-for-christians.

Intelligent Design Theory shares the risks of "god of the gaps" arguments.

Meyer states that ID is more than an argument from ignorance. Yet even if ID theory is not a "god of the gaps" argument per se, it shares the risks of "god of the gaps" arguments: If scientists discover a natural explanation for the phenomenon attributed to design, then the ID argument fails. EC instead argues that the God of the Bible is the sovereign Designer of both the phenomena that science can explain and what science cannot explain.

Intelligent Design arguments have significant scientific weaknesses.

Of the views in this book, ID has the most agreement with EC on science questions, although the two views still have significant scientific disagreements. EC has the same scientific concerns that most biologists have with ID.

Molecular machines could not evolve? Meyer briefly mentions biological structures such as the bacteria flagellum, which was a central ID argument in 1996 with the publication of *Darwin's Black Box* by Michael Behe. The flagellum was argued to be irreducibly complex and thus could not have evolved. Since then, scientists have discovered additional functions of the components of the flagellum, showing that it is *not* irreducibly complex, and found some possible evolutionary precursors.[4]

Specified information can only come from intelligence? EC agrees with ID that DNA contains a pattern of highly specified information.[5] EC disagrees, however, on the source of this information, seeing abundant evidence that this information can and does arise through natural processes. So where does the new information come from? *From the environment.* To illustrate this, imagine a simple computer program written to navigate a maze.[6] At each fork in the maze, the program randomly picks a direction to turn (north, south, east, west). If it hits a wall, the program goes back and tries other combinations of turns, and eventually reaches the end of the maze. The program results in a list of the turns that work, a set of specified information. Where did the information

4. "How Can Evolution Account for the Complexity of Life We See Today?" Biologos .org, http://biologos.org/common-questions/scientific-evidence/complexity-of-life.

5. Randy Isaac "Information, Intelligence, and the Origins of Life" *Perspectives on Science and Christian Faith* 63/4 (Dec 2011).

6. Loren Haarsma and Terry Gray "Complexity, Self-Organization, and Design" in *Perspectives on an Evolving Creation*, ed. Keith B. Miller (Grand Rapids: Eerdmans, 2003).

come from? Not from the computer program, nor from the person who wrote the program. Rather, the information came from the environment of the maze. The information is now embedded in the "organism" (the list of instructions) that "lives" in that environment. Evolution is similar in that organisms incorporate information from their environment as they become more complex and better adapted to it.

Evolution of functional proteins is highly improbable? Meyer cites Axe's claim that only one in 10^{77} proteins is stably folded, and thus that evolution "would have failed to produce even one new functional (information-rich) DNA sequence and protein in the entire history of life on earth" (p. 194). However, Axe's estimate was based on the function of only one specific enzyme; studies examining other enzymatic functions or folded structures have found a far higher proportion of functional proteins, indicating that Axe's work is not an estimate of protein function in general.[7] Additionally, biologists have observed many proteins that formed de novo, i.e., where a functional protein formed via mutation of a sequence that did not previously code for it.[8] One example is a bacterial enzyme that degrades nylon—a man-made chemical. This de novo protein arose within forty years of nylon being introduced to the environment and was the result of a mutation that produced a brand-new protein over three hundred amino acids long.[9] The observation that stably folded, functional, de novo proteins form readily in nature shows that evolution is quite capable of forming new information-rich, functional proteins over very short evolutionary timescales.

Neo-Darwinism is a failed explanation? The term "Neo-Darwinism," as used in this essay, refers to the evolutionary mechanism of natural selection in the context of modern genetics. ID often notes scientists who say that neo-Darwinism is an inadequate explanation for evolution,

7. C. Chiarabelli, J. W. Vrijbloed, D. De Lucrezia, R. M. Thomas, P. Stano, F. Polticelli, T. Ottone, E. Papa, and P. L. Luisi, "Investigation of de novo totally random biosequences, Part II: On the folding frequency in a totally random library of de novo proteins obtained by phage display." *Chem Biodivers* 3 (2006): 840–59; and E. Ferrada and A. Wagner, "Evolutionary Innovations and the Organization of Protein Functions in Sequence Space." *PLoS ONE* 5(11) (2010): e14172.

8. Dennis Venema "Biological information and intelligent design: De novo or ex nihilo," BioLogos.org, Dec 20, 2016, http://biologos.org/blogs/dennis-venema-letters-to-the-duchess/biological-information-and-intelligent-design-de-novo-or-ex-nihilo.

9. Dennis Venema "Intelligent Design and Nylon-Eating Bacteria," BioLogos.org, April 7, 2016, http://biologos.org/blogs/dennis-venema-letters-to-the-duchess/intelligent-design-and-nylon-eating-bacteria.

but this neglects the larger picture. Scientists today are discussing additional evolutionary mechanisms. While the basics of natural selection are not in dispute, new, larger studies point toward additional factors. We now know that the evolutionary process includes a vibrant interplay between environment and living organisms and that it sometimes gives rise to a high degree of cooperation between individual members of a species. We better understand genetic changes that influence the development of embryos and that some of these changes produce significant alterations in body plans. None of this suggests that there is a need for reinterpreting that which has always been at the heart of evolutionary biology.[10] ID calls evolution a theory in crisis,[11] when in fact the scientific consensus for evolution is strong and growing.

First-life could not arise from non-life? As Meyer notes, this is a separate question from the evolution of complex life from simple life, so I will address this only briefly. EC agrees that a complete, satisfactory natural explanation has not (yet) been found for the origin of life from non-life, but EC sees this as an active research field. Many evolutionary creationists are open to God using either natural processes or a miracle to bring about first life but feel it is far too soon to conclude that a natural explanation will never be found.

Evolutionary creation sees God's design and intent in the natural process of evolution.

EC sees God designing evolution in order that new living things can self-assemble via natural processes, all under his governance. Scientifically, it's true that genetic mutations occur without any preference for what is useful, but the selection side of evolution is all about usefulness and purpose, since selection favors those organisms better suited to the environment. More broadly, the history of evolution over a billion years can be seen as having directionality in that it favors development toward greater variety, greater complexity, greater cooperation, and convergence toward useful body plans.

---

10. The BioLogos view is summarized at "Is Evolutionary a Theory in Crisis?" BioLogos .org, http://biologos.org/common-questions/scientific-evidence/is-evolution-a-theory-in -crisis. See also the in-depth blog series, "Reviewing Darwin's Doubt," BioLogos.org, 2014–15, http://biologos.org/blogs/deborah-haarsma-the-presidents-notebook/series/reviewing -darwins-doubt.

11. Michael Denton, *Evolution: Still a Theory in Crisis* (Discovery Institute, 2016).

BioLogos is not the first Christian voice to see evolution as a process governed by God. Meyer's historical overview neglects to mention figures like theologian B. B. Warfield, Christian botanist Asa Gray, and many others. Just as all Christians praise God for the development of a fertilized egg into a healthy human baby (Ps 139:13–14) even though scientists understand all the steps of development, evolutionary creationists praise God for knitting together new species through processes that science can understand.

EC presents Jesus Christ as the intelligent designer.
The Discovery Institute aims to battle atheistic worldviews in our culture, and Meyer opens the essay with an update on this culture war. ID has chosen a strategy that is independent of organized religion, but sadly this means their argument can only convince someone of a deistic god. While Antony Flew accepted the ID argument and left atheism, he did not start believing in the God of the Bible or any organized religion.[12] Another challenge for ID is that their primary arguments are in subtle features unknown outside of modern science and inaccessible to most of the world's population.

EC also aims to counter atheistic worldviews in our culture, especially when militant atheists misuse evolutionary science to argue against God and spirituality.[13] But rather than letting observers speculate about the influence of religion on our approach, EC puts Christianity front and center, drawing on its rich theological framework for intellectual support and on the power of the gospel to change lives. EC invites atheists to view the world through a Christian lens, which brings a greater clarity and unity to our understanding of not only the physical world but of relationships, culture, and spiritual experience. EC's primary arguments for design are in the displays of divine power apparent throughout the natural world (Rom 1:20), not just in scientific details but in the glory of nature that all humans experience. When scientists find natural explanations for the wonders of organisms, evolutionary creationists praise the God of the Bible all the more as our intelligent designer and powerful creator.

---

12. "Antony Flew," Wikipedia.org https://en.wikipedia.org/wiki/Antony_Flew.

13. For example, Ted Davis's blog series "Science, Religion, and the New Atheism," BioLogos.org, 2016–17, http://biologos.org/blogs/ted-davis-reading-the-book-of-nature/series/science-religion-and-the-new-atheism.

STEPHEN C. MEYER

The theory of intelligent design makes a limited, but important, claim: Certain features of the natural world are best explained by an intelligent cause rather than undirected materialistic processes. I have argued here that intelligent design (ID) specifically constitutes the best explanation for the origin of the *functional information* necessary to produce new forms of life (and new protein folds, the smallest unit of structural innovation in living systems).

In the preceding responses, only Haarsma disputes that conclusion. Ross and Ham affirm that functional information in DNA points to intelligent design but critique ID *proponents* for not making other claims. Both criticize ID proponents for: (1) not rejecting the universal common ancestry (though I personally do; see my response to Ross), (2) not identifying the designer as God (though I do in other published writing), and (3) not using scientific evidence as a biblical apologetic (though I appreciate many apologists who do).

Even so, Ham and Ross have correctly understood the limited scope of ID theory (though, perhaps, not my personal views about other issues). Indeed, *the theory* of intelligent design (as opposed to what individual ID proponents may think or do) does not use scientific evidence as a biblical apologetic—though clearly evidence showing that a designing intelligence acted to generate life and the universe does support *a tenet* of biblical faith.

Since Ross and Ham do not dispute the truth of ID, but merely criticize its proponents for failing to address questions beyond its scope, I won't respond to their criticisms here. Suffice it to say, it seems self-evident to me that (1) demonstrating the universe and life are the products of a purposeful intelligence, and (2) establishing a new framework for science that does not presuppose a false materialistic worldview are important endeavors both scientifically and philosophically—even if they do not entail defending everything the Bible teaches.

Instead, I'll focus my response on Haarsma's criticism since she does challenge the validity of my argument, but does so based upon inaccurate characterizations of two scientific studies. Haarsma claims that (1) new studies show that functional proteins are *not* extremely rare (Ross echoes this claim) despite what Douglas Axe's experiments indicate, and (2) the evolution of an enzyme capable of digesting nylon shows that new information can arise by mutation and selection in available evolutionary time.

Both claims are problematic.

First, four other studies using different methods of estimating the rarity of functional proteins[1] have confirmed Axe's multi-year experimental study (cited earlier), showing their extreme rarity in the "sequence space" of possible amino acid combinations. The Italian study[2] Haarsma cites does not show otherwise. That study evaluated how frequently randomly generated amino acid chains organize themselves into stable three-dimensional structures. Unfortunately, the test it used to identify stable three-dimensional structures couldn't distinguish folded functional proteins from non-functional aggregations of amino acids. The group did report two folded structures but discovered that, except in strongly acidic environments, these structures formed insoluble aggregates (not proteins). This means these amino acid chains would not fold in living cells. Thus, this study does not refute Axe's results showing the extreme rarity of protein folds.

Haarsma's claims about nylonase are inaccurate and misleading. I argued that "intelligent activity is *the only known cause of* the origin of functionally specified information, at least *in amounts sufficient to produce a new protein fold* . . ." In response, Haarsma asserts that nylonase "arose within forty years of nylon being introduced to the environment and was

1. K. Durston et al., "Measuring the Functional Sequence Complexity of Proteins," *Theoretical Biology and Medical Modelling* 4 (2007): 47; J. Reidhaar-Olson and R. Sauer, "Functionally Acceptable Solutions in Two Alpha-Helical Regions of Lambda Repressor," *Proteins* (1990): 306–16; S. Taylor, et al., "Searching Sequence Space for Protein Catalysts," *Proceedings of the National Academy of Sciences, USA* 98 (2001): 10596–10601; H. Yockey, "A Calculation of the Probability of Spontaneous Biogenesis by Information Theory" *Journal of Theoretical Biology* 67 (1977): 377–98.

2. C. Chiarabelli et al., "Investigation of de novo totally random biosequences, Part II."

the result of a mutation that produced a brand-new protein . . ." (p. 225). Nevertheless, nylonase is not "a brand new protein" and did not arise de novo via a single frame shift mutation (as her source, Dennis Venema,[3] claims). Instead, the Japanese researchers who extensively studied nylonase postulated that it arose via two-point mutations[4] to the gene for a *pre-existing* 392 amino-acid protein—hardly a de novo origination event.

The Japanese researchers also inferred that the original gene (from which the nylonase gene arose) coded for a protein with limited nylonase function even before nylon was invented. They concluded this because a naturally occurring "cousin" of nylonase—an enzyme with a high degree of sequence similarity to it—has measurable (if weak) nylonase activity and can be converted to full activity with just two mutations.[5] The close sequence identity between nylonase and its cousin suggests the genes for both proteins arose from a common ancestral gene, which also would have produced a protein with nylonase activity. This suggests that the mutations that produced the gene for nylonase did not generate an entirely new functional gene and protein but instead merely optimized a *pre-existing* functional gene for a similar protein.

Most importantly, the evidence indicates that nylonase does not exemplify a new protein fold but instead the same complex three-dimensional (beta-lactamase) fold as its likely ancestral protein. As the Japanese researchers note, "we propose that amino acid replacements in . . . a *preexisting esterase with the beta-lactamase fold* resulted in the evolution of the nylon oligomer hydrolase" (emphasis added).[6] Note the terms "*preexisting*" and "*beta-lactamase fold*." They indicate the mutations responsible for the origin of nylonase did not produce a gene capable of coding a *new protein fold*, but instead a gene coding for the *same* beta-lactamase fold as its predecessor.

Thus, as Axe and I explain elsewhere, the mutation/selection mechanism can *optimize* (or shift) a protein's function provided it does not

---

3. http://biologos.org/blogs/dennis-venema-letters-to-the-duchess/intelligent-design-and-nylon-eating-bacteria.

4. Seiji Negoro et al., "X-Ray Crystallographic Analysis of 6-Aminohexanoate-Dimer Hydrolase: Molecular Basis for the Birth of a Nylon Oligomer-Degrading Enzyme," *The Journal of Biological Chemistry* 280 (2005): 39644–39652.

5. Kato et al., "Amino Acid Alterations Essential for Increasing the Catalytic Activity of the Nylon-Oligomer-Degradation Enzyme of *Flavobacterium* Sp.," *European Journal of Biochemistry* 200 (1991):165–169.

6. Negoro, et al. "X-Ray Crystallographic Analysis," 39644.

have to generate a new fold. Nevertheless, as we also argue, given the extreme rarity of protein folds in sequence space, the number of mutational changes necessary to produce a novel fold (to *innovate* rather than *optimize*) exceeds what can be reasonably expected to occur in available evolutionary time. The nylonase story confirms, rather than refutes, that claim. It also reinforces my claim that intelligent design is the only known cause, and best explanation, for the amount of new information necessary to generate new a protein fold—and, thus, any significant structural innovations in the history of life.

CONCLUSION

J. B. STUMP

I'm grateful for the opportunity to work on this project and with these contributors. By the time the book is released to the public, it will have been well over two years since my initial conversation with Zondervan about it. Of course the work isn't constant, as there are stretches of time when there isn't much to do but wait for contributors to send in their essays. But the project has occupied a prominent place in my mind over this period of time. As I look now at the finished sections, I have a few concluding thoughts about the project—one aspect of which was unsurprising to me, one that disappoints me a bit (but shouldn't be surprising), and one that I take to be the central issue for readers of this discussion moving forward.

Because of my occupation and professional interests, I've been well acquainted with the work of the contributors, and I was not surprised by the content of any of the essays. They are the standard arguments we see for positions in this field. The unique contribution of this book is that the arguments are being articulated (and responded to) by the leaders of the four most prominent origins-related organizations in the country. That adds an interesting twist to the dynamics of a Counterpoints book. I'm sure each of the contributors would affirm their commitment to following the evidence where it leads, but this is no mere academic discussion for them. Their organizations advocate for particular positions, and it seems almost impossible to think that they could be persuaded to shift positions at this stage.

This reminds me of a line from the mid-twentieth century author Upton Sinclair, who ran for governor of California in 1934. He proposed a plan to increase the benefits paid to elderly people in need, but many of his opponents stood to be affected personally by his proposal and claimed it to be without merit. About them Sinclair said, "It is difficult to get a man to understand something, when his salary depends upon his not understanding it!"[1] I'm not suggesting that any of the contributors is crassly guilty of this—or at least no more so than the others (or any of the rest of us); I'm merely noting the fact that there are other factors at work than just the facts. I've heard it is exceedingly rare for contributors to change their positions for any Counterpoints book, and I'd guess it's even more so when the contributors are the public face of their positions like those in the present volume. But it wasn't the goal of the book to change the minds of the contributors. It was to give a snapshot of the state of the conversation about origins among evangelical Christians in America, and I am pleased with the outcome in this respect. I think readers will see fair and accurate representations of the four positions.

Although I wasn't surprised at the arguments put forward or the fact that the contributors didn't appear to change their minds on anything, I'll confess I was hoping this project might display more goodwill and charity than it does. I doubt that readers will come away from this book with the feeling that we are any closer to the goal of Christian unity on topic of origins. I wrote the introduction just as the first essays were coming in, and I mentioned a couple of my hopes for the project. Those hopes now seem too optimistic for a project like this, where the contributors interacted only indirectly through me as the editor, and my own communication with them was almost entirely through email. Add to that the fact that these projects can be stressful with their multiple deadlines, and this results in plenty of opportunities for suspicion about whether everyone was being treated fairly—particularly because in my day job, one of the contributors is my boss! I worked very hard to allay those concerns (probably at the expense of being harder on Haarsma than the others, just to avoid any hint of favoritism). We worked through those issues pretty well, but one remains in the final version that needs some explanation.

All contributors were asked to write their initial essays with a maximum word count of ten thousand words, responses of two thousand words, and rejoinders of one thousand words. It is quite customary for authors to take some liberties with word counts and treat them as suggestions or ballpark figures (I include myself in this propensity!). As the editor, I often had to negotiate about overages with one contributor and

---

1. Upton Sinclair, *I, Candidate for Governor: And How I Got Licked* (Berkeley: University of California Press, 1994), 109.

then go back to the others to recalibrate the "absolute cap." I thought (and continue to think) that it would be most fair to allow the same number of words for all participants in each section. This proved to be more difficult to enforce than it sounds like it should be, and more than once (and with more than one of the contributors) became the grounds for tension and charges of unfairness. Undoubtedly there were aspects of this I could have handled better. The most obvious discrepancy that remains is in the initial essays, where Ham's is noticeably longer than the others. He was unwilling to cut anything further, believing it only fair that he should be given more space than the others since he was the only one defending the young age of the earth and "the authority of Scripture vs. the authority of the scientific majority." Of course each of the other contributors could come up with reasons why they should be entitled to extra space too. But my rationale did not persuade, and I was committed to giving contributors the final control of their words. Readers can judge for themselves what effect this has on the book.

Perhaps it should be seen as a positive sign that these leaders were even willing to appear together in one volume and interact with each other as they have. And perhaps the book will ultimately be seen as a first step that leads to some in-person interaction in the future, where we can get to know each other as fellow believers who have more in common than we have differences. I'm convinced that such interaction is the way to develop the kind of trust and respect required to effect Christian unity.

Speaking of trust, I suspect the central question non-specialist readers will come away with from this book is: Whom do I trust? One contributor says the science clearly points one direction; another says it clearly points the other. One thinks the Bible clearly says this; another thinks it clearly says that. Who is right? How do you determine which one to believe? These issues are complex and we can't sort them out by ourselves.

When I speak to church or school groups about science and the Bible, there invariably comes a point when someone in the audience feels the complexity of biblical interpretation and scientific theories, and says with some despair, "So in order to read my Bible or judge which version of science is correct, I'm going to have to get a couple of PhDs?" My typical response is to affirm two things: (1) Everyone can profit from reading their Bibles every day; God speaks to all of us through his Word—not just to the experts. The same goes for learning more about the natural world through our own observation. We can all cultivate a deeper appreciation for God's handiwork by looking at it more carefully.[2] But this point needs to be balanced by: (2) We all need to rely on experts in our communities to help us read Scripture better and to understand the natural world better. Increased specialization has resulted in the fact that none of us can become experts in all the relevant disciplines. Unless you are fluent in ancient Hebrew and Greek, you are dependent on experts even to simply read the Bible (and if you are fluent in Hebrew and Greek, you were dependent on experts to learn those languages). And how many of us through our own observation could work out the helio-centric solar system or quantum physics? We need experts. But now in this book, we see that experts disagree. That means that the experts can't all be right, and we're back to the question of which ones to trust.

There is no easy formula here, but I'd suggest it starts with regularly subjecting your views to critique. Don't just read the people you agree with, but make an attempt to really understand why others are equally persuaded of different views. Studies show we are hard-wired to see and accept reasons that support what we already believe and to quickly dismiss evidence that challenges our own positions.[3] It takes enormous effort, then, on our part to listen to others and consider their critiques of our own positions. But if we're serious about pursuing the truth in these matters, it is important. And if we ourselves are in the position where others look to us as experts, it is doubly important that we do this with integrity. I think this book makes a good contribution toward that goal. No matter what your perspective on origins, you should be able to find points and questions here that challenge you to examine again what you believe on these matters.

Beyond reading books, trusting experts comes from personal acquaintance. Invite scholars from a variety of backgrounds to come to your church or school group. Get to know them as people and hear their stories. Ask questions about their research to genuinely try to understand what the world looks like to them. Even if you don't come to

2. See Piercarlo Valedsolo, Jun Park, and Sara Gottlieb, "Awe and Scientific Explanation," *Emotion* 16(7) (Oct 2016): 937–40. Commentary on the study by a Christian working in a major scientific research university can be found at http://biologos.org/blogs/deborah-haarsma-the-presidents-notebook/is-science-awesome-for-christians.

3. See, for example, Sara E. Gorman and Jack M. Gorman, *Denying to the Grave: Why We Ignore the Facts That Will Save Us* (Oxford: Oxford University Press, 2017).

accept their perspective, your own perspective will be richer for entering into dialogue not just with a set of ideas, but with a person. In this way, we might move past the rancor and mistrust that characterize too many of our disagreements. I continue to hope that the origins conversation can help the church make strides towards unity, understanding, and love.